STUDIES IN WELSH HISTORY

42

WAGING WAR AND BUILDING PEACE

WAGING WAR AND BUILDING PEACE

MOBILISING INDUSTRY IN WALES, 1934–1947

by

LEON GOOBERMAN

UNIVERSITY OF WALES PRESS
2025

© Leon Gooberman, 2025

All rights reserved. No part of this book may be reproduced in any material form (including photocopying or storing it in any medium by electronic means and whether or not transiently or incidentally to some other use of this publication) without the written permission of the copyright owner. Applications for the copyright owner's written permission to reproduce any part of this publication should be addressed to the University of Wales Press, University Registry, King Edward VII Avenue, Cardiff CF10 3NS.

www.uwp.co.uk

British Library CIP Data
A catalogue record for this book is available from the British Library

ISBN   978-1-83772-270-9
e-ISBN   978-1-83772-271-6

The right of Leon Gooberman to be identified as author of this work has been asserted in accordance with sections 77 and 79 of the Copyright, Designs and Patents Act 1988.

For GPSR enquiries please contact: Easy Access System Europe Oü, 16879218
Mustamäe tee 50, 10621, Tallinn, Estonia.
gpsr.requests@easproject.com

Typeset by Richard Huw Pritchard
Printed and bound by CPI Group (UK) Ltd, Croydon, CR0 4YY

SERIES EDITORS' FOREWORD

Since the foundation of the series in 1977, the study of Wales's history has attracted growing attention among historians internationally and continues to enjoy a vigorous popularity. Not only are approaches, both traditional and new, to the study of history in general being successfully applied in a Welsh context, but Wales's historical experience is increasingly appreciated by writers on British, European and world history. These advances have been especially marked in the university institutions in Wales itself.

In order to make more widely available the conclusions of original research, much of it of limited accessibility in postgraduate dissertations and theses, in 1977 the History and Law Committee of the Board of Celtic Studies inaugurated this series of monographs, *Studies in Welsh History*. It was anticipated that many of the volumes would originate in research conducted in the University of Wales or under the auspices of the Board of Celtic Studies, and so it proved. Although the Board of Celtic Studies no longer exists, the University of Wales Press continues to sponsor the series. It seeks to publish significant contributions made by researchers in Wales and elsewhere. Its primary aim is to serve historical scholarship and to encourage the study of Welsh history.

For Mari, Elen and Gwen

CONTENTS

SERIES EDITORS' FOREWORD   v
ABBREVIATIONS   ix

Introduction   1

Part One: Rearmament and 'Phoney War', 1934–1940   **17**
1 Rearmament, 1934–1938   19
2 Crisis and war, 1938–1940   39

Part Two: Wartime Munitions Industries, 1940–1945   **65**
3 Governing production   67
4 Governing labour   89
5 Factories   106

Part Three: Wartime Natural Resource Industries, 1940–1945   **123**
6 Coal mining   125
7 Metal manufacturing   152
8 Agriculture   175

Part Four: Reconstruction, 1943–1947   **201**
9 Secondary manufacturing   203
10 Natural resource industries   225

Conclusion	**251**
Appendix	263
Bibliography	269
Index	283

ABBREVIATIONS

BNS	British Nylon Spinners
CAEC	County Agricultural Executive Committee
CWAEC	County War Agricultural Executive Committees
GKB	Guest Keen Baldwins
GKN	Guest Keen and Nettlefolds
ICI	Imperial Chemical Industries
NCB	National Coal Board
NECACO	North East Coast Aircraft Company
NFU	National Farmers Union
NUM	National Union of Mineworkers
RAF	Royal Air Force
ROF	Royal Ordnance Factory
TUC	Trades Union Congress
WMIE	Wales and Monmouthshire Industrial Estates Ltd
WRAC	Wales Reconstruction Advisory Council

INTRODUCTION

The shape and governance of territorial economies throughout Britain altered radically between 1934 and 1947, with some of the most dramatic changes taking place in Wales. In 1934 the structure of the Welsh economy had changed little from before the First World War when it had been characterised by scattered industrial concentrations extracting and processing natural resources including coal, metal ore and slate. This economy developed in a 'laissez faire' era when political and commercial elites believed generally that state intervention was counterproductive as it would displace private investment, and barely considered government intervention to boost regional growth. Meanwhile, Wales-specific administrative machinery was absent. The country had been absorbed into England by the sixteenth-century Acts of Union while even its borders were disputed given the anomalous status of Monmouthshire.

The Welsh economy expanded rapidly throughout the nineteenth century, but growth obscured two weaknesses. One was an overdependence on natural resources. In 1911 over half of the occupied male workforce worked in mines, quarries, metals, engineering and transport.[1] Many others depended on the income generated by these activities. Women were disadvantaged in such an industrialised economy and their paid employment concentrated within activities such as domestic service.[2] Wales was so suited to primary production that little diversification occurred, and in the late nineteenth century it was largely bypassed by the second industrial revolution and its focus on newer technologies.

The other weakness was fragmentation. The largest industrial concentration was in south Wales, whose reserves of iron ore, limestone and coal initially prompted the creation of iron and, subsequently, steel-making complexes. However, coal mining emerged in the late nineteenth century as the leading regional activity. Geology endowed the south Wales valleys with abundant coal reserves while geography pointed them towards the coast to ease the construction of railways to facilitate exports. South Wales coal was ideal steam fuel and became the primary energy source for the Royal Navy,[3] helping the number of miners to grow from 73,326 in 1874 to 234,117 in 1914.[4] By 1900 over half of the coal mined in south Wales was exported and the region was central to the globalised Victorian economy. John Davies estimated that at least a quarter of the global energy trade originated from south Wales and compared the Bristol Channel to the Persian Gulf of the 1980s.[5] Meanwhile, industrial concentrations in north Wales expanded although less dramatically. The slate industry employed some 16,000 men in northwest Wales by 1900 as urbanisation drove demand for roof tiles, while 12,629 miners worked in the north-eastern coalfield.[6] Finally, mid-Wales remained predominantly agricultural although some metal mines produced outputs including lead, zinc and gold.

Industrial expansion created employment to such an extent that Wales absorbed population between 1901 and 1910 at rates comparable to the United States.[7] By 1911 its population of 2.4 million was concentrated into two arcs around resource-based industries. One was in the southern counties of Glamorgan and Monmouthshire, home to almost two-thirds of the population.[8] The other was in the north where smaller concentrations existed around coal mining and slate working. Both arcs were separated from each other by a sparsely populated rural upland where population density was low, and out-migration was common. Crucially, an integrated Welsh economy never emerged as it instead became an outward facing natural resource base characterised by the primacy of east–west transport linkages, symbolised by historian Eric Hobsbawm's description of Wales as 'a mining annexe' of England.[9]

These weaknesses barely mattered when demand for resource-based products was high, but the First World War disrupted the global trading system on which these industries depended. Some wartime disruptions persisted while the proportion of the world's merchant shipping fired by coal fell from 96.6 per cent in 1914 to 58.9 per cent by 1930.[10] Moreover, the post-war state shed the responsibilities it had assumed during wartime such as its control over railways and coal mining. Finally, the 'orthodox view' of economic policy reasserted itself while the 1925 restoration of the 'gold standard' at its pre-war level damaged export industries. These dynamics buffeted the economy throughout the 1920s to prompt economic depression and increased unemployment.

This bleak picture worsened during the Great Depression of the early 1930s. Unemployment throughout Wales breached 30 per cent in late 1930 and remained chronic. The nadir was reached in August 1932 when 42.8 per cent of insured males and 15.3 per cent of insured females were unemployed,[11] although a few areas with more diversified economies featured pockets of relative prosperity. One example of depression was the south Wales town of Blaina, where seven out of nine collieries closed, prompting what a later Mass Observation study described as 'extreme hardships' as the town's population fell by a quarter between 1921 and 1935.[12] The number of coal miners in south Wales fell by 40 per cent from 1921 to 1934, while steel production in south Wales collapsed by 40 per cent between 1929 and 1931, although it recovered subsequently.[13] Similar problems beset north Wales, with 4,000 out of Shotton's 6,000 metal manufacturing employees losing their jobs in 1931, while the workforce of the adjacent coalfield fell by 44 per cent between 1920 and 1934.[14] While industrial Wales had once attracted thousands of migrants, population flow reversed as thousands fled to find work elsewhere and the total net inter-war population loss by migration of 450,000 was symbolised by the apocryphal tombstone inscription of 'not departed but gone to Slough'.[15]

Yet the state was not absent in the Welsh economy of the early 1930s. Governments imposed import tariffs on iron and steel, while cross-party campaigning prompted the support of a metal manufacturing plant in Ebbw Vale, closed in 1929 but later reconstructed and reopened as an integrated strip mill producing sheet steel and tinplate.[16] In agriculture, the state gradually extended intervention through imposing import quotas and creating marketing boards.[17] However, governments remained wedded to regional non-intervention, focusing instead on transferring 'surplus' labour through an Industrial Transference Board created in 1928.[18] Political pressure eventually forced the government in 1934 to appoint Commissioners to promote regional industrial development as part of a Regional Policy, but they lacked resources and achieved little.

By 1934 southern England was recovering as Britain divided informally into 'inner' and 'outer' economic regions. In the 'inner' regions of southern and midland England, rising real incomes for workers and their families drove consumer-led growth centred on housebuilding and the consumer goods manufactured in those areas. Yet, although parts of Wales recovered, its industrial areas were mired in deep and persistent depression. Diversification remained elusive as the geography of primary industrialisation that had once benefited Wales was outdated in a new environment of electrical power and road haulage.[19] Secondary manufacturing industrialists tended to see Wales as remote and lacking workforce skills, constructing few factories there.

Wales was, however, transformed by the Second World War as the government mobilised its economy to maximise production of weapons, raw materials and food. Regional data on munitions manufacturing are not available but average weekly output throughout the UK peaked in early 1944 at more than 500 aircraft, eight warships, 700 armoured vehicles, 3,000 tons of bombs, 450 artillery pieces, 1.5 million shells and mines, and 33,000 small arms.[20] Even contemporary observers in Wales pointed to positive impacts. One example was in the Rhondda, one of the areas worst affected by pre-war depression. In 1944 Labour Councillor Iorwerth Thomas argued the war represented a 'new gold rush' of economic activity, while in 1946 MP W. H. Mainwaring claimed that 'this last terrible catastrophe in the world's history was actually a relief to south Wales, because the ghastly thing relieved us of unemployment'.[21] Later observers agreed. In 1960 economist Brinley Thomas argued that war 'twisted the Welsh economy into an unfamiliar mould', eliminating unemployment, establishing manufacturing industry, and enabling many women to join the workforce.[22]

Despite the wartime fears of many as to a post-war return to slump, state intervention evolved and continued under the post-1945 Labour government. The state constructed new factories and converted wartime munitions factories for peacetime occupation, while a new iteration of Regional Policy influenced many industrialists to locate their factories in Wales. The government also nationalised the steel and coal industries, while enveloping agriculture in controls and subsidies. The result was a far more diversified if state dependent economy where unemployment stabilised at levels far below those of inter-war years.

This book explores how governments mobilised key industries in Wales, namely, munitions manufacturing, coal mining, metals manufacturing and agriculture to achieve their goals during war and peace between 1934 and 1947. It has three aims. The first is to map mobilisation. How and why were munitions factories employing thousands of workers established at unlikely sites, including a slate quarry in Llanberis in mountainous Snowdonia, and how did mobilisation impact agriculture, metals manufacture and coal mining? The second is to detail the governance of mobilisation. How did governments develop governance across and within different industries, how did these approaches differ and how effective were they? The third is to assess the extent to which wartime governance influenced the formulation and implementation of post-war industrial policy. What lessons were learned from wartime governance and how were they implemented?

Wales has two merits as a regional case study of Britain's industrial mobilisation. One is that its lack of administrative autonomy meant that structures developed in Wales to coordinate production were generally mirrored throughout other British regions and there were few 'Wales only' aspects. The main exception is Northern Ireland, where most aspects of domestic governance were subject to the politically devolved Northern Ireland Parliament and were not directly comparable with other parts of the UK. A similar comparability also applies for post-war developments although some institutional dynamics in Scotland differed. The other is that the inter-war depression created surplus labour capacity formed from unemployed people and unoccupied females. Labour availability meant that Wales became a focus for state-governed industrial mobilisation, while its existing concentrations of metal manufacture, coal mining and agriculture were subject to varying forms of state-led governance. Finally, the legacy of inter-war experiences meant that it became a focus for the regional and industrial policies of the post-1945 Labour government.

There is no shortage of literature on rearmament, the war, and the economic policies of the post-war Labour government but significant gaps exist on the governance of regional industrial mobilisation.

The literature on the governance of pre-war rearmament is formed from two strands. One is service specific where Forbes, Gordon and Miller explored factors including the state's reluctance to manage armaments factories and abandon normal commercial approaches to procurement.[23] The other is general governance, where Shay, Rollings and Gibbs each examined continued financial rationing and how governance was often improvised and incoherent.[24] Nevertheless, regional impacts have been neglected and although econometric studies by Thomas, and Crafts and Mills, estimated regional employment created by rearmament, their results differ and lack disaggregated data on Wales.[25]

Although there is an enormous literature on Britain during the Second World War and researchers such as Peden, Broadberry and Howlett have explored national economic strategies,[26] the state's approaches to governing production are less commonly considered. However, state intervention within some industries have been examined: Howlett explored its allocation of capacity within the steel industry from 1939 to 1945, Edgerton analysed its marshalling of aircraft manufacturing from 1935 to 1948, while others have examined its control over wartime agriculture.[27] Moreover, industrial surveys such as Burn's study of the steel industry between 1939 and 1959, and Supple's exploration of coal mining between 1914 and 1946,[28] include data on wartime governance. Both highlighted the complexity of governance processes, with Burn arguing that it is difficult for 'outsiders to pierce … to the heart of [wartime] administrative activity'.[29] Yet overall processes are neglected. Although Todman argued in his surveys of Britain's wartime experiences that industrial governance developed in 'fits and starts' and the 'organisers, not the improvisers' eventually prevailed, the broad scope of his work precluded more detailed analysis.[30] Finally, other studies incorporating analyses of production tend to focus on topics other than governance. Examples include Coombs's exploration of tank technology and Jeffreys's analysis of the coalition government.[31]

Nevertheless, researchers have explored the broader national environment surrounding mobilisation. Edgerton argued that Britain was a 'warfare state' for much of the twentieth century, questioning the 'standing alone' narrative and 'people's war' arguments of which the latter emphasised the labour market role of the Ministry of Labour and National Service.[32] He argued instead that a broader 'warfare state' prompted science and technological innovation while deploying governance machinery to enable large-scale munitions production. Administrative strength enabled domestic mobilisation while military strength maintained international trading links enabling domestic production to be complemented with imports.[33]

There are three explanations as to the relative neglect of wartime production governance. The first is that studies of relations between state and business focus on the Board of Trade. Despite the Board's responsibilities over many commercial activities throughout the economy, three supply ministries contracted businesses to manufacture munitions, governed their activities and often financed their capital expenditure, and revitalised regions by guiding their dispersion. Yet works including those by Wren and Parsons focus on the Board's planning for post-war reconstruction and neglect its other activities such as licensing regional industrial floorspace.[34] Finally, the activities of government bodies controlling raw materials are barely analysed outside official histories or survey works.

The second is that mobilisation depended on administrative processes described by historians as 'unglamorous' and 'immensely complex'.[35] Neglect is highlighted by the Lord President's Committee created in 1940 to mediate between ministries on home front topics. Despite its importance, Crowcroft argued that there was 'no integration of [the Committee] into the historiography'.[36] Meanwhile, memoirs often lack detail. One example is Oliver Lyttleton, Minister of Production from 1942 to 1945, whose autobiography contains little on what he described as 'tedious' governance processes.[37]

The final factor is that official wartime histories remain dominant as secondary sources although they were published some seventy years ago. The primary reason for this dominance is their depth and quality. Their production began remarkably early. By December 1941 historians had interviewed civil servants within the Board of Trade and in the subsequent year were seconded to ministries to prepare narratives of selected activities.[38] These narratives informed the series of twenty-eight civil history volumes published from 1949, including seven on war production appearing from 1953. Yet these volumes feature weaknesses often found within official research such as reflecting official views and focusing on central ministerial activities at the expense of regional and private actors. The only sustained critique has been that mounted by agricultural historians who argued that the relevant volume overstated the importance of rising crop yields in prompting production increases, also noting how its author was influenced by his civil service sponsors to remove references to friction between farmers and the county committees governing the industry.[39]

The neglect of the overall processes and achievements of production governance is even more apparent at regional levels, where Ollerenshaw observed 'very few studies of the regional experience of mobilisation'.[40] Exceptions include his works on Northern Ireland, and sector-specific studies on Wales including journal articles by the present author.[41] The chapters in this book on governing wartime munitions production, coal mining, and the reconstruction of secondary manufacturing, draw on material from these articles. In general terms, the coal mining industry illustrates the paucity of research. While regional unions including those in south Wales have been studied,[42] other works tend to treat the industry as if it was nationally organised, obscuring regional mechanisms and organisations. National organisations representing employers and employees existed but were dominated by autonomous regional members that interacted with the state's regional functions during wartime.[43]

Similarly, there is a large literature on the economic policies of the post-1945 Labour government but studies of its economic governance tend to feature national foci.[44] Further gaps exist on Regional Policy which research views as having been developed in wartime for subsequent implementation. Booth argued that wartime controls offered 'radical new solutions' to regional employment problems that were accepted by policymakers and industrialists before their implementation by the 1945 Distribution of Industry Act.[45] Studies of peacetime events focus on how the national machinery set out by this Act operated and its efficiency. As examples, Scott and Rosevear argued that post-war implementation focused on creating jobs immediately and failed to prompt self-sustaining industrial expansion.[46] Meanwhile, similar themes are also prominent in surveys examining Regional Policy from the 1930s,[47] while evaluations of its post-war impacts begin in 1950 or 1951 after its peak effectiveness had passed.[48]

The aim of this book is to address these gaps. It does this by examining the course and consequences of state-led industrial mobilisation in Wales between the initial acceleration of rearmament in 1934, and the ending of the most effective phase of post-war Regional Policy in 1947. It is divided into four parts.

The first is formed from two chapters. One deals with the beginnings of mobilisation through rearmament from 1934 to 1938, and the other with its steadily increasing if inconsistent and uneven pace until the formation of the coalition government in May 1940. The second part focuses on munitions production after 1940. Its first chapter explores the gradual and contested development and implementation of governance to coordinate competing ministries, and the businesses to whom they contracted production, to drive greater output. Its second chapter explores the processes behind labour force mobilisation. Both chapters begin with a discussion of Britain-wide governance structures, reflecting the extent to which activities in Wales were part of a broader effort. They then focus on the development and implementation of regional administrative structures, before discussing the development and operation of munitions factories throughout Wales.

The third part is formed from chapters covering manufacturing, coal, steel and agriculture from 1940 to 1945. Each chapter begins with a discussion of Britain-wide governance structures, then examines regional administrative structures before ending with explorations of development of each industry in Wales. The final part of the book focuses on the post-war impact of wartime mobilisation by exploring the extent to which reconstruction was planned during the war, and its subsequent implementation. It comprises two chapters. One explores linkages between the wartime governance of munitions manufacture and post-war Regional Policy that sought to influence industrial location, and the other examines the approaches taken to the post-war governance of agriculture, metals manufacture and coal mining, and how these approaches flowed from wartime experiences.

Most of the source material for this book was obtained from the UK's National Archives at Kew. The lack of administrative autonomy in Wales means that records of its governance were retained centrally in the regional files of the various ministries. Yet there is one exception, the south Wales coal industry where governance was contested. The National Archives hold records generated by the state but the National Library of Wales in Aberystwyth holds those of the coal owners' regional employers' association, while the South Wales Miners' Library at Swansea University holds those of the regional union. Archives in Wales contain economic data relating to union branches, as well as oral histories gathered from workers, but those on industrial governance are largely absent with only a few exceptions. These include Glamorgan Archives' data on the government body responsible for some government-owned factories and industrial estates constructed in the 1930s and from 1944. Finally, records of metal manufacturing and coal mining businesses exist, such as those on the GKN Cwmbran mining and metal complex held by Gwent Archives. Yet those on munitions businesses are conspicuous by their absence given the generally short-lived nature of such factories, or their status as branch factories of larger concerns.

Three arguments are made. Briefly, the first is that mobilisation was ultimately successful but was protracted as pre-war rearmament barely impacted on the Welsh economy, while peak output throughout Britain was not reached until 1944. The second is that the development of wartime industrial governance featured piecemeal and pragmatic advances driven by force of circumstances around individual industries, each subjected to different approaches. The third is that wartime governance was a crucial influence on the creation of the post-war regional economic settlement and its flagship achievement of full employment.

In sum, rearmament was slow to impact on Wales, while the subsequent wartime public governance of businesses producing munitions, raw materials and agricultural produce was improvised and inconsistent, but also pragmatic and effective in all industries apart from coal mining. Wales was marginalised as a location for munitions manufacture until 1940, but it subsequently became a focal point for a large-scale, state sponsored, migration and mobilisation of business while its agricultural sector was transformed. There was less impact on metals manufacture given its pre-war relative efficiency, while coal mining remained mired in crises. Nevertheless, war legitimised state intervention throughout Britain, especially within once depressed regions. Such success prompted arguments that, if the state could create full regional employment in wartime, it could and should achieve similar success in peacetime. Business historians such as Scranton and Fridenson have characterised the state's role in relation to businesses as being 'always in' given its role in shaping markets, business and law.[49] This study reflects this characterisation by demonstrating how the threat, necessities and lessons of war shaped the state–business relationship in a once neglected region, ultimately prompting the creation of a state-dominated post-war economy.

Notes

1. J. Williams, *Was Wales Industrialised?* (Gomer, 1995), p. 307.
2. C. Howell, 'Hidden Labours: The Domestic Service Industry in South Wales, 1871–1921', in L. Miskell (ed.), *New Perspectives on Welsh Industrial History* (University of Wales Press, 2020), pp. 75–102 (p. 81).
3. S. Gray, *Steam Power and Sea Power, Coal, The Royal Navy and the British Empire, c. 1870–1914* (Palgrave Macmillan, 2018), p. 73.
4. L. J. Williams, *Digest of Welsh Historical Statistics 1700–1974, Volume 1* (Welsh Office, 1985), p. 300. Hereafter *DWHS, vol. 1*.
5. J. Davies, *A History of Wales* (Penguin, 1994), p. 470.
6. D. Gwyn, *Welsh Slate, Archaeology and History of an Industry* (Aberystwyth: RCAHMW, 2015), p. 9; Williams, *DWHS, vol. 1*, p. 299.
7. B. Thomas, 'Wales and the Atlantic Economy', in B. Thomas (ed.), *The Welsh Economy: Studies in Expansion* (University of Wales Press, 1962), pp. 1–30 (p. 9).
8. Williams, *DWHS, vol. 1*, p. 7, pp. 8–24.
9. E. Hobsbawm, *Industry and Empire* (Penguin, 1969), pp. 283–4.
10. *South Wales Coalfield, Regional Survey Report* (Ministry of Fuel and Power, 1946), p. 48.
11. Williams, *DWHS, vol. 1*, pp. 143–4.
12. TNA, BD 11/1465, Letter from Clerk of Blaina UDC, 5 December 1934; Mass Observation, *Mining Town*, 1942, 2.
13. Williams, *DWHS, Vol. 1*, p. 300; J. Driscoll, 'Steel', in Thomas (ed.), *The Welsh Economy: Studies in Expansion*, pp. 114–37 (p. 115).
14. *Western Mail*, 'Welsh Steel Sensation', 25 April 1931; G. Smith, *A Century of Shotton Steel* (British Steel, 1996), p. 26; Williams, *DWHS, vol. 1*, p. 299.
15. Thomas, 'Wales and the Atlantic Economy', p. 9; C. Harris, *Redundancy and Recession in South Wales* (Basil Blackford, 1986), p. 13.
16. D. E. Pitfield, 'Regional Policy and the Long Run: Innovation and Location in the Iron and Steel Industry', *Business History*, 16/2 (1974), 160–74 (162–5).
17. A. F. Wilt, *Food for War: Agriculture and Rearmament in Britain before the Second World War* (Oxford University Press, 2001), p. 32.
18. *Reports of Investigations into the Industrial Conditions in Certain Depressed Areas*, p. 182.
19. N. Crafts, *Forging Ahead, Falling Behind and Fighting Back* (Cambridge University Press, 2018), p. 67.
20. M. Harrison, 'A Volume Index of the Total Munitions Output of the United Kingdom, 1939–1944', *Economic History Review*, 43 (1990), 657–66 (665–6).
21. Hansard (Commons), 28 October 1946, vol. 428, col. 390; *Pontypridd Observer*, 'A New Rhondda is Being Born!', 16 September 1944.
22. B. Thomas, 'Post-war Expansion', in Thomas (ed.), *The Welsh Economy: Studies in Expansion*, pp. 30–50 (p. 31).
23. G. Gordon, *British Seapower and Procurement Between the Wars: A Reappraisal of Rearmament* (Springer, 1988), p. 264; C. Miller, *Planning and Profits: British Naval Armaments Manufacture and the Military-Industrial Complex 1918–1941* (Liverpool University Press, 2018), p. 222.

24 R. Shay, *British Rearmament in the Thirties* (Princeton University Press, 1977), p. 289; N. Rollings, 'Whitehall and the Control of Prices and Profits in a Major War, 1919–1939', *The Historical Journal*, 44/2 (2001), 517–40 (538–9); N. Gibbs, *Grand Strategy* (HMSO, 1956), p. 767.

25 M. Thomas, 'Rearmament and Economic Recovery in the late 1930s', *The Economic History Review*, 36/4 (1983), 552–79; N. Crafts and T. C. Mills, 'Rearmament to the Rescue? New Estimates of the Impact of "Keynesian" Policies in 1930s' Britain', *Journal of Economic History*, 73/4, 1077–104. Thomas estimates that multipliers of around 1.6 created employment for over a million people throughout the UK by 1938, but Crafts and Mills estimate between 0.3 and 0.8, implying far fewer.

26 S. Broadberry and P. Howlett, 'The United Kingdom: "Victory at All Costs"', in M. Harrison (ed.), *The Economics of World War II: Six Great Powers in International Comparison* (Cambridge University Press, 1998), pp. 43–80; P. Howlett, 'New Light Through Old Windows: A New Perspective on the British Economy in the Second World War', *Journal of Contemporary History*, 28/2 (1993), 361–79; G. Peden, *Arms, Economics and British Strategy: From Dreadnoughts to Hydrogen Bombs* (Cambridge University Press, 2007), pp. 164–228.

27 D. Edgerton, 'Technical Innovation, Industrial Capacity and Efficiency: Public Ownership and the British Military Aircraft Industry, 1935-48', *Business History*, 26/3 (1984), 247–79; P. Howlett, 'Resource Allocation in Wartime Britain: The Case of Steel, 1939-45', *Journal of Contemporary History*, 29/3 (1994), 523–44; B. Short, C. Watkins and J. Martin (eds), *The Front Line of Freedom: British Farming in the Second World War* (British Agricultural History Society, 2006).

28 D. Burn, *The Steel Industry, 1939–1959* (Cambridge University Press, 1961); B. Supple, *History of the British Coal Industry, Volume 4* (Oxford University Press, 1987).

29 Burn, *The Steel Industry, 1939–1959*, p. 12.

30 D. Todman, *Britain's War: Into Battle, 1937–41* (Penguin, 2016), pp. 593, 617.

31 B. Coombs, *British Tank Production and the War Economy, 1934–1945* (A & C Black, 2013). K. Jeffreys, *The Churchill Coalition and Wartime Politics, 1940–1945* (Manchester University Press, 1995), pp. 61–84. See also D. Todman, *Britain's War: A New World, 1942–1947* (Penguin, 2016), pp. 261–8.

32 A. Calder, *The People's War, Britain 1939–1945* (Random House, 2012).

33 Edgerton, 'Technical Innovation'; D. Edgerton, *Britain's War Machine* (Penguin, 2012); Edgerton, *Warfare State: Britain, 1920–1970* (Cambridge University Press, 2005), pp. 59–88.

34 D. Parsons, *The Political Economy of British Regional Policy* (Routledge, 1988), pp. 47–68; C. Wren, *Industrial Subsidies: The UK Experience* (Springer, 1996), pp. 29–31.

35 R. Crowcroft, '"Making a Reality of Collective Responsibility": The Lord President's Committee, Coalition, and the British State at War, 1941–42', *Contemporary British History*, 29/4 (2015), 539–62 (540); Edgerton, *Britain's War Machine*, p. 200.

36 Crowcroft, 'Making a Reality of Collective Responsibility', 540.

37 O. Lyttleton, *The Memoirs of Lord Chandos* (The Bodley Head, 1962), p. 286.
38 TNA, BT 138/28, *Note of Talk with Miss Elroy and Sir C. Weir, Board of Trade*, Professor Hancock, 23 December 1941.
39 J. Martin, 'The Structural Transformation of British Agriculture: The Resurgence of Progressive High-Input Arable Farming in Wartime', in *The Front Line of Freedom*, pp. 16–35 (p. 31).
40 P. Ollerenshaw, 'War, Industrial Mobilisation and Society in Northern Ireland, 1939–1945', *Contemporary European History*, 16/2 (2007), 169–97 (171). See also P. Ollerenshaw, *Northern Ireland in the Second World War: Politics, Economic Mobilisation and Society, 1939–45* (Manchester University Press, 2013).
41 L. Gooberman, 'Public governance of private munitions businesses in regional Britain, the case of Wales, 1938 to 1945', *Business History* (2021), 1–20; L. Gooberman, '"Revolution in the Coalfields": Industrial Relations in Wartime South Wales, 1939–45', *Labor History*, 63/1 (2022), 55–72; L. Gooberman (2023), 'The Emergence of Regional Industrial Policy in Britain: The Case of Wales, 1939 to 1947', *Enterprise and Society*. Published online before print. See also: L. Gooberman, *From Depression to Devolution, Economy and Government in Wales, 1934–2006* (University of Wales Press, 2017), pp. 22–32; R. Moore-Colyer, 'The County War Agricultural Executive Committees: The Welsh Experience, 1939–45', *Welsh History Review*, 22 (2005), 558–87.
42 H. Francis and D. Smith, *The Fed* (Lawrence & Wishart, 1980).
43 D. Howell, '"All or Nowt": The politics of the MFGB', in A. Campbell, N. Fishman and D. Howell (eds), *Miners, Unions, and Politics 1910–1947* (Routledge, 1996), pp. 35–58.
44 O'Hara, '"What the electorate can be expected to swallow": Nationalism, Transnationalism and the shifting boundaries of the state in post-war Britain', 501–28; J. Tomlinson, *Democratic Socialism and Economic Policy: The Atlee Years, 1945–1951*; Morgan, *Labour in Power*.
45 Booth, 'The Second World War and the Development of Modern Regional Policy', 1–21.
46 Scott, 'British Regional Policy 1945–51: A Lost Opportunity', 358–82; Rosevear, 'Balancing Business and the Regions', 77–99.
47 Parsons, *The Political Economy of British Regional Policy*; McCallum, 'The Development of British Regional Policy', pp. 3–42; McCrone, *Regional Policy in Britain*, p. 106.
48 Moore and Rhodes, 'Evaluating the Effects of British Regional Policy', 87–110; Moore, Rhodes and Tyler, 'The Effects of Government Regional Economic Policy'; Moore, Rhodes and Tyler, 'Urban/Rural Shift and the Evaluation of Regional Policy', 139–57; Scott, 'The Worst of Both Worlds: British Regional Policy, 1951–1964', 41–64.
49 Scranton and Fridenson, *Reimagining Business History*, p. 17.

PART ONE

REARMAMENT AND 'PHONEY WAR',
1934–1940

1
REARMAMENT, 1934–1938

PLANNING REARMAMENT

Victory in the First World War prompted defence expenditure to fall rapidly, a trend that continued throughout the 1920s as policymakers interpreted victory as precluding the possibility of another general war. In 1919 the government enshrined this view into a 'ten-year rule' stating that war was unlikely over a rolling ten-year period and rearmament was unnecessary. The rule was initially temporary but was made permanent in 1928 by Chancellor Winston Churchill. Meanwhile, governments saw low expenditure and a balanced budget as necessary to reduce inflation and enhance the UK's financial standing, while the abolition of conscription in 1919 restricted the size of the armed forces. By the early 1930s the defence apparatus had withered. While the navy remained the world's largest if measured by number of vessels, the air force had slipped to the world's fifth largest by 1933 and was equipped with obsolete aircraft. The weakest service, however, was the regular army whose 1933 complement of 206,000 men was fewer than before the First World War, while most of its equipment was of pre-1918 vintage.[1]

Yet the prospect of war gradually re-emerged. In 1931 Japan's invasion of Manchuria threatened Britain's far eastern territories and the 'ten-year rule' was cancelled in March 1932. However, finance remained influential as the cabinet's decision to cancel was accompanied by their acceptance of a memorandum from Chancellor Neville Chamberlain stating that the 'financial and economic risks are by far the most serious and urgent that the country has to face' and the cancellation had little impact on defence expenditure.[2]

The international outlook darkened further as Hitler took power in Germany and Japan further developed its navy. A turning point was reached in 1933 when the Geneva Disarmament Conference collapsed, followed by Germany's withdrawal from the League of Nations. The dual danger from Germany and Japan then became a triple threat from 1935 as Italy prepared to invade Abyssinia. Discussions on rearmament gained more urgency and in 1935 the government's Statement Relating to Defence argued that the UK was 'approaching a point when we are not possessed of the necessary means of defending ourselves against an aggressor'.[3] Although military expenditure quadrupled in the four years after 1934, it was from a low base. When Germany reoccupied the Rhineland in 1936, service chiefs told the Cabinet that the UK could deploy only a small and 'purely symbolic' force of five partially equipped brigades to 'show the flag'.[4] By 1938 the UK had increased defence expenditure to 7 per cent of national income, a substantial amount but far less than Germany's 17 per cent.[5] However, competing peacetime demands in the UK combined with widespread residual horror as to the carnage of the First World War to restrict politicians' readiness to consider war and prepare accordingly. While the German dictatorship simply ordered its armed forces in 1935 to ignore all financial limits, this was politically impossible in the UK.[6]

Much of the relative slowness of the UK's rearmament was attributable to financial concerns. Crucially, Prime Minister Stanley Baldwin, in office between 1935 and 1937, lacked an overall concept to shape the programme.[7] The vacuum was filled partially by Chamberlain, Baldwin's Chancellor and successor who supported some rearmament but wanted to continue peacetime approaches to prudent procurement.[8] Two options to fund rearmament existed. One was borrowing but Chamberlain believed that excessive borrowing would prompt inflation and a loss of confidence in the UK's financial standing. The other was tax increases, but he saw these as economically damaging. The government ruled out both while its desire to maintain peacetime economic conditions prompted its discounting of statutory controls that would divert civilian industrial capacity towards military production.[9]

The cautious approach had some opponents. The most notable was Churchill, who kept up a barrage of criticism throughout his 'wilderness years' outside government. A typical example was his letter to Sir Thomas Inskip, Minister for Co-ordination of Defence, in 1936 arguing that efforts to develop air defences were 'dilettante futility ... delays are dreadful'.[10] Nevertheless, the government held firm and the budgetary balance between income and expenditure remained broadly level from 1934 to 1938.[11] Restraint was illustrated in 1936 when Chamberlain warned the Cabinet that the cost of rearmament was 'mounting at a giddy rate ... our resources were not unlimited',[12] and the government dismissed increasing borrowing or taxation until late 1937.

Although the pace of rearmament lagged behind Germany, large-scale programmes emerged. The most dramatic were linked to the air force whose financial allocations increased seven-fold between 1934 and 1938. Increases were prompted by an 'air panic', given fears that the new technology of aviation could allow the enemy to launch 'knock-out' blows by destroying cities.[13] Baldwin famously argued in 1932 that 'the bomber would always get through', while in 1938 Chamberlain stated that:[14]

> When war starts today, in the very first hour, before any professional soldier, sailor, or airman has been touched, it will strike the workman, the clerk, the man-in-the-street or in the bus, and his wives and children in their homes ... people

burrowing underground, trying to escape from poison gas, knowing that at any hour of the day or night death or mutilation was ready to come upon them.

These fears prompted increasingly ambitious schemes. In 1934 the first set out plans to manufacture 2,400 aircraft over two years, while the Air Ministry invited proposals against specifications that eventually led to the Spitfire and Hurricane. In 1935 the second scheme proposed the annual manufacture of 2,000 aircraft. The productive capacity of existing factories was, however, reached by 1936 when a third set out plans to construct 8,000 aircraft over three years.[15] Although annual aircraft production grew from 893 in 1935 to 2,218 in 1937,[16] the RAF was not fully equipped for war. In 1937 Chamberlain asked officials to outline the 'exact position in which we should be if we were attacked on January 1st, 1938'. Their pessimistic answer was that the air force was in an 'unsatisfactory position in respect of the number of squadrons that can be mobilised'. Limited production meant that 'we should not be able to maintain ... squadrons for very long if our present estimates of war wastage are correct', and only 'eighteen of the thirty [fighter] squadrons are equipped with aircraft which could compete with modern bombers'.[17]

The second priority was the navy, which, despite its imperial scale, risked being unable to contain its enemies. The Admiralty's plans for expansion aimed for a 'two power standard' enabling the navy to wage war simultaneously against Germany and Japan. By late 1935, however, the government decided that the standard was too expensive, although it agreed to accelerate shipbuilding. Admiralty attempts at further acceleration foundered within Whitehall committees, given the government's determination to maintain peacetime approaches to procurement,[18] but a quarter of the navy's effective strength of two million tons was either newly built or renovated between 1935 and 1938,[19] and by 1937 shipyards were at capacity.

While rearmament proceeded in the air force and to a lesser extent in the navy, the army was what the official history described as a 'Cinderella service'.[20] Financial allocations grew from 1934 but the army's share of all defence expenditure was less than a quarter until 1938. Meanwhile, some additional resources were absorbed by anti-aircraft defences whose construction was a prolonged process. In 1935 the government's home defence sub-committee observed that a 'partial defence' for London and adjacent areas would not exist until 1940, while the rest of the UK would have to wait until 1950.[21] Although preparations were accelerated subsequently, air defences remained incomplete in 1938.

The secondary importance accorded to the army was justified by the 'limited liability' concept that emphasised imperial defence, not continental war. In 1937 the government developed the implications of this concept through a sliding scale of priorities: air defences, preserving sea trading routes, and defending overseas British territories. The final and least important was the defence of allied territories, prompting the army to be tasked with defending 'imperial commitments including anti-aircraft defence at home'.[22] It was not to be rebuilt but was instead to receive 'deficiency' programmes to fill gaps. Yet activity remained modest as only seventy-four tanks were produced between March 1936 and December 1937, while none were imported.[23] By 1938 the army remained unequipped to fight a large-scale land war.

PLANNING MANUFACTURING CAPACITY

While the UK's rearmament lagged behind Germany, it was a significant programme directed from Whitehall via a labyrinthine committee system. The apex was the Committee on Imperial Defence, chaired by the Prime Minister and tasked with overall coordination. Its most important sub-committee was the Chiefs of Staff committee that advised on defence policy, but it was joined by the mid-1930s by many other standing sub-committees such as Principal Supply Officers, Manpower, Defence Plans (policy), Defence Plans (requirements), and Food Supply in Time of War. Many sat atop their own pyramid systems, such as the Principal Supply Officers sub-committee which from 1933 began to identify firms that could be called on in an emergency to produce war material.[24] It drew on subordinate bodies including a Supply Board to estimate deficiencies between wartime requirements and production forecasts, as well as an inter-service Contracts Co-ordinating Committee.[25]

Meanwhile, task-specific committees were convened. As an example, the Food Supply in Time of War Sub-Committee appointed one headed by Sir William Beveridge to examine food rationing. Others, such as those directing the location of factories created by rearmament, drew on private sector expertise. The system was administratively strengthened in 1936 by the appointment of Sir Thomas Inskip as Minister for the Co-ordination of Defence, while Cabinet Secretariat civil servants provided committees with secretariats. All these committees began to plan rearmament, but the government remained determined to control expenditure and avoid large-scale industrial planning.

Two factors meant that Welsh interests were poorly represented within Whitehall. One was the absence of a devolved territorial government department. Yet concern as to the social impacts of depression throughout Britain's peripheral areas forced the government to designate such areas as 'Special Areas' in 1934 and appoint Commissioners to stimulate growth in such areas. Nevertheless, South Wales Special Areas Commissioner Malcolm Stewart could do little but build a few factories and commission small schemes to alleviate social distress. He lobbied for munitions factories to be placed in the region but the desperate tone of an appeal to the Ministry of Labour in 1935 highlighted his limited influence. He argued that 'unless the government show their own confidence in south Wales' by establishing a munitions factory 'what chance have I to persuade any private employer to go there?'[26] His appeals were ignored as in 1935 factories opened in London numbered 213 compared to none in the South Wales Special Area, and he resigned in the subsequent year.[27]

Commissioners' powers were enhanced by a second Special Areas Act in 1937 that extended their ability to construct factories and offer financial support. However, these powers did not equate to state industrial planning and although Commissioners did achieve some successes through their South Wales and Monmouthshire Trading Estates subsidiary that constructed an industrial estate at Treforest and factories including those in Merthyr Tydfil, their overall impact was marginal. Commissioners in south Wales helped to create perhaps 5,000 jobs on their sites by 1938, while persuading industrialists to open plants elsewhere created a further few thousand.[28] Many delegations of MPs and councillors asked Whitehall for greater support to bring munition and civilian factories to Wales but were rebuffed.

The other factor hampering the representation of Welsh interests was how the lack of industrial diversification prompted a paucity of manufacturing leaders of status sufficient to lobby creditably in Whitehall. In contrast, the more advanced institutions of Scotland enabled its interests to be articulated effectively. The most important was its territorial government department, the Scottish Office, that was headed by a Cabinet level Secretary of State whose membership of many Whitehall committees such as that on Food Supply in Time of War enabled ready access to the governing machine.[29] The more diversified and integrated nature of Scotland's economy also meant that the Scottish Office could draw on the support of leading business figures. One example was the Glasgow engineering magnate Lord Weir chairing a sub-committee instrumental in dispersing aircraft factories to the benefit of Scotland. The presence of powerful Scottish industrialists also meant that the Scottish Office could support a new Scottish Economic Committee formed from such figures, which enthusiastically lobbied for contracts to be awarded to Scottish firms.[30] Both factors combined to ensure that Welsh interests were marginalised throughout the 1930s, while the state itself was reluctant to involve itself in any activity that resembled planning, a view that changed only gradually as rearmament gained momentum.

CREATING MANUFACTURING CAPACITY IN WALES

The munitions industry divided broadly into government owned and operated plants, and privately owned factories working under contract. Crucially, uncertainty as to whether war would break out meant that the government could not rely on the private sector to create new production capacity, as demand and financial returns were uncertain. Some private sector activity existed, such as the Curran metal works in Cardiff producing cartridge cases from 1937, but these firms were few. Uncertainty prompted the government to develop and disperse its own industrial capacity, with the Committee for Imperial Defence arguing apathetically in 1936 that 'little can be done [in peacetime] to alter the location of industry'.[31] Rearmament was conceived partly as a response to potential enemy air action, prompting interest in Wales. In 1934 the Government's Air Council divided the UK into safe, unsafe and dangerous zones based on proximity to the continent. Unsurprisingly, London and eastern England were 'dangerous', the midlands was 'unsafe' while Wales was 'safe'.[32] Wales suddenly became a potentially suitable location for munitions factories, and the government began to steer these to Wales although the process was protracted and uneven.

The most important mechanism was expanding the state-owned Royal Ordnance Factories (ROFs). These were divided into filling factories to load cartridges with cordite and produce fuses, explosives factories to make material to be used by filling factories, and engineering factories producing items such as gun barrels and artillery shells. Three such factories existed in 1936, in Woolwich, Enfield and Waltham Abbey.[33] All were in 'dangerous' southeast England and were dispersal priorities, although departmental and budgetary tensions complicated the processes of site selection and factory construction. The first step in establishing new factories was the establishment of an inter-departmental Committee chaired by Sir Douglas Hacking to propose locations. It considered south Wales, but service chiefs argued that the region was vulnerable to enemy air action given proximity to the continent and the navigational marker of the Severn estuary. They also argued that transferred workers 'might not like the class of house (miners etc.) available' in Wales.[34] A location near Wrexham was also rejected as too close to built-up areas.[35] The committee instead proposed locations including Oswestry in Shropshire and former explosives factories at Gretna in Scotland and Queensferry in north Wales.[36]

In April 1935, however, the government rejected these recommendations as impractical and ordered a further review of the potential of Special Areas to host new factories. But this review also dismissed south Wales given its distance from midlands shell case manufacturers and exposure to air raid risk. The government instead chose a site in Chorley in Lancashire. Chorley was not in a Special Area and its local unemployment was lower than in Bridgend,[37] although skilled labour was available including women used to factory work. Nevertheless, politicians felt obliged to make a gesture to south Wales. Chamberlain supported siting a factory south Wales for political reasons, most likely linked to the national debate over regional economic and social distress,[38] even though its 'liability to flooding' was raised as a barrier in the Cabinet meeting approving the Chorley factory.[39]

Concerns led to the creation of another committee, chaired by Sir Arthur Robinson, to consider south Wales.

This committee eventually settled on a flat site with good rail connections at Bridgend, where in March 1936 the government approved a filling plant initially to employ some 500 workers on a 900-acre site.⁴⁰ The political importance of the plant was symbolised by its announcement during a parliamentary debate on the Special Areas. Lord President of the Council Ramsey MacDonald, charged with coordinating government business, outlined the government's aim to 'plan new industries within those areas' when rearming.⁴¹ The Bridgend factory became the largest factory in employment terms ever seen in Wales, but its gestation reflected the piecemeal nature of rearmament. The site was bought in July 1936, but construction was held back for a year as the Treasury withheld approval. It argued that Bridgend could be delayed, saving money, as Chorley could satisfy current requirements.⁴² Construction finally began in mid-1937 and almost 900 construction workers were employed by mid-1938 prompting the virtual elimination of male unemployment and what the *Western Mail* reported as 'jubilation' in the surrounding area.⁴³

The Robinson committee also examined sites for a smaller explosives factory, recommending one at Pembrey used similarly in the First World War. It offered advantages including isolation, existing buildings on a large site and proximity to unemployed labour.⁴⁴ The proposal was, however, rejected in late 1936 by the Treasury given the absence of a comprehensive armaments programme from the War Office but, once a plan appeared, it was approved in June 1937.⁴⁵

Meanwhile, the navy argued that the new factories were insufficient to meet its demands for specialised munitions and, after prolonged inter-service dispute, a site at Glascoed in Monmouthshire was selected for a ROF in July 1937. Approving construction took a leisurely three months, as did obtaining land access for surveys. Construction finally began in spring 1938.⁴⁶ The final filling factory authorised was a Royal Navy Propellant Factory whose selection criteria included access to a railway line, labour availability and water supply. Caerwent in Monmouthshire was selected in April 1938, primarily because of its proximity to a pumping station evacuating water from the Severn rail tunnel.[47] Nevertheless, large ships were not to be constructed in Wales, where there were no large private shipyards and the only Royal Dockyard, at Pembroke, had closed in 1926.[48] As well as filling and explosive factories, the government constructed engineering ROFs in Lancashire and Nottingham but officials tended to see Wales as unsuitable given its lack of precision engineering traditions. Factory managers agreed; those responsible for an engineering ROF in Newport constructed after 1938 argued initially that they would struggle to obtain suitable labour given the lack of such factories in the surrounding area.[49]

The other state mechanisms building industrial capacity were the overlapping shadow and agency factory schemes, with both reflecting a reluctance to consider state-run factories apart from the ROFs and Admiralty facilities.[50] Rearmament was instead characterised by cooperation between the government and private sector, an early indicator of which was the shadow factory programme. It was conceived in 1934 when the government asked industrialists Lord Weir, Sir Arthur Balfour and Sir James Lithgow to review armaments production. One of their recommendations was that automobile companies should also build aircraft, through a process of 'shadowing' aircraft manufacturers to gain skills and knowledge. After a slow start, the programme evolved and by 1938 'agency factories' were provided at government expense to be managed by aircraft companies receiving fixed fees, and bonuses linked to production.[51]

The expanding aircraft industry was mostly located in the south and midlands of England and the prospect of attracting advanced manufacturing to Wales enticed politicians. However, the location of new factories was influenced by company managements who preferred sites near to existing concentrations of industry. Special Areas were neglected but their demands reached national prominence in 1937 when the government announced a site near Reading for an airframe factory to be managed by the Bristol Aeroplane Co. and Rootes. The government had tried to persuade their management to locate the new factory elsewhere, but the Cabinet heard that Rootes had 'definitively declined to run the factory if it was situated in south Wales on account of their fear of labour trouble'.[52] A furious political reaction prompted the government to review the decision, but Wales was again discounted in favour of Lancashire.

The exception to the generalised reluctance to locate more advanced factories in Wales was the Vickers Armstrong plant at Broughton in northeast Wales. Production of the Wellington twin engine medium bomber was concentrated at Weybridge in Surrey but this factory reached capacity by mid-1936. Vickers Armstrong then approached the government with plans to construct a new factory close to engineering concentrations in northwest England. The government accepted the company's proposals and construction commenced in November 1937 at Broughton in northeast Wales, with the factory located adjacent to the border with England.[53]

The final mechanism to increase production was agency factories. These used private sector expertise at public expense, so were state-owned factories under commercial management as were most shadow factories by 1938. Their justifications were to ensure public control of some strategic production, and to attract more firms to participate by removing the requirement for them to contribute working capital.[54] The programme focused initially on chemical and explosives production, mostly by Imperial Chemical Industries (ICI). ICI's Billingham plant was the UK's most important manufacturer of the ammonia vital to manufacturing explosives but was located on England's east coast where it was vulnerable to air raids. A government sub-committee headed by ICI Chair John Rodgers argued in

1935 that the loss of Billingham's capacity would have 'very serious' consequences. It recommended the construction of four ammonia plants in locations including south Wales to take 'into consideration the requirements of the distressed areas'.[55] Merthyr Tydfil was considered but reluctance from ICI management combined with the emergence of expansion plans at Billingham to delay any decision.

PREPARING THE RESOURCE-BASED INDUSTRIES FOR WAR

The extent to which the three resource-based industries of coal, steel and agriculture were the subject of planning for war varied. The government was reluctant to plan any intervention in the coal mining industry given its turbulent history. Coal mining had been gradually and unevenly brought under government control in the First World War amidst friction between owners and unions.[56] The fractious industry, however, was soon returned to private ownership but the state was gradually pulled towards some intervention amidst depression and industrial unrest. From 1930 it mandated industry-led cartels to set prices and impose production quotas before announcing plans to stimulate amalgamation. Nevertheless, the fragmented industry struggled while the south Wales coalfield was beset by turbulent industrial relations and geological problems. By 1938 the proportion of coal cut mechanically in south Wales was the lowest in the UK, as was its productivity.[57]

In 1936 the government's Mines Department argued that the industry could meet the UK's estimated annual wartime demand of 267 million tons, even though production in that year was only 228.4 million tons.[58] Their overall assumption was that peacetime ownership and control methods would suffice during wartime, although such assumptions conveniently masked the government's reluctance to intervene. Some reluctance was attributable to how its control of prices and wages during the First World War had embroiled the state in the chronic problems characterising the industry. Moreover, the torrid inter-war years had prompted endemic distrust amongst the well-organised workforce as to the motivations and behaviour of mine owners and governments; the latter viewed the industry and its turbulent politics with wary distrust. The industry struggled as increased demand from rearmament was insufficient to offset export markets lost during the First World War. A survey of the south Wales coalfield stated in 1937 that while there had been 'a measure of recovery', a 'mass of chronic unemployment' remained in place, 'peculiar to this and other regions which have not developed large new industries to compensate for contraction of basic industries'.[59]

The government, however, was more favourable towards metal manufacturing, whose modernisation, prompted in part by the demands of newer industries such as car manufacturing, was embodied in the new or expanded plants opened by the late 1930s. Ebbw Vale hosted Britain's first continuous hot strip mill that was far more efficient than the unmechanised and labour-intensive hand mills that had dominated tinplate production, while a steelworks at Cardiff became one of the most modern medium-sized works in Europe.[60] Meanwhile, increased domestic demand enabled the tinplate industry, whose UK activities were clustered in south Wales, to mitigate its falling share of the global export trade, although demand was prompted by the popularity of tinned foods and not by rearmament.[61] The privately owned industry voluntarily coordinated its activities through the British Iron and Steel Federation, created in the mid-1930s as a cartelised trade association in return for extended import tariffs.[62] By this time, the government was considering how to control wartime raw materials production. It planned to convert trade associations into control functions although exceptions were made within industries partially covered by associations or where trade was controlled by one firm.[63]

Within agriculture, the government was determined to extend planning given institutional and popular memories of food shortages in the First World War, and the scale of the gap between domestic production and consumption. Planning began in 1935 when Minister of Agriculture Walter Elliot appointed a committee representing his England and Wales Department, and those of Scotland and Northern Ireland, to consider wartime food production. In 1936 it reported on production deficiencies, the worst of which was flour where the UK imported 85 per cent of its calorific requirements. The committee warned against repeating the delayed response of the First World War and proposed swift action to secure supplies of labour, machinery and fertiliser, conclusions accepted by the Food Supply Sub-Committee of the all-powerful Committee of Imperial Defence.[64]

Over the next two years, the government readied systems to ration food and boost output, assisted from 1936 through a decentralised and Treasury-funded Farm Management Survey, with Wales data collected by staff at University College of Wales, Aberystwyth.[65] Food rationing was discussed by the 1936 Beveridge Report, while in early 1937 the Ministry of Food and Agriculture proposed that an assumed 25 per cent decrease in food imports could be offset by 'ploughing up' pastures for reuse as arable. Such ambitions required administrative machinery to ensure that central policy was implemented by the thousands of farms throughout the UK. The government planned to realise its aims through more powerful versions of the county level committees that had coordinated and managed agriculture during the First World War.[66]

These new committees were to be known as County War Executive Committees. They were comprised, at least in theory, of farmers, farm workers, local officials and those active within bodies such as the Women's Institute. In mid-1937 the Ministry wrote to prospective chairmen inviting them to apply for such posts, although committees were not to be constituted until the outbreak of war. Although there was no territorial government department in Wales, some administrative devolution existed as the Ministry's Welsh Department at Aberystwyth was responsible for Wales-specific administrative issues. Its secretary, Cadwaladr Bryner Jones, exerted considerable influence as the Agricultural Commissioner for Wales responsible for administration of government schemes within livestock improvement and education.[67] Nevertheless, he held less authority than his equivalents in Scotland, where an administratively devolved government department used its autonomy to design more centralised systems.[68]

CONCLUSION

Appeasement did not rule out rearmament, but instead restricted it within a limited and largely defensive programme. The volume of employment throughout the UK created by rearmament is subject to conflicting estimates,[69] but most direct jobs were created in industries with little presence in Wales and few in the areas most impacted by economic depression. The long-lasting nature of economic weaknesses in much of Wales were illustrated in August 1936 when the Minister of Health and the Minister for Labour submitted a memorandum to the cabinet asking for 'additional and immediate assistance' for Merthyr Tydfil, many of whose inhabitants 'were giving up hope ... as they see themselves destitute in the midst of returning and increasing prosperity in the country generally'.[70] Nevertheless, some impacts were apparent through employment in new factories or their construction and supply chains, and in supplying factories elsewhere while the construction of the ROFs and Admiralty facilities created many construction jobs. All this meant that although unemployment in Wales declined from its peak in August 1932 of 39.9 percent, it still stood at

24.4 per cent in March 1938, almost double the UK level and equivalent to 160,524 people.[71]

The most important explanation for the limited impact of rearmament in Wales was its slow pace. Delays were partly attributable to the difficulty of persuading governments or industrialists to choose it as a factory location, especially for activities such as engineering and aircraft that required higher level skills. Industrialists and officials tended to view Wales as an unsuitable location and were unwilling to locate there unless compelled, while factories constructed by the end of the decade were usually basic manufacturing facilities requiring fewer skills than elsewhere. Moreover, the lack of home-grown secondary manufacturing industrialists and the absence of territorial governance structures meant that Welsh interests were often excluded from Whitehall considerations.

Partial economic recovery in Wales was not driven by rearmament but instead by rapid growth in 'inner Britain' where rising real incomes in these areas drove demand for household goods, cars and housing. Although new manufacturing industries were generally located in such areas, they often turned to Wales for raw materials. Moreover, a start had been made in using Wales as a state-driven production location, while the speed at which Europe reached the brink of war in 1938 was soon to transform the attitude and approaches of government, and its impact on regional economies.

Notes

1 G. Peden, *British Rearmament and the Treasury, 1932–1939* (Scottish Academic Press, 1979), pp. 6–7.
2 TNA, CAB 24/229/5, *Note by the Treasury on the Annual Review for 1932 by the Chiefs of Staff Sub-Committee.*
3 *Statement Relating to Defence* (Cmd 4827) (HMSO, 1935), 5.
4 TNA, CAB 24/261/11, *Possible Despatch of an International Force to the Rhineland*, 18 March 1936, 2.
5 Wilt, *Food for War*, p. 54.

6   A. Tooze, *The Wages of Destruction: The Making and Breaking of the Nazi Economy* (Penguin, 2007), pp. 208–9.
7   Shay, *British Rearmament in the Thirties*, p. 88.
8   Shay, *British Rearmament in the Thirties*, p. 289; Rollings, 'Whitehall and the Control of Prices and Profits in a Major War, 538–9.
9   Shay, *British Rearmament in the Thirties*, pp. 132–3; Peden, *British Rearmament*, p. 3.
10 TNA, CAB 64/5, *Winston Churchill to Sir Thomas Inskip*, 25 May 1936, 2.
11 Peden, *British Rearmament*, p. 207.
12 TNA, CAB 23/86/4, *Cabinet Conclusions*, 4 November 1936, 18.
13 Peden, *British Rearmament*, 205; B. Holman, 'The Air Panic of 1935: British Press Opinion between Disarmament and Rearmament', *Journal of Contemporary History*, 46/2 (2011), 288–307.
14 Hansard (Commons), 10 November 1932, vol. 270, col. 632; 6 October 1938, vol. 339, col. 545.
15 W. Hornby, *Factories and Plant* (HMSO, 1958), p. 200.
16 *Statistical Digest of the War* (HMSO, 1951), p. 152.
17 TNA, CAB 64/9, *Air Defence Position at 1st January 1938*, 1–2,4.
18 G. A. H. Gordon, *British Seapower and Procurement Between the Wars* (Naval Institute Press, 1988), p. 264; C. Miller, *Planning and Profits: British Naval Armaments Manufacture and the Military-Industrial Complex, 1918–1941* (Liverpool University Press, 2018), p. 222.
19 M. M. Postan, *British War Production* (HMSO, 1952), p. 27.
20 Postan, *British War Production*, p. 27.
21 TNA, CAB 3/6/205, *Memorandum by the Home Defence Sub-Committee the Committee for Imperial Defence*, 1935.
22 TNA, CAB 24/273/41, *Defence expenditure in Future Years: Interim Report by the Minister for Coordination of Defence*, December 1937, 7, 10.
23 *Statistical Digest of the War*, p. 148.
24 TNA, BT168/18, *Note on Capacity Allocation Register*, 10 May 1943, 1.
25 J. D. Scott and R. Hughes, *The Administration of War Production* (HMSO, 1955), p. 54.
26 TNA, LAB 25/6, *Letter from Commissioner Stewart to Ministry of Labour*, 21 October 1935.
27 *Third Report of the Commissioner for Special Areas* (Cmd 5303) (HMSO, 1936), 8; T. Rowlands, *'Something Must Be Done': South Wales V Whitehall, 1921–1951* (TTC Books, 2000), pp. 95–7.
28 L. Gooberman, *From Depression to Devolution: Government and Economy in Wales, 1934–2006* (University of Wales Press, 2017), pp. 15–22.
29 TNA, CAB 16/156, *Minutes of Sub-Committee on Food Supply in Time of War*, 1 July 1936.
30 A. MacKenzie, '"Public-spirited men": Economic Unionist Nationalism in Inter-War Scotland', *The Scottish Historical Review*, Volume XCVI, 1/242 (2017), 87–109 (103).
31 *The War Effort at the Curran Works* (Curran: 1945), p. 3; TNA, CAB 3/6/262, *Committee of Imperial Defence, Air Raid Precautions*, August 1937.

32 P. Scott, *Triumph of the South: A Regional Economic History of Early Twentieth Century Britain* (Ashgate, 2007), p. 276.
33 Hornby, *Factories and Plant*, p. 77.
34 TNA, LAB 25/6, *Removal of Ordnance Factories*, 7 November 1935, 3.
35 TNA, CAB 102/625, *The Histories of 22 Royal Ordnance Factories 1881–1944*.
36 TNA, CAB 3/6/208, *Report of the Committee of the Removal of the Royal Ordnance Factories*, December 1934, 15.
37 Rowlands, *Something Must Be Done*, p. 147.
38 TNA, CAB 102/625, *The Histories of 22 Royal Ordnance Factories 1881–1944*, 1.
39 TNA, CAB 23/82, *Cabinet Papers*, 31 July 1935, 6.
40 TNA, CAB 3/6/233, *Report of the Interdepartmental Committee on the Removal of parts of the Royal Ordnance Factories*, February 1936, 11; LAB 25/6, *Committee on Removal of Ordnance Factories*, 7 November 1935, 5.
41 Hansard (Commons), *2 March 1936, vol. 309, col. 1041*.
42 TNA, CAB 102/627, *Construction of Filling Factories*, 6.
43 Hansard (Commons), *23 May 1938, vol. 336, col. 871–2W*; *Western Mail*, 'Bridgend Pleased', *4 March 1938*.
44 TNA, CAB 102/625, *Histories of 22 ROFs*, 2.
45 TNA, CAB 102/628, *Construction of Explosives Factories*, 13.
46 TNA, CAB 102/625, *Histories of 22 ROFs*, 5.
47 *Western Mail*, 'Farm Land as Factory Site', 8 April 1938.
48 L. Phillips. *Pembroke Dockyard and the Old Navy: A Bicentennial History* (The History Press, 2014), pp. 46–8.
49 TNA, CAB 102/629, *ROF Newport*, 1.
50 N. Forbes, 'Democracy at a disadvantage? British rearmament, the shadow factory scheme and the coming of war, 1936-40', *Economic History Yearbook/Jahrbuch für Wirtschaftsgeschichte* (2014), 49–70 (67).
51 W. Ashworth, *Contracts and Finance* (HMSO, 1953), p. 150.
52 TNA, CAB 23/82, *Cabinet Papers*, 25 January 1937, 11.
53 D. Berryman, *North Wales Airfields in the Second World War* (Countryside Books, 2013), p. 44; D. Smith, *Hawarden: A Welsh Airfield, 1939–1979* (Clarington Press, 1980), p. 1.
54 Hornby, *Factories and Plant*, p. 157.
55 TNA, CAB 16/168, *Letter to the Air Ministry, 14 August 1936*.
56 G. Holmes, 'The First World War and Government Control', in C. Baber and L. J. Williams (eds), *Modern South Wales: Essays in Economic History* (University of Wales Press, 1986), pp. 206–21 (p. 219).
57 Supple, *The History of the British Coal Industry, Volume 4*, p. 317.
58 W. H. B. Court, *Coal* (HMSO, 1951), p. 29; Supple, *The History of the British Coal Industry, Volume 4*, p. 8.
59 Wales National Industrial Development Council, *The Second Industrial Survey of Wales, Volume 1* (University Press Board, 1937), p. 388.
60 B. S. Keeling and A. E. G Wright, *The Development of the Modern British Steel Industry* (Longmans, 1964), p. 15; E. Jones, *A History of GKN, Volume 2, 1918–1945* (Macmillan, 1990), p. 133.

61 W. E. Minchanton, *The British Tinplate Industry* (Clarendon Press, 1957), pp. 182–3.
62 J. C. Carr and W. Taplin, *History of the British Steel Industry* (Basil Blackwell, 1962), pp. 499–500.
63 Keeling and Wright, *The Development of the Modern British Steel Industry*, p. 31; J. Hurstfield, *The Control of Raw Materials* (HMSO, 1953), pp. 68–9.
64 TNA, CAB 16/157, *Sub-Committee on Food Production in Time of War, Report*, April 1936; Wilt, *Food for War*, p. 68.
65 R. Moore-Colyer, *Farming in Wales, 1936–2011* (Y Lolfa, 2011), pp. 92–3.
66 B. Short, *The Battle of the Fields* (Boydell Press, 2014), p. 56.
67 J. M. Jones, Sir Cadwaladr Bryner Jones. *Dictionary of Welsh Biography*. Retrieved 1 Jun 2020, from *https://biography.wales/article/s2-JONE-BRY-1872*.
68 K. A. H. Murray, *Agriculture* (HMSO, 1955), p. 322.
69 Thomas, 'Rearmament and Economic Recovery in the late 1930s', 552–79; Crafts and Mills, 'Rearmament to the Rescue?', 1077–104.
70 TNA, CAB 24/264/4, *Joint Memorandum by the Minister of Health and the Minister of Labour*, 2 September 1936.
71 *DWHS 1700–1974, vol. 1* (ed. by Williams), pp. 144–5.

2
CRISIS AND WAR, 1938–1940

REARMAMENT ACCELERATES AND WAR BEGINS

The international situation worsened throughout 1938. Germany annexed Austria in March before claiming the Sudetenland borderlands of Czechoslovakia. Tension escalated as France was bound by treaty to assist Czechoslovakia if Germany attacked, while Britain was bound similarly to support France. War seemed imminent until September when the leaders of Britain, France, Germany and Italy met in Munich, where a German annexation of the Sudetenland was accepted in return for an assurance of no further territorial claims. Chamberlain returned to the UK declaring 'peace for our time', while public support for appeasement was widespread but not universal. Divergent opinions were apparent in Cardiff where Lord Mayor Oliver Purnell ordered that the swastika be hoisted above City Hall to fly alongside the flags of Britain, France and Italy as 'a gesture of jubilation'. Outraged councillors swiftly removed the swastika, but it was reinstated before public anger forced a second and permanent removal.[1]

The UK was not prepared for war. In October 1938 the Chiefs of Staff argued that the army could deploy two divisions to the continent but these were 'deficient of the many types of modern equipment, e.g., tanks and modern medium artillery, necessary for successful offensive operations' while the Royal Air Force (RAF) had 'practically no reserves and [was] deficient of trained personnel'.[2] Deficiencies flowed from the government's earlier decisions to ration expenditure while the Treasury remained determined to enforce restraint. In January 1939 it argued that spending more on defence would in practice reduce the UK's ability to defend itself because such expenditure would imperil economic stability and endanger subsequent budgetary allocations.[3] Yet such assumptions were soon threatened when German forces occupied Prague and the remaining Czech lands in March 1939. The occupation breached understandings reached in Munich and two weeks later Chamberlain guaranteed Polish independence. Appeasement had failed but its spirit persisted; in June 1939 the Prime Minister told a Cardiff audience that he could still help to 'establish a peaceful world in which each nation can pursue its own occupations with security and confidence'.[4]

Yet darkening international prospects had already forced the government to accelerate rearmament to the immediate benefit of the RAF. Shortly after the seizure of Austria, the Cabinet approved a new production programme, Scheme L. It proposed the manufacture of 12,000 aircraft over two years, equivalent to a doubling of the previous annual target and was the first to be conceived regardless of financial limits.[5] The aircraft industry was ordered to maximise production and even the Treasury agreed that 'the basis of this programme is now the productive capacity of this country'.[6] Monthly output rose from fewer than 200 aircraft in early 1938 to 630 in early 1939, reaching 780 in September 1939.[7] While there was much anguish about the relative strength of the air force, the removal of financial constraints combined with improving manufacturing capacity and technology to enable Britain to produce more aircraft in 1940 than Germany.[8] The pace of technological change meant that aircraft manufactured a few years earlier were outdated but, crucially, the newer Spitfires and Hurricanes could match German aircraft. Nevertheless, only one of the thirty fighter squadrons operational in late 1938 possessed Spitfires, while only five were being equipped with Hurricanes.[9]

The dismemberment of Czechoslovakia meant that the need to prepare the army for continental deployments could no longer be avoided. In October 1938 the government instructed the army to prepare five divisions for potential deployment to France. The army then asked the Treasury for sufficient funding, and the request was assessed over many subsequent weeks. The Cabinet finally approved funding in January 1939 and tight financial restraint over the army ended, although the Treasury did not release its grip fully.[10] In April the government introduced conscription and decided to construct a field force of thirty-two divisions.

Meanwhile, the Admiralty had long pressed for a 'two-power standard' to enable the navy to fight simultaneously in European and far eastern waters. While these attempts failed, the strategic importance of the navy prompted large-scale construction and refitting, although a limited capacity to produce naval armour meant that programmes were briefly dependent on imports from Czechoslovakia, while in mid-1939 attempts were even made to purchase armour plate from Germany.[11] Inter-departmental negotiations in mid-1939 over financial allocations were brutal as the Admiralty pressed to be released from rationing, during which First Sea Lord Earl Stanhope told Chancellor of the Exchequer John Simon that 'the country is dependent on its seaborne trade ... without imported petrol the RAF cannot fly. Without imported food all our air raid precautions will not protect the country from starving'.[12] Nevertheless, the navy was the last service to escape the tight financial restraints that applied until shortly before the outbreak of war.

Germany invaded Poland on 1 September 1939 and Britain declared war two days later. To the surprise of many, a devastating aerial assault on cities did not materialise. While the British Expeditionary Force was immediately dispatched to France, late 1939 and early 1940 became known as the 'phoney war'. Calmness extended to economic planning, with the official war history observing that 'the needs of war did not yet dominate the life of the nation, and economic resources were not yet fully mobilised'.[13] Calls for full economic mobilisation such as those made by John Maynard Keynes were ignored. In January 1940 he argued in 'How to Pay for the War' that compulsory savings levies were needed to divert more financial resources into the war effort. These proposals were rejected, prompting his prophetic retort in *The Times* that 'how little the country understands what sacrifices victory will require'.[14]

Although the government remained reluctant to assume powers over finance, industry and labour, it did accelerate rearmament. Continuing concerns as to the offensive potential of the Luftwaffe meant that the greatest beneficiary was again the RAF. On 22 September 1939, the War Cabinet approved a monthly production target of 2,550 aircraft by 1942 and actual production of Hurricane and Spitfire fighters increased from a peak monthly average of, respectively, 64 and 46 in 1939 to 258 and 160 in 1940.[15] Efforts to bolster the army were less successful and reflected the earlier failure to develop productive capacity and the difficulty of building wartime production without full state direction. In the first meeting of the Land Forces Committee of the War Cabinet of 7 September 1939, Churchill, appointed First Lord of the Admiralty a few days previously, proposed to create an army of at least forty divisions within a year and fifty-five over two years. However, the requirements of the army of thirty-two divisions announced in April 1939 was testing the limits of industrial capacity and Churchill's proposals were rejected as impractical.[16]

Yet the urgency of war meant that production for the army was increasing. Tank production, for example, doubled from 419 in 1938 to 969 in the following year and, by the first four months of 1940, British production matched that of Germany in numeric terms.[17] Nevertheless, the low priority given to developing new models meant that most were markedly inferior to their German counterparts. In sum, the territorial and regular armies of 1939 were poorly equipped. While the British Expeditionary Force by early 1940 comprised ten well-equipped mechanised infantry divisions and a tank brigade,[18] equipment and supplies elsewhere were in short supply. Deficiencies suffered by army units in Wales were exposed by county-level welfare organisations established by the government to channel public support. That for Glamorgan contacted army units stationed locally to ask what they needed, only to receive a reaction described as 'overwhelming and almost alarming' with a 'limitless appeal for woollen comforts, wireless sets, furniture, stoves ... and the hundred and one items that could not be supplied from official sources'.[19] Finally, while the navy at last received permission to plan for a two-power standard, it concentrated on constructing smaller vessels to escort merchant convoys helping the UK to import goods to supplement domestic production.

The outbreak of war inevitably eclipsed regional policies, although the Royal Commission on the Distribution of Industrial Population, created in 1937 and known as the Barlow Commission, continued to work. It reported in January 1940 and argued that the 'drift of the industrial population to London and the home counties' was 'a social, economic, and strategic problem which demands immediate attention'.[20] The Commission's majority report proposed a national decentralisation authority with functions including the control of industrial location and the development of garden cities.[21] This identification of a national problem as opposed to separate regional difficulties was the culmination of inter-war thinking on the topic, but government was unsurprisingly preoccupied.

The 'phoney war' ended with the military catastrophes of mid-1940. In April German forces invaded Denmark and Norway, while a shambolic British attempt to hold Norwegian ports failed. Chamberlain was blamed even though Churchill as First Lord of the Admiralty was responsible. The House of Commons turned against Chamberlain during the Norway debate of 8th May and Churchill became Prime Minister two days later.

PLANNING MANUFACTURING CAPACITY

The outbreak of war prompted high-level administrative change as the government replaced the Committee of Imperial Defence and its sub-committees with a War Cabinet. It also created new ministries, including one for food to control all aspects of production and distribution. The Ministry of Food needed a large bureaucracy in a safe location, and plans were prepared to evacuate its headquarters to Colwyn Bay. The government also established a Ministerial Priority Committee to adjudicate resource allocations. Decisions on other matters were taken by sub-committees established to adjudicate demands for production, manpower, labour, works, buildings and transport. Yet the new system symbolised the problems of continuing peacetime approaches to production and procurement as, while the sub-committee on materials and production had met forty times by April 1940, the government's reluctance to control labour supply meant that the Labour Sub-committee had little to do and never met.[22] Meanwhile, sub-committees were comprised of representatives of competing interests, hampering their ability to act as adjudicators. Finally, the entire system was cumbersome with Churchill aptly describing it as a 'fearsome array'.[23]

The transitional nature of rearmament was matched by the tentative emergence of planning. The crucial debate was whether Britain required a Ministry of Supply to enforce priority for munitions. Secretary of State for Labour Ernest Brown claimed in January 1939 that preparations were inadequate as only 35 per cent of Britain's engineering capacity was engaged in defence work. Although Chamberlain was reluctant to abandon the fundamentals of a peacetime economy, by mid-1939 action to tackle production bottlenecks was necessary. A compromise emerged in April when a Ministry of Supply was established to supply the army with all its requirements, provide 'common stores' to all services including small arms, ammunition and wheeled vehicles, as well as supervise raw materials production and use throughout the economy.[24]

Yet the government remained unwilling to assume full powers of direction over industry, instead preferring to retain standard commercial approaches to procurement whenever possible.[25] The Ministry of Supply assumed the War Office's procurement responsibilities for army supplies and many items common to the three services, but the Admiralty and the Air Ministry argued successfully that they should retain procurement responsibilities as their specialist knowledge would be diluted if these were subsumed into a common function.[26] The Ministry of Supply collated a '392' register of engineering contractors, their production load, and the Ministry supplied by them,[27] but while this database helped identify potential contractors, it was no substitute for central direction. Finally, the low status of the new Ministry of Supply was reflected by its Minister, Leslie Burgin, a little-known former Transport Minister.

All this meant that the outbreak of war barely impacted on production governance even as the army risked being unable to obtain sufficient uniforms for its conscripts.[28] Meanwhile, around thirty production directorates within the three supply ministries procured goods but were what officials described as 'watertight concerns' competing with one another to source goods.[29] Regional structures later became essential components of the planning system but had inauspicious beginnings. The initial Britain-wide structure subsumed Wales into a West of England Area directed from an office in Bristol. By the start of 1940 the *Western Mail* reported that Welsh firms seeking munitions contracts had 'found it most difficult to establish any real contact with the Ministry', while Ministry staff were 'only ... able to suggest a visit to inspect certain samples on view at Bristol with a view to tendering'. An editorial concluded glumly that there was 'nothing comparable with the war purposes activity of 1914–18 ... hundreds of small firms wait on the doorstep for orders'.[30]

In late 1939, however, the government had divided the UK into twelve civil defence regions including Wales, and in January 1940 the Ministry of Supply established concurrent Area Boards. Boards were comprised from regional representatives of the three supply ministries as well as the Ministry of Labour, supported by Advisory Committees whose members were nominated by the Trades Union Congress (TUC) and employer bodies.[31] They were to coordinate manufacturing but had little access to information and even less authority, while their secretariats usually comprised one retired civil servant. Their initial activities included arranging exhibitions of sample goods that could be inspected by firms who could propose their manufacture, but the samples covered a narrow range of goods and 80 per cent of the manufacturing offers made were for wooden boxes. Boards were supported by twenty-member advisory committees including employer representatives, but these cumbersome bodies lacked purpose and most expired in a few months. Finally, the Ministry of Supply and the Air Ministry employed Regional Officers, but they lacked authority over ministerial staff in their own regions.[32]

As rearmament accelerated, so too did localised labour shortages and poaching of skilled workers.[33] Shortages could in theory be addressed by directing labour into priority industries, creating new skilled labour through training, and diluting workplace demarcations agreed between employers and unions. But the government did not want to direct labour, and training would take time. The alternative was dilution, but the government was reluctant to imperil industrial peace and unions guarded their hard-won demarcations; the TUC argued in October 1939 that women should not be allowed to work in factories at night.[34] Meanwhile, Air Ministry attempts to instruct aircraft manufacturers to break the Factory Acts limiting working hours were firmly rebuffed by the Home Office given their fear of industrial unrest.[35] In general, the government was reluctant to act, apart from a Schedule of Reserved Occupations introduced in 1938 that excluded some skilled workers from conscription. The state remained wedded to pre-war concepts of non-interference and wanted to avoid conflict with unions, and little was done to marshal labour throughout the 'phoney war'.

FACTORIES IN WALES

Despite rearmament's fitful nature, momentum was apparent in Wales by 1938 even if the Merthyr Express observed in June that rearmament had 'not helped south Wales much so far'.[36] From 1933 to 1938, the Board of Trade estimated that new factory projects in Wales comprised 1.6 per cent of the UK total, but this average obscured an improving performance that reached 4.5 per cent by 1938.[37]

The most visible impact was the construction of three types of government owned ROFs. The first and largest was vast ammunition filling factories. Each featured up to twenty miles of light railways, forty miles of roads, and several thousand buildings or underground facilities including textile factories, locomotive sheds, joinery shops, engineering facilities, power stations, administration blocks, hostels and warehouses.[38] Construction was, however, characterised by delay, acceleration once war broke out, and continual confusion. Delay was illustrated by the Bridgend ROF, although its 3,600 construction labourers prompted unemployment in the surrounding area to halve by November 1938. This construction workforce rose to 4,600 by April 1939 but carpenters and bricklayers were in short supply, while the lack of national planning prompted uncertainty as to how 30 million bricks could be sourced.[39] The Treasury, however, remained determined to restrain expenditure. In June 1939 the Ministry of Supply argued that 'full emergency powers' could enable the factory to be completed by the end of the year. Weeks passed until the proposal was, remarkably, rejected in August given the cost of overtime labour. This mistaken decision was exposed by the outbreak of war when the government finally prioritised construction as 'before all other government departments whatsoever'.[40]

Yet prioritisation meant little as peacetime approaches to labour still prevailed, typified by farcical attempts in October 1939 to recruit labour. A contractor needed 300 carpenters and sent a foreman to London to obtain them. He placed an advert in the *Daily Herald* for a well-paid 'government job' inviting applicants to apply in person at a local office. Staff at this office were promptly overwhelmed by 1,400 men and were forced to close early after selecting 350. However, 500 then arrived at the train station expecting to be taken to Wales but officials at the station could not identify those selected and all 500 were transported to lodgings in Porthcawl. These men then discovered that their accommodation and travel costs were not to be paid by their new employer as had been promised. All refused to work, negotiations failed, and they returned to London.[41]

Recruitment problems aside, construction accelerated. Seven thousand construction workers were on site by November 1939 while 2,350 production employees had been recruited by mid-1940.[42] Recruiting production labour was straightforward, as the official war historian observed that Bridgend had the least recruitment difficulty of any filling factory in the UK given localised unemployment. This contrasted with other sites such as those in Lancashire where surplus labour had been absorbed into new engineering and aircraft factories of a type yet to reach Wales in volume.[43]

The construction of the second filling factory in Wales, Glascoed, followed a similar sequence. In April 1938 ROF management proposed to depart from normal processes by awarding a contract to an on-site firm without an open tender. The Treasury then leisurely considered the request for four months before granting approval.[44] Nevertheless, 6,000 construction workers were active by August 1939 and production commenced in March 1940.[45]

The second type of state-owned factories produced explosive. Three were in Wales. The first, and largest, was ROF Marchwiel, located within a few miles of Wrexham to manufacture cordite propellant for the army. Site selection illustrated how the imminence of war reversed attitudes to industrial location. The site at Wrexham was rejected in 1934 but, by 1939, a prime factor in site selection was labour availability,[46] and Wrexham was chosen. Preliminary work began in June 1939, but the Ministry of Agriculture objected to the 'sterilisation' of 2,000 acres of agricultural land and delayed construction for four months, before granting consent two days before the outbreak of war. Nevertheless, the shortage of raw materials impacted construction as railway tracks intended for internal transport were taken by the army in early 1940, prompting managers to improvise transportation using cement runways and canvas wheels. Construction restarted and was well-advanced by mid-1940. The second, smaller, explosives factory was located at Pembrey on a secluded 500-acre site. Construction commenced in early 1938 and production began in November 1939 even though the factory was incomplete. The number of production staff reached 571 in November 1939 even as 1,000 construction workers scrambled to complete the factory.[47]

The final explosives factory was the Royal Navy's propellant factory at Caerwent. The initial gestation of this factory was again leisurely. The Cabinet approved construction in November 1937 but the 1,580-acre site was not acquired until December 1938. Surveyors finally arrived on site in mid-1939 and construction commenced in September. The outbreak of war meant that work began the day after the award was awarded without agreed final costings, an approach unthinkable a few weeks earlier. The 1,300 construction workers on site by February 1940 made quick progress, helped by the Director of Navy Contracts waiving requirements for competitive tenders for machinery and plant.[48]

The third type of ROFs were engineering, created as firms involved in automotive and aircraft production lacked capacity to produce other types of war materials, while smaller companies lacked volume and efficiencies of scale. These problems prompted the creation of engineering ROFs to produce shells, cartridge cases and fuses. In total, twenty-five factories were constructed throughout the UK, twenty of which were approved between the outbreak of war and the fall of France. Most were close to concentrations of engineering activity in England, but two were approved in Wales up to mid-1940. One was in Cardiff to produce munitions including anti-tank gun barrels, a process that required advanced machining skills. The Treasury approved the factory in November 1939 and construction was underway by the following March.[49] The other was sited in Newport to produce guns, although it was incomplete by mid-1940. Crucially, the need to increase production meant that the concerns as to labour that had precluded south Wales as a location for skilled factories no longer applied. Both factories were to make heavy usage of initially unskilled labour, with the factory in Cardiff located by a main road between the city and the valleys to enable commuting. Meanwhile, skills deficiencies were resolved through intensive training, with technicians at engineering ROFs elsewhere breaking the production process into up to 100 sub-processes to enable skills acquisition.

The expansion in aircraft manufacturing also impacted on Wales even though none of the ten aircraft factories approved between mid-1938 and mid-1940 were located there.[50] In 1939 the Air Ministry listed forty factories it had contracted to provide aircraft or their components, but only three were in Wales. Moreover, two of these tended towards lower skill requirements as they comprised a bomb factory in Cardiff and an aluminium factory near Newport that had been approved although construction had yet to commence.[51]

The third factory was the Vickers plant at Broughton in northeast Wales. It produced Wellington bombers and benefited from government financial support of £1.07 million on construction and £432,560 on equipment.[52] Yet this exception demonstrated the reluctance to locate factories in Wales that required labour with secondary manufacturing skills. The plant's location in Wales was a geographic quirk as it was within a few hundred yards of the border and had been selected for its proximity to engineering concentrations in northwest England, prompting it to be known as the 'Chester factory'. In addition, employee skills levels were less than elsewhere as, unlike factories such as the main Vickers plant at Weybridge, Broughton was an assembly plant where 80 per cent of each aircraft was stitched together from components and sub-assemblies manufactured elsewhere,[53] supplied on a 'just in time' basis.

Nevertheless, the factory was an important industrial concern. Its core was an open-plan assembly area 1,200 feet in length and 1.5 million square feet in area, reputed to be the largest unsupported single span roof in Europe.[54] It was greeted enthusiastically by local residents, and in November 1938 the *Western Mail* reported that construction caused 'hundreds of men seeking employment [to gather] around the site … many had walked or cycled many miles in the hope of being first on the spot for a job'.[55] The first contract was placed in May 1939, for 750 aircraft. Assembly commenced in a temporary hangar before the factory was complete and the first aircraft flew in August 1939. All sub-contractors to the privately managed plant were also private. Some employed just a handful of staff and struggled financially, as demonstrated by their owners visiting the factory weekly to collect cheques.[56] The factory was fully operational by September 1939, only nine months after construction had commenced. By January 1940 it employed 1,156 people.[57]

Aside from aircraft manufacturing, the government identified companies vital to war production and ordered them to increase production through agency factories. By 1940, British Industrial Solvents, for example, was constructing a calcium carbide plant at Kenfig in south Wales. The most prominent company, however, was ICI, which received annual agency fees for its management services of between 0.5 per cent and 1.5 per cent of fixed capital cost borne by government.[58] The prominence of ICI derived from the government's aims to disperse ammonia production and be seen as addressing regional unemployment. In early 1939 it instructed ICI to locate an agency factory in Dowlais to produce ammonia, adding a methanol facility a few months later.[59] Eighty per cent of the factory was completed by September 1939 when 710 construction workers were employed, and production commenced in the following January. ICI was also ordered to construct an ammonia factory at Pembrey adjacent to the new ROF.[60] As well as conventional weapons, the government wanted to increase chemical warfare stocks to ensure that any enemy use could be met in kind. In August 1939 it approved an ICI mustard gas factory and storage facility at an isolated rural site at Rhydymwyn in northeast Wales. Work began on a complex of underground storage tunnels as well as a hundred buildings and a rail network linked to an adjacent mainline, although gas was not produced until 1941.

Finally, rearmament prompted greater activity in existing factories. A few were long established, such as the Cookes explosives plant in Penrhyndeudraeth that replaced its production of mining explosives with hand grenades, but others had been attracted by the government's fitful regional policies. By mid-1939 these included 64 businesses on the Treforest Industrial Estate occupying factories constructed by the Commissioner for Special Areas,[61] some of whom supplanted their production of clothing and luxury goods with military uniforms and badges. War demand meant that estate employment grew from 2,510 in 1939 to 6,141 in 1940, while the continuation of peacetime approaches offered opportunities and threats to the estate. The relative safety of Treforest prompted estate managers to view war as a marketing opportunity and deploy 'put your factory out of harm's way' as an advertising slogan to entice firms to relocate.[62] Businesses, however, often had other ideas. One was the Marconi Wireless Company, which considered occupying a large factory in October 1939 but subsequently withdrew citing a lack of skilled labour.[63]

Finally, rearmament benefited engineering firms given their ability to switch from producing peacetime goods to munitions manufacture with relative ease, prompting what the *Western Mail* called an 'exceptional impetus'.[64] But there were few such factories in 1940, although those contracted by the Ministry of Supply included an ICI (Metals) plant in Swansea manufacturing cartridge cases from 1939 and Metal Pressing's Caldicot factory producing bomb casings from the subsequent year.[65]

CONTROLLING RESOURCE-BASED INDUSTRIES

The patchwork nature of governance continued within the resource-based industries. The steel industry was taken under indirect state control in September 1939 through absorbing most of the British Iron and Steel Federation into the Ministry of Supply as the Iron and Steel Control.[66] It formed one of twenty-three raw materials controls, although its operational autonomy was reflected by its staff being paid by federation members, not the government. The national union representing metal manufacturing employees observed correctly that the Control's approach to industrial governance was 'voluntary' but it could nevertheless decide to impose Iron and Steel Orders to fix maximum prices and direct the type and volume of production.[67] While the Control was operated centrally from London, from February 1940 it was headed by Sir Charles Wright, Chair of the Baldwins company that operated plants throughout south Wales.[68]

Two factors were apparent within the governance of steel. One was the continuation of peacetime approaches around existing levies on steel consumers that subsidised the high costs of imported ore and machinery to reduce price distortions, prompting Ministry of Supply Permanent Secretary William

Brown to tell a parliamentary Committee of Public Accounts that the system was one 'to which the industry was accustomed, and it was working'.[69] The other was trial and error. A licensing system enabled companies to purchase steel for self-declared 'essential' categories, but such purchases accounted for 80 per cent of demand by early 1940 to prompt the near breakdown of the distribution system. Moreover, steel requirements were estimated using service requirements without any consideration of production capacity. Difficulties mounted to prompt the development of a new distribution scheme in early to mid-1940.[70]

Yet governance was helped by the modernised nature of much of the industry with, for example, large plants in Cardiff reconstructed and modernised by 1938. War saw capacity utilisation in south Wales grow from 65 per cent in October 1938 to 97 per cent in July 1939 when the union reported 'much greater activity in virtually every section' as the region vied with the northeast of England as the UK's leading producer of steel ingots and castings.[71] One source of demand was corrugated galvanised sheets for Anderson air raid shelters. The initial order in late 1939 was for 400,000 shelters to be supplied in thirteen weeks. Production was split between nineteen manufacturers, two-thirds in south Wales, and by early 1940 one thousand wagon loads of sheeting were being dispatched weekly to London.[72] Meanwhile, from 1938 the Bank of England part-funded the creation of a new continuous strip mill at the John Summers plant at Shotton. Machinery was shipped from the United States throughout 1939, and the plant entered production in November.[73] It was soon producing sheets for Anderson shelters, although the occasionally ad hoc nature of war production was reflected by product testing. A 'volunteer' sat inside a shelter and a large concrete ball normally used to break up foundry slag waste was dropped on the roof.[74] Finally, relatively calm industrial relations were reflected by the conclusion of wages agreements in late 1939 and early 1940.[75]

Other metal manufacturing was also subjected to state governance, although improvisation was apparent. Much of this was inevitable. A. G. Charles, Controller of Non-Ferrous Metals from 1940 observed that although the outline of his control was in place before war broke out, 'much that was strange and new had to be tackled' and governance 'took time to settle down'.[76] Some improvisation, however, resulted from poor planning, such as, within the production of light alloys, including the aluminium that was vital for aircraft production. The Ministry created a voluntary control formed from controllers representing the key activities of strip and sheet, extrusion, castings and forgings. Yet, instead of a central office, each operated from their own factory and held different opinions about their role. One, for example, wanted to control all orders within his remit while another wanted to minimise such intervention.

Unsurprisingly, the light metal supply position deteriorated and, by early 1940, the Society of British Aircraft Constructors asked the government to 'reorganise and strengthen' the control, prompting the May 1940 creation of a unified and statutory control.[77] In the absence of a suitable trade association, the Ministry of Supply established an Aluminium Control using the staff and organisational capabilities of a leading commercial agent, the British Metals Corporation.[78] Imports from north America increased, while domestic producers such as the Dolgarrog aluminium plant, long established in rural north Wales to take advantage of hydroelectric power, increased output. Labour availability combined with a tradition of metal manufacture to prompt Wales being favoured for new factories such as the aluminium alloy plant at Rogerstone in south Wales constructed by Northern Aluminium of Canada from 1939 to supply the aircraft industry. It was located on the site of a steelworks closed in 1934, while other favourable factors included proximity to docks and railway links to the aircraft factories of the Midlands.[79] Other plants under construction included a smaller British Aluminium Company plant in Newport, and an aluminium works at Resolven.

While the government assumed indirect control over metal manufacturing, it was far more reluctant to act within the coal industry given its long history of industrial conflict.[80] Difficulties were symbolised by thirteen strikes in south Wales during August 1939. Two of these were underway when war broke out, including one at West Blaina colliery where a dispute over piece work payments prompted 130 miners to strike for twelve days before work resumed.[81] Meanwhile, the government feared the consequences of close involvement in governing the fractious industry, and mine owners wanted to preserve their property. The government therefore left the marketing and distribution cartels it had encouraged in the 1930s largely unchanged. The mines remained privately owned and managed, the Mines Department was left untouched under the Board of Trade, and the unions were kept at arm's length even as the industry lost labour to the armed forces with one mine in Caerphilly reporting in September 1939 that 91 of its 1,000 workers had been called up.[82] The government's approach was demonstrated in October 1939 when Arthur Horner, President of the South Wales Miners' Federation sought government help to sustain a colliery. The Mines Department responded simply that it could not compel a mine owner to work a colliery at a loss or provide subsidy.[83]

Nevertheless, the government appointed officials to monitor coalfields, consuming areas and ports, and in April 1940 created two advisory mechanisms. One was a Coal Production Council comprising representatives of the industry, unions and the Mines Department. Regional Consultative Committees were also created, including one for south Wales.[84] The other was a system of district and pit production committees, formed from worker and management representatives. However, both mechanisms were advisory, meaning that the industry saw little change and employment numbers were stable. Complacency reigned in early 1940 as the Ministry of Labour noted the lack of labour supply problems throughout the Welsh coalfields, while the Board of Trade observed 'strong demand' from overseas markets.[85] Yet industrial relations were ominous as south Wales miners rejected a national settlement covering flat rate additions to their wages by a majority of nine to one.[86] Although the miners' national federation later approved the settlement, the Executive Committee of the South Wales Miners Federation noted 'considerable misunderstanding' within the workforce and ordered 20,000 copies of a speech given by Horner to be distributed to its members.[87]

While state control was indirect within metal manufacturing and absent in coal, intrusive intervention was apparent within agriculture given the need to maximise food production. The aim was not to eliminate imports but instead to conserve shipping space by boosting domestic production of arable crops by 'ploughing up' grassland. Detailed governance plans were set in motion before war broke out. The Czech crisis had prompted the Ministry of Agriculture to alert the chairs of the County War Agricultural Executive Committees (CWAECs), the Agricultural Development Act of 1939 set ploughing up subsidies, while the government contracted to buy as many tractors as Ford could produce.[88] Finally, the Women's Land Army that had served as a volunteer labour force during the First World War was reformed in June 1939.

On the day war was declared, the government instructed CWAEC chairs to activate their committees. Each comprised up to twelve members and a chair. All were unpaid and government appointed, while chairs tended to be prominent figures within agriculture recommended by the Lord Lieutenant of each county.[89] The committee in Glamorgan, for example, was headed by Hubert Alexander, an agricultural surveyor who was a magistrate, the secretary of the Glamorgan Chamber of Agriculture, a previous Chair of the South Wales and Monmouthshire Auctioneers and Estate Agents Association and had been the armed forces' recruitment officer for Barry during the First World War.[90] Committees spawned many district and topic sub-committees, prompting the *Cambrian News* to observe prophetically in early 1940 that the 'regiment of officials who have been given temporary commission to run the country will soon develop into a permanent army of occupation'.[91]

The most important initial function of the CWAECs was the 'ploughing up' campaign to convert 10 per cent of grassland into arable to produce crops such as wheat and potatoes. Each committee was allocated a quota totalling 180,000 acres throughout Wales. Farmers were encouraged by government grants of £2 per acre but were coordinated through orders issued by CWEACs to each farm. The campaign was effective, ploughing up 224,500 acres by May 1940.[92] Local variations in governance, however, appeared quickly. Some committees were known for their willingness to adjust to suit local conditions such as the Montgomeryshire district sub-committee that held a public meeting in October 1939 to explain how it would adjust targets to take account of farm conditions.[93] Yet other committees, such as those for Cardigan and Carmarthen, were less flexible and quickly became mistrusted.[94]

CWAECs held other extensive powers. Under the 1939 Defence of the Realm Act, they could inspect farms to persuade farmers to adopt techniques to maximise production. They also controlled tractors and other machinery acquired by the government, allocating them to farms where they were needed most, although very few were available in 1940.[95] If farmers failed to respond adequately to instructions, committees could evict them, although such powers were rarely used. Their powers over labour supply were embryonic, but the call-up age for agricultural workers was raised in spring 1940 and CWAECs directed Women's Land Army members to farms. Meanwhile, County Wage Committees formed from employer and employee representatives, and government appointed independent members, agreed minimum wages for agriculture before their confirmation by a Central Wages Board. Yet, by April 1940 agricultural wages were dropping behind other occupations, prompting the government to endow the Central Wages Board with powers to set minimum wages for England and Wales from April 1940, below which County Wage Boards could not set wages without permission.[96]

However, mobilisation was not yet total as the crops to be planted on ploughed up lands were not specified, prompting the Welsh Department of the Ministry of Agriculture to argue in February 1940 that 'normal peace-time activities have been continued to the maximum extent compatible with a state of war'.[97] Nevertheless, the Ministry of Food began to purchase agricultural produce from farmers at fixed prices, before selling their purchases to the retail trade at lower prices. Yet Britain-wide policy was inconsistent and occasionally counterproductive: one example was fixing wool prices at a low level to reduce the costs of manufacturing uniforms, an approach that reduced costs while exacerbating the economic plight of hill farmers.[98]

CONCLUSIONS

The governance of war production from 1938 to 1940 was fragmented and its effectiveness varied. Although *The Economist* argued in 1939 that rearmament was 'the greatest public works programme ever devised in time of formal peace',[99] its impact on Wales was belated and insufficient to undo the lingering impacts of depression. Unemployment throughout Wales grew from 1937 to 1938, falling quickly only from the middle of the subsequent year.[100] As late as March 1939 unemployment in the south Wales coalfield remained elevated at 41.5 per cent in Ferndale, 39.7 per cent in Tonypandy and 35.5 per cent in Porth.[101] Crucially, the ROFs were still under construction and only a few factories produced munitions. Subdued activity during wartime prompted the *Western Mail* to editorialise in February 1940 that 'the women are waiting, as are the unemployed men, where are the jobs?'[102] Nevertheless, rapid expansion elsewhere prompted demand for raw materials that caused capacity problems within metal manufacturing although coal mining benefited less.

The problem was that Wales remained disadvantaged by an outdated industrial structure. Manufacturing accounted for only 13 per cent of all employment, less than half that of mining, meaning that the country was not seen as a location suitable for more advanced manufacturing processes. Few factories were opening in the south Wales coalfield, although some arrived elsewhere. However, rural areas benefited as CWAEC ploughing up quotas and the beginnings of mechanisation drove increased activity. Overall, the economy remained peripheral and struggling but rapidly falling unemployment in 1939 signalled change, as geographic remoteness and abundant reserves of labour were to give Wales a central role in the all-encompassing, centrally planned economy created after 1940.

Notes

1 *Western Mail*, 'Nazi Flag Hauled Down at Cardiff City Hall', 1 October 1938.
2 TNA, CAB 16/183A, *Committee of Imperial Defence, the Czechoslovak Crisis*, October 1938.
3 Shay, *British Rearmament in the Thirties*, pp. 242–3.
4 *Western Mail*, 'Full report of the Prime Minister's Cardiff Speech', 26 June 1939.
5 J. D. Scott and R. Hughes, *The Administration of War Production* (HMSO, 1955), p. 38.
6 TNA, T161/ 905, *Proposals on Air Strength*, 28 October 1938.
7 Postan, *British War Production*, p. 66.
8 Egerton, *Britain's War Machine*, p. 66.
9 Postan, *British War Production*, p. 55.
10 Shay, *British Rearmament*, pp. 236–7.
11 Scott and Hughes, *The Administration of War Production*, p. 95.
12 TNA, T161/ 905, *First Sea Lord to Chancellor of the Exchequer*, 21 June 1939, 6.
13 Postan, *British War Production*, p. 53.
14 R. Skidelsky, *John Maynard Keynes* (Penguin, 2005), pp. 597–8.
15 Postan, *British War Production*, p. 69; W. Hornby, *Factories and Plant* (HMSO, 1958), p. 395.
16 Postan, *British War Production*, p. 74.

17 Egerton, *Britain's War Machine*, p. 60.
18 D. French, *Raising Churchill's Army: The British Army and the War against Germany 1919–1945* (Oxford University Press, 2001), p. 159.
19 *How Glamorgan Helped the Fighting Services in the World War* (Western Mail and Echo Ltd, 1946), p. 6.
20 *Royal Commission on the Distribution of the Industrial Population* (Cmd 6153) (HMSO, 1940), 202.
21 G. McCrone, *Regional Policy in Britain* (George Allen and Unwin, 1971), p. 103.
22 *Tenth Report from the Select Committee on National Expenditure* (HMSO, 1941), 4.
23 Scott and Hughes, *The Administration of War Production*, p. 409.
24 TNA, 102/272, *Ministry of Supply, Note on Responsibility for Production and Labour Supply*, 4 December 1942.
25 Shay, *British Rearmament*, p. 274.
26 Scott and Hughes, *The Administration of War Production*, pp. 16–18, 77.
27 TNA, BT168/18, *Note on Capacity Allocation Register*, 10 May 1943, 1.
28 Scott and Hughes, *The Administration of War Production*, p. 218.
29 TNA 102/613, *The Regional Organisation of the Ministry of Supply*, 2, 4.
30 *Western Mail*, 'Wales not Neglected, say Ministry', 23 January 1940; 'Wales and the Ministry of Supply', 23 January 1940.
31 *Report of the Committee on Regional Boards* (Cmd 6360) (HMSO, 1942), 2.
32 TNA, 102/503, *The Regional Organisation of the Ministry of Supply*, 1–2, 4; TNA, CAB 102/613, *Notes on the Development of Regional Organisation*, 2–3; *Report of the Committee on Regional Boards*, 5.
33 H. M. D. Parker, *Manpower* (HMSO, 1957), pp. 85–6.
34 TNA, CAB 102/275, *Report on Relaxation of the Factory Acts*, 7 October 1939.
35 TNA, CAB 102/275, *Extract from Letter from Sir Alexander Maxwell of the Home Office*, 7 October 1939.
36 *Merthyr Express*, 'Merthyr's Great Opportunity', 4 June 1938.
37 TNA, CAB 64/3119, *Nuffield College Social Reconstruction Survey, Interim Report on Location of Industry*, 1942, 56.
38 TNA, CAB 102/627, *Construction of Filling Factories*, 19.
39 M. J. Clubb, *The Welsh Arsenal* (Bridgend, 2007), pp. 40, 44.
40 TNA, CAB 102/625, *The Histories of 22 Royal Ordnance Factories 1881–1944*, 9–10.
41 TNA, LAB 8/256, *Ministry of Labour, Wales's Divisional Office to Ministry of Labour, London*, 20th October 1939. Cited in Gooberman, *From Depression to Devolution*, p. 23.
42 TNA, LAB 12/82, *Ministry of Labour Monthly Report, Wales*, 13 November 1939, 4; LAB 12/82, *Ministry of Labour Monthly Report, Wales*, 17 June 1940, 5.
43 Hornby, *Factories and Plant*, p. 102.
44 TNA, CAB 102/625, *The Histories of 22 Royal Ordnance Factories*, 6.
45 *Western Mail*, 'Local Labour First', 2 August 1939; CAB 102/625, *The Histories of 22 Royal Ordnance Factories*, 7.
46 TNA, 102/273, *The Siting of Explosives Factories*, 1.

47 TNA, CAB 102/625, *The Histories of 22 Royal Ordnance Factories 1881–1944*, 2; CAB 102/272, *Employment at ROFs, 1939–1943*; LAB 12/82, *Ministry of Labour Monthly Report, Wales*, 12 February 1940, 5.
48 R. Medwyn Parry, *A History of the Royal Navy Propellant Factory, Caerwent*; TNA, LAB 12/82, *Ministry of Labour Monthly Report, Wales*, 12 February 1940, 5.
49 M. Christensen, 'Royal Ordnance Factory, Cardiff, Llanishen, Part 1', *Quarterly Journal for British Industrial and Transport History*, 33 (2002) 31–42 (33).
50 Hornby, *Factories and Plant*, p. 224.
51 TNA, CAB 102/59, *List of Air Ministry Factories*, 1939.
52 TNA, CAB 102/274, *Government Owned Factories Operated by Contractors on Agency/Commercial Terms*, 1945.
53 Hornby, *Factories and Plant*, p. 230.
54 Berryman, *North Wales Airfields*, p. 45.
55 *Western Mail*, 'Hundreds of Men Seek Work on Factory Site', 22 November 1938.
56 Smith, *Hawarden*, pp. 3, 53–36.
57 TNA, 102/275, *Labour in Aircraft Industries*, 9 January 1940; Berryman, *North Wales Airfields*, pp. 47–8.
58 Ashworth, *Contracts and Finance*, p. 155.
59 TNA, 102/270, *Agency Explosive Factories* (undated).
60 TNA, CAB 16/168, *Committee on Imperial Defence, Sub-Committee on Billingham*, 28 April 1938; Rowlands, *Something Must Be Done*, pp. 151–2.
61 GLA, DIEC 3, *South Wales and Monmouthshire Trading Estates Limited, Report of Directors, 1938–1939*, 3.
62 *Western Mail*, 'Put Your Company out of Harm's Way', 28 February 1939.
63 G. Percival, *The Government's Industrial Estates in Wales 1936–1975* (WDA, 1978), p. 35.
64 *Western Mail*, 'South Wales and New Industries', 3 April 1939.
65 TNA, CAB 102/270, *Ministry of Supply Agency Factories, Production Branch*, 25 August 1945.
66 J. Hurstfield, *The Control of Raw Materials* (HMSO, 1953), pp. 68, 414.
67 Glamorgan Archives, DITSC/23, *Iron and Steel Trade Confederation Reports*, 31 December 1939, 262; Keeling and Wright, *The Development of the Modern British Steel Industry*, p. 31.
68 Birmingham Gazette, 'Baldwins Ltd, Review of Past Year's Operations', 30 March 1940.
69 Burn, *The Steel Industry, 1939–1959*, p. 30.
70 TNA, BT 131/88, *Iron and Steel Narrative*, 1952, 14–15; BT 131/28, *Priority and Allocation*, 27; *Western Mail*, 'Steel supplies to be rationed', 20 March 1940.
71 S. Parry, 'History of the Steel Industry in the Port Talbot Area' (unpublished doctoral thesis, Leeds University, 2011), 111; Glamorgan Archives, DITSC/23, *Iron and Steel Trade Confederation Reports*, 30 June 1939, 131, 141.
72 J. Hutton, *An Illustrated History of Cardiff Docks, Volume 3: Cardiff Railway Company and the Docks at War* (Silver Link Publishing Ltd, 2008), p. 113.

73 B. Redhead and S. Goodie, *The Summers of Shotton* (Hodder and Stoughton, 1987), pp. 132–4.
74 G. Smith, *A Century of Shotton Steel* (British Steel, 1996), p. 32.
75 Glamorgan Archives, DITSC/23, *Iron and Steel Trade Confederation Reports*, 31 December 1939, 265; DITSC/24, 31 March 1940, 49.
76 TNA, AVIA 12/85, *History of the Non-Ferrous Metal Control*, 1947, 7.
77 Hurstfield, *The Control of Raw Materials*, p. 400.
78 Hurstfield, *The Control of Raw Materials*, p. 68; TNA, 10/298, *Light Metals Control Organization*, 28 September 1943, 1.
79 J. Elliot and C. Deneen, 'Iron, Steel and Aluminium', in C. Williams and A. Croll (eds), *The Gwent County History* (University of Wales Press, 2013), pp. 59–74 (p. 72).
80 Gooberman, 'Revolution in the Coalfields', 55–72.
81 TNA, LAB 34/54, *Trade Disputes*, 1939.
82 TNA, LAB 12/82, *Ministry of Labour Monthly Report, Wales*, 13 November 1939, 2.
83 TNA, POWE 22/124, *Note of the Under-Secretary for Mines Meeting with Mr Arthur Horner*, 20 October 1939, 2.
84 *Western Mail*, 'South Wales Will Dig', 16 April 1940.
85 TNA, LAB 12/82, *Ministry of Labour Monthly Report, Wales*, 16 January 1940, 2.
86 R. P. Arnot, *The Miners in Crisis and War* (Allen and Unwin, 1961), p. 290.
87 SWML, *SWMF Executive Committee Minutes*, 14 November 1939.
88 Wilt, *Food for War*, pp. 113, 115.
89 R. Moore-Colyer, 'The County War Agricultural Executive Committees: The Welsh Experience, 1939–45', *Welsh History Review*, 22 (2005), 558–87 (568).
90 *Western Mail*, 'Britain's War-Time Food Production Plans', 4 May 1939.
91 *Cambrian News*, 19 January 1940, cited in Moore-Colyer, p. 569.
92 Murray, *Agriculture*, 73; *Western Mail*, 'Welsh Farmers Praised', 18 April 1940.
93 TNA MAF 80/5002, *Minutes of Public Meeting, Llanfyllin*, October 1939.
94 Moore-Colyer, 'The County War Agricultural Executive Committees', 571.
95 *Western Mail*, 'Tractors for Ploughing', 22 September 1939.
96 Murray, *Agriculture*, pp. 83–4.
97 *Western Mail*, 'Work of the Ministry of Agriculture in Wales', 26 February 1940.
98 J. Martin, *The Development of Modern Agriculture; British Farming Since 1931* (Palgrave Macmillan, 2000), p. 40.
99 *The Economist*, 'British Budgets', 22 April 1939.
100 Williams, *DWHS 1700–1974, vol. 1*, p. 145.
101 Williams, *A Forgotten Army*, p. 50.
102 *Western Mail*, 'Mobilising Nations' Resources', 27 February 1940.

PART TWO

WARTIME MUNITIONS INDUSTRIES, 1940–1945

3

GOVERNING PRODUCTION

THE UNITED KINGDOM AND REGIONS

Churchill's coalition government was determined to grip war production. It quickly passed an Emergency Powers Act to obtain more control over people and property before reforming the cumbersome committee structure directing the economy. The focus was on physical planning as symbolised by the initial exclusion of the Chancellor of the Exchequer from the War Cabinet. Although Churchill controlled strategy, governing war production centrally was hampered by the need to find compromises acceptable throughout his coalition government, and how a transparent chain of command over all munitions production might prompt the appearance of a leader comparable in status to the Prime Minister.[1]

These factors meant that the new committee system struggled to control the munitions industries. The lynchpin of the system was the Lord President's Committee. It was tasked with coordinating the war economy but was hampered by the illness of its Chair, Chamberlain, and became preoccupied instead with minor issues. The government created a Production Council to coordinate eponymous activity, but it was a committee including the three supply ministers and the Minister of Labour and National Service, Ernest Bevin. Its structure prompted a lack of authority, effectiveness and impact. One problem was caused by the personality of Minister of Aircraft Production Lord Beaverbrook, a Canadian newspaper tycoon and confidante of Churchill. He disliked committees and refused to attend the Production Council after its first meeting, instead remaining in his office where a prominent notice stated that 'committees take the punch out of war'.[2]

Meanwhile, the Area Boards created in early 1940 barely functioned as they lacked authority and access to information, while their secretariats tended to be a solitary, retired civil servant. Each Board possessed a regional advisory committee, but these were irrelevant and quickly fell out of use. The Production Council took responsibility for the boards in July 1940 and asked Ministry of Supply junior minister Harold Macmillan to review their operation. He concluded that they were 'enfeebled' by the subordination of their members to their ministries while a lack of authority had 'disabled' their advisory committees.[3] Inter-departmental tensions meant, however, that the central problem of production directorates within supply ministries ignoring Area Boards and their own regional officers when procuring was not solved.[4] Instead, only minor reforms were made. These included folding advisory committees into the Area Boards, to be led by employee or employee representatives, and creating 'capacity clearing centres' to match firms with capacity with those that were overloaded.[5]

The absence of regional coordination was symbolised by the inability to stem disruptive flows of businesses fleeing air raids on London. In October 1940, the Midlands Area Board argued that allowing non-essential industries to move there was 'suicidal' while the North West Area Board objected to a new arrival from London as 'knitwear hardly sounds important [to the war effort]'. The Production Council responded by creating a sub-committee to investigate the problem, but it ludicrously reported three arguments in favour of regulating industrial movement and six against. Arguments against included 'control should not be imposed unless it is really necessary' and a 'control would have to be set up'. The sub-committee concluded by making 'no definite recommendation' before referring the matter back to the Production Council.⁶ The Area Boards' continued lack of impact then prompted a second review, in December 1940, but this met the fate of its predecessor as reflected by plaintive recommendations including 'giving the boards specific tasks to perform'.⁷

The key governance defect was that the three supply ministries remained largely autonomous, while labour availability in some regions meant that they were not incentivised to coordinate their activities. The largest supply ministry was the sprawling Ministry of Supply whose work began when a service identified a munitions requirement. The Ministry then prioritised and allocated the requirement to one of its forty directorates that decided which company should be contracted, often using the '392 Register'.⁸ It also housed autonomous raw materials controls and controlled the ROFs whose governance reflected broader trends of improvisation. Despite their rapid growth, no over-arching administrative plan emerged. Instead, the small central management structure at the Ministry of Supply subdivided itself by appointing new directors as its responsibilities expanded. A specialist directorate to supervise the filling factories was not created until April 1941 and, although it incorporated a regional structure dividing the UK into three administrative areas, it employed only 101 technical officers to cover factories featuring 90,000 workers.⁹

The second supply ministry was Aircraft Production, created in May 1940 as an emergency measure. It inherited Air Ministry functions and was headed by the impulsive and unpredictable Beaverbrook, who seconded managers from business to spur increased production during the Battle of Britain. The final supply ministry, the Admiralty, traced its history to the Middle Ages and resisted structural changes. Its ships were built and repaired in the five state-owned royal dockyards in England and Scotland,¹⁰ or in privately owned yards throughout the UK. Other Admiralty procurement was 'inland', where it either competed with the other two supply ministries to source munitions from private companies or its own factories that produced items like those made at the ROFs. The Admiralty managed its operations through divisions based on nationwide patterns of the industrial activity from which each drew their contractors, meaning that their boundaries differed from each other and did not match those of the civil defence regions that shaped regional administration in other ministries.

Parliamentary concern at dislocated production governance helped prompt reforms in late 1940 and early 1941. One revitalised the Lord President's Committee to adjudicate disputes between ministries, endowing it with authority to review and amend home front decisions.[11] Board of Trade President Oliver Lyttleton described the committee's workings in relation to his scheme to ration civilian clothing. He appeared before the committee members, who 'frisked the scheme, took it apart, fitted it together again and asked every sort of question', making amendments before allowing it to proceed subject to Prime Ministerial approval.[12] Yet a second reform was less successful. In January 1941 the Production Council was replaced with a Production Executive. Bevin argued that the 'basic principle' of the new organisation was that 'the whole process of production' should be 'gripped and controlled … by a small and compact directing body'.[13] Nevertheless, the Executive was another committee lacking authority. It was formed from the three supply ministers under Bevin and became little more than a debating forum, although even this proved difficult as Beaverbrook, Minister of Supply from June 1941, refused to attend meetings.[14]

The Production Executive attempted to address the problem of Regional Coordination. Macmillan revisited the Area Boards for a third review to find disillusioned members who saw the Boards as a waste of time. His report entitled 'Matters of policy requiring an early decision by the Production Executive' made depressing reading, arguing that the failure to plan industrial location had left some regions overloaded and others underused, creating a 'serious situation' at risk of 'deteriorating still further'.[15] The subsequent reorganisation followed familiar themes. Board membership was extended to include other ministries relevant to munitions production, smaller executive commitees were formed to direct operations while boards assumed responsibility for updating the '392' capacity register. However, this reorganisation achieved little and was hindered by the Board of Trade's refusal to allow its Factory and Storage Control Function to be represented on the boards.[16] Even Macmillan's attempt to rename the Area Boards as 'regional production boards' was resisted by Whitehall as it 'might lend the members to expect powers and opportunties which it would not in fact prove possible to give them' and they were instead renamed the 'Production Executive's Regional Boards'.[17]

Regional Boards searched for a worthwile function throughout 1941. Supply ministries ignored them while the role of the Production Executive was unclear; a London and South Eastern Regional Board officer cabled the Executive head office in November 1941, stating that:[18]

> One of the Technical Officers came to me the other day for a heart-to-heart talk about the recent meeting of the [regional board] Advisory Committee Chairman and the Technical Officers. He said that one of the questions asked was "what exactly is the Production Executive" – and nobody knew. Do you think that you could let me have a short note?

Although the Production Executive floundered, progress was made elsewhere. One problem addressed successfully was 'factory snatching' where each ministry was requisitioning factories only to find that occupying businesses were contracted to another ministry.[19] After Churchill overruled opposition from Beaverbrook, a Factory and Storage Control Function was created in early 1941. The Function could not be housed by one of the feuding supply ministries and was placed instead within the Board of Trade to carry out what Controller General Cecil

Weir argued was the 'cruel work' of requisitioning factories from their occupiers before allocating them to other firms as munitions manufacturing bases.[20] This work had three components. The first was registering factories and storage space: the Function eventually listed 34,400 factories totalling 1,025 million square feet and other properties with 67 million square feet of storage. The second was licensing firms taking floor space: the Function eventually issued 34,000 orders covering 220 million square feet, either directly to ministries or to businesses sponsored by them. The final responsibility was approving requisition requests: the Function only granted a 'nil certificate' for construction when space was unavailable.[21]

Concern as to mobilisation intensified throughout 1941 and early 1942 as military setbacks continued. The loss of Crete in June 1941 prompted *The Times* to argue that 'production is one of the master keys of victory' but the 'parallel plans' produced by various ministries were 'in danger of clashing'.[22] In January 1942 the newspaper criticised a 'loose and often chaotic' production system while *The Economist* argued that the Production Executive was a 'battleground rather than a place of decision'.[23] By mid-1942 production worries combined with further setbacks such as the fall of Singapore to prompt a political 'production crisis'. Mass Observation studied war production in early 1942, arguing that 'people are more worried and concerned about the future of the war now than at anytime since it began'.[24] In a parliamentary censure debate on the direction of the war Labour MP for Ebbw Vale Aneurin Bevan argued that 'the Prime Minister wins debate after debate but loses battle after battle ... the country is beginning to say that he fights debates like a war and the war like a debate'.[25] Yet, despite such concern, the UK was mobilising quickly as munitions production increased by half between the first quarters of 1941 and 1942. Later in the war, Lyttleton, a Minister responsible for production, observed that the capital equipment of the armed forces was 'virtually complete' by the end of 1942 as production switched to new weapons.[26]

Nevertheless, criticism of ROF management inevitably formed part of the 'production crisis'. In April 1942 the House of Commons's Select Committee on National Expenditure released a typically scathing report on what it described as an inefficient and 'strangely lopsided' headquarters structure lacking detailed data on factory-level operation. The Committee questioned the effectiveness of the filling factory regional structure, identified many overlapping functions such as the separate quality inspectorates maintained by each service in the same factories, before recommending a 'single organisation that possess all the functions ... necessary to their operation' including labour supply and welfare.[27]

Yet Minister of Supply Sir Andrew Duncan did not want to intervene as 'lopsided things sometimes work very well, and this has produced very excellent results'.[28] These results meant that the impact of the 'production crisis' on the ROFs was fleeting as the problem was not lack of output, but overproduction. Factory planners had underestimated the time needed to reach full production, military planners had overestimated the amount of ammunition needed, production capacity was available in Canada, and labour efficiency by the end of 1941 was 40 per cent higher than eighteen months earlier.[29] Efficiency growth was driven by payment by results, modern management techniques such as 'time and motion' studies, and moving from two long shifts to three shorter shifts in the larger ROFs, reducing the hours worked by individuals from 60 to 48 hours with no loss of pay.[30] The Ministry of Supply responded by reducing output and employment at filling and explosive factories, although employee numbers at engineering ROFs grew.

The ROFs accounted for only one, if a vital, part of munitions output and a prominent debate during the 'production crisis' was over the need to create a Ministry of Production to coordinate munitions industries throughout the war economy. Impetus flowed from how poor coordination hampered the mobilisation of private industries while the entry of the United States to the war offered the potential to obtain vast quantities of supplies, but one organisation was needed to coordinate a prioritised list of requirements. Mass Observation explored war production to argue that the 'most difficult' aspect of its study was understanding the 'extremely complicated machinery that links the industrial unit with the [contracting] Government unit'.[31] The government finally responded in February 1942 by creating a Ministry of Production, headed by Beaverbrook. However, Bevin threatened to resign rather than cede authority over labour, viewing such authority as underpinning Labour's participation in the coalition government.[32] In response, the government confirmed that the new Ministry had only 'supervision and guidance' roles and that the responsibilities of Supply Ministers were 'unaltered'.[33] Unsurprisingly, Beaverbrook resigned immediately.

On his appointment, the central problem faced by the subsequent Minister of Production, Lyttelton, remained the supply ministries, which 'would not take readily to interference'.[34] Difficulties were heightened by their vast scale, with the Ministry of Supply ROFs alone employing 351,400 people by October 1942.[35] These formed part of the 1,391,200 employed on Ministry of Supply contracts, within a broader munitions industry (excluding shipbuilding) that employed three million by June 1943.[36] Such activity prompted huge volumes of administration within what Ministry of Supply Permanent Secretary Oliver Franks called a 'vast organ of central planning and control'.[37] Meanwhile, each supply ministry guarded their autonomy and focused on ensuring that their own procurement needs were met. Finally, and unsurprisingly given the traditional hostility of many industrialists towards government administrators, Mass Observation recorded that it could 'fill a second volume … with instances of alleged official inefficiency' related to them by those in industry.[38]

After much discussion, the Ministry of Production created an Industrial Division to control the supply ministries, but it faltered amidst Whitehall infighting. Nevertheless, some effective inter-departmental mechanisms existed. One was a Headquarters Preference Committee that designated items prioritised for production, with the Ministry of Production having the final say. Another was a Location of Industry Committee chaired by a Ministry of Production representative that designated 'crowded areas' where further industrial development was barred unless approved by the committee.[39] Yet problems continued as ministries struggled to control industrial minutiae in locations far removed from London, while ministerial governance needed to be coordinated to ensure greater efficiency, and output, of munitions by businesses. The answer had always been effective regional governance, but supply ministries lacked any incentive to cooperate as sufficient labour capacity still existed in many regions.

Ineffective regional structures were inevitably caught up in the 'production crisis'. In March 1942 Lyttelton argued that 'if there is one thing about which I am sure a change is desirable … it is in the regional organisation of production'.[40] He ordered another inquiry. This was the fourth inquiry into regional governance but his determination to acheive change was reflected in the choice of those forming the commission of inquiry. It was chaired by TUC General Secretary Sir Walter Citrine and most members were Regional Board Chairs. In May 1942 the Citrine Commision reported on what it described as a 'melancholy list of frustrations and disappointments'. It observed a 'strange' lack of effective regional structures governing production to argue that 'an efficient regional organisation is an essential element in the effective prosecution of the war'.[41]

A primary annoyance was that supply ministries ignored regional structures. The Minstry of Aircraft Production admitted that its regional organisation was 'functioning … largely independently of the Regional Boards'.[42] Meanwhile, regional officers of the supply ministries sat on Regional Boards but did not know what contracts their own ministries were placing. The Admirality had grudgingly appointed retired personnel as regional officers to sit on Regional Boards but loftily told the commission that it would 'be a needless duplication of work' to give them notice of Admiralty contracts. Simultaneously, the Ministry of Supply admitted that production officers within its central directorates rarely sought advice from regional officers. Yet both ministries rebuffed any suggestion of reform; the Admiralty argued laconically that its approach 'seems the logical way of doing it'.[43]

In response, the Citrine Commission made recommendations including the appointment of a 'Regional Director of Production' to supervise supply departments, giving regional officers the right to enter and inspect factories, and authorising boards to gather comprehensive information on production contracts and unused capacity. Data were to be gathered by local offices that would absorb capacity clearing centres.[44] The government accepted these recommendations, although the sensitivities of supply ministries meant that the 'Regional Director of Production' title was downgraded to 'Regional Controller' to 'coordinate' rather than 'supervise' ministries.

This continuation of a largely voluntary approach might have repeated earlier failures, but circumstances finally delivered a solution to poor regional coordination. Lyttleton captured these circumstances and their impacts in October 1942 when he argued that a 'general expansion in productive capacity' throughout Britain was almost complete and that continued growth needed a 'readjustment and reallocation of resources'.[45] Capacity shortages incentivised supply ministries to cooperate through exploiting the few remaining pockets of capacity. The extent to which the remaining labour reserves were scattered throughout the regions gifted a role to the Ministry of Production's recently strengthened regional structures. This Ministry immediately focused on the benefits that regional governance could unlock, arguing that it needed 'some means of keeping ourselves informed in factories to enable us to exercise our general role as co-ordinator … a capacity organisation ... over the whole country' was the best means of doing this.[46]

Full time Regional Controllers were in post by June 1942 as regional staff in the supply and production ministries were obliged to share offices to foster cooperation, while more district offices were established to gather local capacity data.[47] Yet Regional Boards were not tasked with controlling the three supply ministries. In any case, this would have been a mammoth task as, for example, the Ministry of Supply was processing 41,600 contracts in mid-1942.[48] They were instead to coordinate ministerial relationships with contractors by identifying companies most able to fulfil specific contracts, authorising floorspace and tracking regional capacity. Importantly, executive committees expanded to include the Board of Trade's Regional Controllers of its Factory and Storage Control Function although only after more inter-departmental dispute, reflecting the later comment of Ministry of Production Chief Executive Sir Robert Sinclair that 'the establishment of the Ministry ... in a position of leadership in the regional organisation was not an easy thing to effect in 1942'.[49]

Administrative reform meant that, as production increased, regional machinery was finally established to ensure capacity was evenly and fully utilised. Capacity was assessed by monthly visits or telephone calls to companies that gathered data for collation by machine readable cards.[50] A National Production Advisory Council was also created to grant regional controllers enhanced access to central governing structures. By 1943 the Ministry of Production possessed what the official history argued correctly was 'an instrument capable of ascertaining, recording and ... advising on minute fluctuations on which Britain's ability to surmount the manpower famine so greatly depended'.[51] Yet administrative devolution was never all-encompassing. In early 1943 Regional Controllers argued for full control over local activities of supply ministries but were firmly rejected.[52] Nevertheless, by the end of 1943 the Ministry of Supply's

Director General of Regional Organisation noted that effective working was finally in place, symbolised by increased 'confidence and goodwill' between regional and national functions.[53] The system worked relatively smoothly in the last eighteen months of war as ministries cooperated to wring productive capacity out of a fully mobilised economy.

WALES

Production coordination was embryonic in 1940 as the Wales Area Board searched for a meaningful role. The search was reflected in plaintive communications with the Ministry of Supply in Whitehall as the board asked fruitlessly to be informed when large production contracts were placed in Wales, to receive guidance as to the direction of production, and recommended that the 'numerous' departments collecting data on factories suitable for dispersed production should be coordinated.[54] By the end of 1940 other Area Boards established clearing centres to redistribute production within their regions but none were created in Wales where there was no surplus.[55]

The irrelevance of the Wales Area Board and the lack of consideration given by the supply ministries to coordinating regional procurement was reflected by their regional officers in Wales acting independently and informally. Ministry of Supply Regional Controller Percy Thomas initially took the post on an honorary basis and continued his architectural practice. He travelled throughout the country to find capacity 'at unexpected little factories', while, when asked to find capacity for larger contracts, he simply asked the leading contractors 'to come to his office and see [if] they could meet the requirements'.[56] Meanwhile, the government's mid-1941 rebranding of the Area Boards to the Production Executive's Regional Boards achieved little. Advisory panels were created in west and north Wales to help 'ensure the continuous co-ordination of government officials',[57] but these officials were not impressed. Regional staff in the supply ministries promptly told Regional Board Secretary Denis Morgan that such panels were 'eyewash and a waste of time' before condemning the Production Executive's recommendations on disabling factories during an invasion as 'impractical as most of the[ir] instructions'. The secretary wearily compared inter-departmental tensions to the Libyan theatre of conflict before informing his Whitehall superiors that 'we plod on, saddened but undismayed'.[58]

Regional production coordination in Wales was mired in inertia. Macmillan noted that regions such as the Midlands and the North-West of England suffered from 'congestion and overload', while for others including south Wales the 'problem is still that of discovering uses for unused capacity'.[59] Such problems needed coordination but the lack of effective regional structures prompted civil servants to inform him in December 1941 that 'the lack of precise information on questions of capacity is crippling our discussions … causing an appalling waste of time'.[60] Problems faced by the Regional Board in Wales throughout 1941 were symbolised by its fraught relationship with Richard Walters, the Regional Controller of the Board of Trade's Factory and Storage Control Function. Walters owned a toffee manufacturing company, and ran the function from offices in Cardiff and Ruthin as what his Assistant Controller Emrys Price described as a 'vast estate agency, armed with powers to take what we wanted'.[61] Yet the Board of Trade was determined to remain autonomous from other ministries, refusing to join the Regional Board as it would be a 'waste of time'.[62] Refusal was significant as the control was the main instrument coordinating munitions businesses.

Discontent mounted and in December 1941 Wales Regional Board chair Herbert Hiles told his superiors in London that regional staff within other government ministries saw his board as little more than a 'channel of information' whose 'powers of initiative should be limited'. He was sufficiently concerned to consider resignation, arguing that 'the prestige of certain individuals and departments should mean nothing in days like these'.[63] In early 1942 problems were confirmed by a Regional Board investigation on questions raised frequently by war workers, including 'why should we be slack, even idle, when there is all this call for more production'. The Board's defensive answer was that it was not always easy to allocate production efficiently and that 'bottlenecks' were inevitable.[64]

However, administrative tensions and inertia were unsustainable as a steady flow of businesses arrived in Wales. While arrivals in mid-1940 were chaotic and unplanned, the government noted later that by 1941 the 'labour situation in England grew tighter', prompting it to 'progressively exert [influence] toward the creation of more industrial capacity in Wales'.[65] Greater direction meant that the Factory and Storage Control Function allocated more floorspace in Wales to firms. The percentage of such allocations grew from only 1.2 per cent of the UK total in mid to late 1941 to 8 per cent in the first three months of 1942.

The need to exploit regional capacity inevitably prompted more interest in regional governance and in July 1942 Lyttleton attended a Wales Regional Board meeting to argue as to the 'vital importance at the present time of additional regional devolution in production administrative matters'.[66] He achieved greater administrative devolution by implementing the Citrine Commission's recommendations. The Board was reconstituted under chair Percy Thomas who presided over a three-tier structure. A regional board was comprised of representatives from each supply ministry, the Board of Trade, the Ministry of Labour and National Service, as well as employer and union representatives. Meanwhile, an executive to implement the board's decisions was formed from the same ministerial representatives but fewer from employers and unions. Finally, three area advisory committees were created from representatives of both sides of industry and were linked to new district offices.[67] Although the Ministry sought to prompt cooperation by encouraging the regional staff of all ministries to share offices, problems remained as the Admiralty refused initially to release office space in Cardiff, an act described by the Regional Board as 'threatening to neutralise the whole value of [our] work'.[68]

Nevertheless, the Wales Regional Board lacked formal authority over supply ministries. Its chair attempted to 'remove feelings of jealousy between departments' by obtaining such authority in March 1943 but failed.[69] The Board instead took advantage of circumstances to assume a clearing function for factory expansions and arrivals. The most important success factor was that supply ministries now saw advantages in mutual cooperation given capacity constraints. The Board opened new district offices, staffed by officers who visited at least two firms per day to collect data on their production load and capacity remaining for further work.[70] Finally, the Regional Board absorbed and deployed the authority held by the Board of Trade whose Regional Controller of Factories and Storage Space finally joined the Regional Board in late 1942,[71] after which floorspace allocations were usually agreed on a collective basis. Crucially, the controller told the Regional Board that he saw Wales as a 'reception area for small units of production' and that 'where pockets of available labour existed, he would ... make every effort to secure the necessary premises for production'.[72]

As mobilisation intensified and more factories opened in Wales, a Nuffield College survey observed how many industrialists were keen to come to south Wales but were struggling to find premises as almost all floorspace suitable for production had been requisitioned.[73] By late 1942 the Board was inundated with enquiries for new factories. Greater demand was prompted by the Britain-wide construction of a strategic bomber fleet requiring the development of manufacturing supply chains to provide components and sub-assemblies. Meanwhile, floorspace available for requisition became scarce or non-existent, prompting the Factory and Storage Control

Function to authorise the construction of new factories by issuing Nil Certificates.

Demand enabled the board to direct location. One example was at Treforest Industrial Estate, where combined rents payable by tenants increased from £55,737 in 1940–1 to £68,634 by 1944–5.[74] By 1943, however, labour shortages prompted employment to be diverted elsewhere. Estate employment peaked at 15,781 in 1943 before declining even as UK-wide munitions production peaked in early 1944.[75] Nevertheless, two problems prompted difficulties when dealing with demand. One was that an outdated industrial structure prompted a shortage of manufacturing space. Assistant Factory and Storage Space Controller Emrys Pride observed that 'the trouble was that we had comparatively few factories in South Wales and so many were in poor shape' while in north Wales 'all we had was scenery'.[76] The few factories built before the war were soon occupied for war work, prompting frantic requisitioning, as reflected by premises released during one week in 1945 as the war in Europe ended. The Ministry of Supply released a Gymnasium Hall in Neath and a brickworks in Penhros, the Ministry of Aircraft Production released a garage in Bangor, and the War Department released an automotive showroom in Llandrindod Wells.[77]

The other problem was the tendency of ministries to use premises in Wales for the storage of food, raw materials and munitions, not production. Between the creation of the Factory and Storage Space Control in 1940 and September 1942 it allocated 1.2 million square feet throughout Wales for production, but 5.3 million for storage. These figures were equivalent to 3.9 per cent of the UK totals for production space but 6.6 per cent of storage. This high usage of floorspace for storage was reflected by property requirements requests from ministries in September 1942. These comprised 768,000 sq. ft. for storage in south Wales but only 104,000 square feet for production, while requests within north Wales were for storage of 318,000 square feet but no production.[78] Imbalances were largely prompted by the lack of space suitable for production although traces of the pre-war reluctance to locate factories in Wales remained.

The inevitable result was disquiet in locations such as Merthyr Tydfil. In November 1942 Labour MP S. O. Davies complained to the Ministry of Supply that the lack of production directed to the town, and the use of premises for storage, meant that a thousand men rejected for military service as unfit were idle, as were many women.[79] A delegation including the Mayor travelled to London but achieved nothing while a prolonged and fruitless correspondence ensued between the Regional Board and the Ministry of Supply as to the suitability of buildings in Merthyr for production. One focus was the Market Hall, used as a food storage facility by the Navy, Army and Air Force Institutes, which refused to vacate the premises. By June 1943 the town council had lost patience and passed a resolution protesting the 'delay in providing factory work in the buildings available for production in the borough'.[80]

Pressure to be allocated more work intensified through questions in the House of Commons and resolutions from trade union branches and the local Labour Party.[81] Another delegation to London met with little success when Ministry of Production Parliamentary Secretary Garro Jones argued that, although his Ministry could 'tell firms and departments that they could not develop in certain areas' and 'forcibly' bring Merthyr to their attention, it was not possible to 'force development into certain places'.[82] The reality was that the Ministry was content to use existing factories and requisitioned premises for production or storage, while it was reluctant to vacate existing storage space or press for the construction of factories unless vital for war production. The Ministry believed correctly that concern in Merthyr Tydfil emanated from fears as to post-war employment, yet to emerge as a government priority, and not wartime employment as by 1943 over 4,100 people were manufacturing munitions in three factories.[83] While the Regional Board could refuse industrial projects and order them to choose another location, it could do little to guide production to a selected area without suitable premises. Towards the end of the war, however, the board increasingly focused on managing the process of transition to peacetime manufacturing and managed an inflow of such firms as central government prioritised the recreation of regional manufacturing economies.

CONCLUSION

Munitions production was governed through complex and evolving series of interlocking mechanisms across many ministries. The system initially retained the shape inherited in May 1940 except for the creation of a Ministry of Aircraft Production. Nevertheless, total war necessitated wholesale reform to drive greater efficiency but successfully achieving such reform was remarkably difficult and protracted. Extensions of state control were reactive solutions as the government initially preferred voluntaristic approaches even though the administrative bodies they created lacked sufficient coordinating authority. More authoritative mechanisms tended not to be created unless voluntaristic approaches failed.

This preference for administrative voluntarism meant that the many elements of governance developed fitfully in an occasionally farcical manner. By late 1940 the obvious risk to production as the supply ministries competed to occupy the same factories prompted government to impose the Factory and Storage Control Function on the feuding ministries. Yet while floorspace constraints had forced such intervention, continued labour availability meant that these ministries had little incentive to coordinate their regional activities. Instead, they ignored repeated attempts within government to obtain their mutual cooperation, prompting four ineffectual reviews between mid-1940 and mid-1942. However, by mid-1942 labour constraints finally incentivised the supply ministries to accept cooperation, and the newly created Ministry of Production orchestrated a cross-departmental regional structure that played a critical role in enabling peak mobilisation. Nevertheless, administrative voluntarism prevailed as Regional Boards such as those in Wales lacked formal authority over the supply ministries, instead sharing information to enable munitions businesses to be coordinated, while identifying and exploiting the remaining pockets of capacity that had assumed a national importance. All this meant that 173 new factories were created in Wales between September 1942 and December 1944.[84]

Britain-wide debates on munitions production receded as the economy headed towards peak mobilisation, the fortunes of war shifted in favour of the allies, and large-scale imports arrived. Boards played an important role in enabling peak mobilisation, but they inevitably lacked influence over national production priorities and programmes, operating instead through consent in a fluid administrative environment. In August 1945, Stafford Cripps, the new Labour government's President of the Board of Trade thanked regional controllers for their 'excellent work done during the war'.[85] This was more than a formality as the boards had played a crucial part in eventually enabling almost all localities to contribute towards the war effort. It was the neglected regions of 'outer Britain' such as Wales that benefited most as businesses orchestrated by regional structures combined with state-owned operations to transform regional economies.

Notes

1 Jeffreys, *The Churchill Coalition and Wartime Politics*, p. 67. Parts of this chapter draw on material within Gooberman, 'Public Governance of Private Munitions Businesses in Regional Britain', *Business History* (2021), 1–20.
2 A. J. P Taylor, *Beaverbrook* (Hamish Hamilton, 1972), p. 421.
3 TNA, CAB 102/613, *Notes on Regional Organisation*, 4.
4 TNA, CAB 102/503, *The Regional Organisation, and its use, of the Ministry of Supply*, 5.
5 *Report of the Committee on Regional Boards*, 6; TNA, CAB 102/613, *Notes on Regional Organisation*, 4.

6. TNA, BT168/135, *Reports from Area Boards: Industrial Capacity Committee: Report on Removal of Factories*, October 1940.
7. TNA, CAB 102/613, *Notes on Regional Organisation*, 5–6.
8. TNA, BT 168/125, *Memorandum by the Ministry of Supply*, 24 March 1942, 1.
9. TNA, CAB 102/630, *The Filling Factory Organisation*, 33; CAB 102/272, *Regional Administration of Filling Factories*; Hornby, *Factories and Plant*, pp. 142, 136.
10. Hornby, *Factories and Plant*, pp. 66, 69.
11. Crowcroft, 'Making a Reality of Collective Responsibility', 543–4.
12. O. Lyttleton, *The Memoirs of Lord Chandos*, p. 204.
13. Hansard (Commons), *21 January 1941, vol. 368, col. 81*.
14. D. R. Thorpe, *Supermac, the Life of Harold Macmillan* (Pimlico, 2011), p. 154.
15. TNA, BT 168/32, *Matters of Policy Requiring an Early Decision by the Production Executive: Memorandum*, Harold Macmillan, 1–2.
16. TNA, CAB 102/100, *Regional Controllers of Factory and Storage and Regional Board Organisation*, 41.
17. TNA, CAB 102/613, *Notes on Regional Organisation*, 8.
18. TNA, BT 168/111, *Cable from London and South Eastern Regional Board to Production Executive*, 14 November 1941.
19. TNA, BT 131/28, *Talk with Miss Elroy and Sir C. Weir, Board of Trade*, Professor Hancock, 23 December 1941.
20. C. Weir, *Civilian Assignment* (Methuen, 1953), p. 48.
21. *Western Mail*, 'Warehouse Storage Order', 31 October 1942; TNA, CAB 102/100, *The Control of Factory and Storage Premises*, 56–7, 72.
22. *The Times*, 'Production Drive', 12 June 1941, 5.
23. *The Times*, 'Brakes on Production', 3 January 1942, 5; *The Economist*, 'Inquest on Production', 17 January 1942, 58.
24. Mass Observation, *An Enquiry into British War Production, Part 1, People in Production* (Penguin, 1942), ix.
25. Hansard (Commons), 2 July 1942, *vol. 381, col. 528*.
26. TNA 168/12, *Production Plans for 1944, Statement by Oliver Lyttelton, Minister of Production*, 9 March 1944, 1.
27. *Eleventh Report from the Select Committee on National Expenditure, Royal Ordnance Factories* (HMSO, July), 8, 19.
28. Hansard (Commons), *5 August 1942, vol. 382, cols 1071–154*, 1083.
29. Postan, *British War Production*, p. 180.
30. Clubb, *The Welsh Arsenal*, p. 119.
31. Mass Observation, *An Enquiry into British War Production*, 1.
32. Jeffreys, *The Churchill Coalition and Wartime Politics*, p. 91.
33. *Office of the Minister of Production* (Cmd 6337) (HMSO, 1942), 1.
34. Lyttleton, *The Memoirs of Lord Chandos*, p. 284.
35. *Statistical Digest of the War*, p. 30.
36. TNA, 102/272, *Ministry Labour Survey of Employment in Munitions*, June 1943.
37. O. Franks, *Central Planning and Control and War and Peace* (London School of Economics, 1947), p. 9.
38. Mass Observation, *An Enquiry into British War Production*, 297.

39 Scott and Hughes, *The Administration of War Production*, pp. 466, 484.
40 Hansard (Commons), *24 March 1942, vol 378 col.* 1849.
41 *Report of the Committee on Regional Boards*, 7, 21.
42 TNA, BT 168/127, *Ministry of Production to Secretary of the Regional Boards Committee*, 20 March 1942.
43 TNA, BT 168/125, *Ministry of Supply Memorandum*, 24 March 1942, 1–2; BT 168/126, *Admiralty Regional Organization*, 19 March 1942.
44 TNA, CAB 102/613, *Regional Organisational Division and Regional Boards*, 103.
45 *The Times*, 'Strengthening the Controls', 15 October 1942.
46 TNA, BT 168/13, *Note from Sir Robert Sinclair on the Regional Capacity Organisation*, 7 June 1944, 1.
47 TNA, CAB 102/613, *Regional Organisational Division and Regional Boards*, 105.
48 Ashworth, *Contracts and Finance*, p. 76.
49 TNA, BT 168/13, *Note from Sir Robert Sinclair on the Regional Capacity Organisation*, 7 June 1944, 1.
50 TNA, CAB 102/613, *Regional Organisational Division and Regional Boards*, 107–8.
51 Scott and Hughes, *The Administration of War Production*, p. 488.
52 TNA, CAB 102/613, *The Crisis of the Regional Boards*, Annex II.
53 TNA, CAB 102/503, *The Regional Organisation, and its use, of the Ministry of Supply*, October 1943, 13.
54 TNA, BT 168/116, *Notes on Suggestions by Area Boards for the Greater Utilisation of Industrial Capacity*, 29 October 1940.
55 TNA, BT 168/32, *Clearing Centres*, 3.
56 P. Thomas, *Pupil to President, Memoirs of an Architect* (F. Lewis, 1963), p. 42.
57 *Flintshire County Herald*, 'Co-ordination in North Wales', 5 September 1941.
58 TNA, BT 168/41, *Letter from Secretary of Wales Regional Board to the Production Executive*, 2 December 1941.
59 TNA, BT 168/32, *Matters of Policy requiring an early decision by the Production Executive*.
60 TNA, BT 168/2, *Note to Parliamentary Secretary*, 5 December 1941.
61 E. Pride, *Tinman's Progress* (University College Swansea, 1959), p. 27.
62 TNA, BT 168/32, *Summary of Regional Board Matters for the consideration of Mr Bevin*, 12 September 1941.
63 TNA, BT 168/41, *Letter from the Chair of the Wales Regional Board to Production Executive*, 3 December 1941.
64 *Western Mail*, '"Whys" of Welsh War workers answered', 29 January 1942.
65 *Wales and Monmouthshire: A Summary of Government Action 1st August 1945–31st July 1946* (Cmd 6938) (HMSO, 1946), 5.
66 TNA, BT 168/29, *Regional Board Minutes*, 3 July 1942.
67 *Western Mail*, 'District Offices for Welsh Production', 3 September 1942.
68 TNA, BT 168/29, *Regional Board Minutes*, 28 September 1942.
69 TNA, BT 168/12, Wales Regional Board, Suggestions for Regional Organisation, 26 March 1943.
70 TNA, BT 168/13, *Regional Controllers Conference*, 8–9 November 1944.

71 TNA, CAB 102/100, *Regional Controllers of Factory and Storage, and Regional Board Organisation*, 41.
72 TNA, BT 168/29, *Regional Board Minutes*, 23 November 1942.
73 TNA, BT 64/3153, *Nuffield College Reconstruction Survey, South Wales Report*, 1941, 11.
74 GLA, DIEC 4, *South Wales and Monmouthshire Trading Estates Limited, Report of Directors, 1940–1941*, 3; DIEC 6, *1944–1945*, 2.
75 Percival, *The Government's Industrial Estates in Wales*, Appendix.
76 Pride, *Tinman's Progress*, p. 27
77 TNA, BT 170/215, *Regional Board Minutes*, 9 April 1945, 6.
78 TNA, BT 168/29, *Regional Board Minutes*, 26 October 1942, 4.
79 TNA, BT 168/5, *S. O. Davies to Garro Jones*, 20 November 1942.
80 TNA, BT 168/5, *Merthyr Town Clerk to Ministry of Production*, 4 June 1943.
81 Hansard (Commons), 10 June 1943, vol. 390, col. 818; TNA, BT 168/5, *Merthyr Tydfil Trades Council and Labour Party*, 24 June 1943; *Letter from National Union of Railwaymen*, 5 September 1943.
82 TNA, BT 168/5, *Meeting between Mr Garro Jones and a Deputation from Merthyr Tydfil*.
83 TNA, BT 168/5, *Letter from Wales Regional Board*, 20 July 1943, 3.
84 TNA, BT 131/28, *Control of Factory and Storage Space*, annexes.
85 TNA, BT 168/13, *Minutes of Regional Controllers Conference*, 22 August 1945, 1.

4

GOVERNING LABOUR

UNITED KINGDOM AND REGIONS

In mid-1940 the most obvious priority for the Ministry of Labour and National Service was securing sufficient labour throughout the UK to enable industrial mobilisation. Moreover, governing labour throughout the economy was smoother than controlling manufacturing as, while production authority was divided between ministries, the Ministry of Labour and National Service had undisputed authority over its area of activity. It also benefited from the political weight of Bevin, Minister for Labour and National Service. Yet while Bevin was determined to mobilise labour, his role as the General Secretary of the Transport and General Workers Union prompted him to favour voluntarist approaches over state compulsion. Such voluntarism reflected how unions sought to avoid legal jurisdiction over industrial relations given their fear of judicial bias, and his belief that industrial conscription would impede the war effort by antagonising workers. Such determination meant that Bevin initially opposed conscription, proposing instead that labour should be sourced voluntarily through employment exchanges or unions. The war cabinet, however, disagreed and the Emergency Powers bill of May 1940 declared that anybody could be compelled to place 'themselves, their services and their property' at the government's disposal.

Nevertheless, Bevin told his advisory council that 'with the goodwill of ... unions and the employers federation ...

we could maintain to a very large degree intact the peacetime circumstances, merely adapting them to suit these extraordinary circumstances'.[1] Such views meant that industrial conscription was slow to develop. In June 1940 the Ministry of Labour and National Service issued an Undertakings (Restriction on Engagement) Order that forced the engineering, construction and civil engineering industries to source labour only through employment exchanges or unions. Yet skilled workers evaded these restrictions to move to better paid jobs as ministries argued furiously over the loss of skilled labour from businesses with whom they had contracted to produce war material.[2] Overall, the overriding need for defensive weapons meant that there were no labour allocations, but instead a simple priority system that gave designated weapons first claim on labour and material. Nevertheless, poor planning prompted what Ministry of Supply Assistant Under-Secretary of Labour Douglas Jay described as 'internecine war' in late 1940 between supply ministries over labour resourcing.[3]

By early 1941 the need to plan and direct labour was clear as the armed forces and munitions industries required a further 3 million men and women. Meanwhile, 49 per cent of the workforce was employed on government work and easily accessible labour reserves had been utilised.[4] Over a twelve-month period the government subsequently and gradually extended labour governance across four legislative measures. When combined with adjustments to the system of 'reserved occupations' exempting workers from military service, these measures enabled the Ministry to control nationwide labour supply and demand through what became known as 'manpower budgeting', coordinated with the assistance of Anderson, Lord President of the Council and, from September 1943, Chancellor.[5]

The first measure was the Essential Work Order of February 1941 that prevented workers from leaving scheduled companies, or places of work. The earliest concerns scheduled were those within aircraft engineering, but 4.5 million workers across many industries were covered by December. The second was the Registration of Employment Order of March 1941 that compelled men above military age and women, eventually up to the age of 50, to register at employment exchanges to identify those of most use to the war effort.[6] This order was important primarily as a means of mobilising women as most men registering were already engaged on war work. The third was the National Service Act of December 1941 that finally began conscription, although Bevin preferred to instead deploy it as a threat to drive voluntary take up. The fourth was the Employment of Women (Control of Engagement) Order in February 1942 that prohibited women from taking up work unless organised through employment exchanges. Single, childless women aged between twenty and thirty were classed as 'mobile' and could be transferred to work elsewhere in the UK, while married women were 'immobile' and were exempt from transfer.[7]

Although these measures corralled labour supply, machinery to prioritise labour demand was also needed. The first step was to prioritise labour requirements within the supply ministries. Within the Ministry of Supply Jay noted a 'babel' of conflicting approaches from its many production directorates towards the Ministry of Labour and National Service as each directorate was 'professing its own product to be of supreme and unique priority'. Yet by 1941 he headed a Labour Supply Department deploying an 'urgency list' of priorities channelling all Ministry of Supply requests to the Ministry of Labour and National Service for workers to fulfil production contracts.[8]

The second step was to coordinate and prioritise labour demand across the three supply ministries. In late 1941 fortnightly meetings between representatives of the Ministry of Labour and National Service and the supply ministries began and a centralised 'preference procedure' gradually emerged over the subsequent year. The process began when regional Labour Supply Officers at the Ministry of Supply and Production Officers at the supply ministries proposed first-priority labour demands. These were complemented by a list of priority items formed generally from those suggested by either the Ministry of Production following inter-departmental discussions, or one of the services citing operational requirements.[9] These lists were then combined and evaluated by the fortnightly Headquarters Preference Committee formed from central representatives of the supply ministries and the Ministry of Labour, with the Ministry of Production having the final say. Agreed Labour priorities were immediately teleprinted to every Ministry of Labour and National Service Office in the UK.[10] Nevertheless, inter-departmental tensions still hampered mobilisation, as demonstrated in 1942 when a Parliamentary Select Committee found that the Ministry of Supply often failed to cooperate with the Ministry of Labour and National Service when recruiting; the former responded by promising to cooperate.[11]

The success of labour mobilisation hinged on women. It was their inflow that enabled men to be drafted into the services or from peacetime industries to munitions. Government analysts divided the workforce into industrial groups (see Table 2 in Appendix), identifying that almost 1.7 million women were added to the workforce between 1940 and 1943, mostly to Group I (munitions) industries, enabling 2 million men to join the services. Meanwhile, Group II industries (such as agriculture, mining and utilities) received 625,000 new female employees and lost 216,000 male employees. The greatest change, however, occurred within Group III (non-essential industries and services) where employment fell by 1.9 million men and 432,000 women. Peak labour mobilisation was achieved by September 1943, some three years after the establishment of the Ministry of Labour and National Service.

'Manpower budgeting' on this scale necessitated a vast administration to survey labour patterns, estimate requirements of supply ministry programmes, and match labour supply with demand.[12] Yet compulsion was still balanced with voluntarism. Legal proceedings were reserved as a last resort to deal with those refusing to follow regulations. In mid-1943 Bevin declared that although 6.5 million people were subject to Essential Work Orders, legal proceedings had been taken against only one in 10,000 of these, and one in 50,000 had been imprisoned, of whom 15 were women.[13] He also argued that compulsory directions made under all measures within his remit were relatively few given the scale of the war effort: fewer than 250,000 men (outside building and civil engineering) and 90,000 women.[14] Finally, negotiations on pay and conditions within munitions enterprises were generally left to voluntary collective bargaining between unions and employer associations. Bevan strongly supported this approach, although government intervened where necessary to maintain production.[15]

Continuing with voluntarism, Bevin developed joint consultative machinery as he believed that discussing policies with unions before implementation was necessary to obtain their cooperation. Consultative procedures operated at three levels. The first was national, where joint consultative and advisory bodies such as the Joint Consultative Committee formed from the Employers' Confederation and the TUC discussed major decisions on labour policy before their implementation. Others included a Factory and Welfare Advisory Board, and a Women's Consultative Committee. The second was sub-regional: labour within some industries was preserved through a 'ring-fence' where transfers between businesses were decided by local committees of employer and worker representatives, and a Ministry of Supply representative, chaired by a Ministry of Labour and National Service Official.[16]

The final level was factory-based Joint Production Committees. By 1940 a variant of these existed in the coal industry through Pit Production Committees, and in 1942 unions and employer bodies reached agreement to create similar structures within Ministry of Supply factories, as well as in privately operated munitions businesses. The agreement covering the latter set out their aim as 'to consult and advise on matters relating to production and increased efficiency [...] in order that maximum output may be obtained from the factory'. By July 1943 there were 4,169 in existence throughout the UK.[17] However, their effectiveness varied widely and depended on factory-specific factors such as management attitudes. Although supply ministries encouraged the formation of committees in munitions factories, they generally distanced themselves from their operation and rarely obtained minutes to understand how they impacted industrial activities.[18] Nevertheless, the Ministry of Labour and National Service improved welfare throughout the munitions industries by enhancing, wherever possible, employment terms and conditions. Munitions work was well paid relative to many other occupations; the Ministry prioritised issues such as housing and transport, and assumed responsibility from the Home Office over the Factory Acts governing health and safety.

While protracted departmental infighting hampered the development of regional production governance, governing labour was far less fraught. Crucially, the Ministry of Labour and National Service already possessed an effective regional structure through its 1,620 offices scattered throughout the UK. Half were fully staffed employment exchanges while the remainder were branch offices. All sat within one of eleven regional divisions managed by a Regional Controller. These controllers were the most important element within the Ministry's labour supply organisation and represented the Ministry within the evolving regional production structures. Regional Controllers and their Regional Supply Labour Officers were expected to understand industrial labour needs before using instruments such as Essential Work Orders to fulfil the requirements of industries within their regions, albeit following centrally mandated priorities.[19]

All these instruments were put in place gradually and the Ministry of Labour's regional staff struggled to control labour in their absence. Yet, once controls were tightened, a mammoth programme began of registering workers at employment exchanges before using interviews to match them to vacant posts. Compulsion was reserved as a threat to incentivise their acceptance of such jobs. Regional structures were further empowered in 1942 when District Manpower Boards were created to examine whether individuals should be granted deferment from military call-up if their work was important to war production. These boards assessed 5 million applications by the end of the war, rejecting 885,000. As well as identifying suitable people to fill vacancies, regional divisions played an important role within intra-regional transfers. Transfers of 'mobile' labour, generally young childless women, was planned by dividing the UK into 'scarlet', 'red', 'amber' and 'green' areas depending on their labour surpluses or deficiencies.[20] Regions with surpluses were linked with those with deficiencies, and labour was directed accordingly. Nevertheless, voluntary transfers were preferred and even these were used sparingly given the hostility they often provoked.

As the war progressed, generalised shortages of labour in much of Britain accelerated amidst a 'manpower famine'. By 1943, the operations of the Headquarters Preference Committee were supplemented and eventually largely replaced by a system within which the supply ministries submitted items of the greatest importance to the Ministry of Production. Those agreed by the Ministry became 'designated items' whose manufacturers could claim preference over other firms in their locality for labour, with such items amounting to over a quarter of all production by early 1943. Central functions sought to divert production activity from 'scarlet' areas to areas that still had pockets of labour availability, necessitating more regional devolution of authority; Regional Controllers were sent lists of priority items and then communicated their local requirements to labour exchanges, while the volume of administration meant that Regional Preference Committees were established in November 1943 to decide on labour allocations to produce items, or carry out activities, that were not 'designated'.[21]

In 1944 the Ministry of Labour observed that administrative devolution to the regions was advanced and that Regional Controllers were responsible for 'all executive action relating to the mobilisation of man and women power for the services, industry and civil defence' through the 'administration of various war time orders'.[22] By this time, they worked closely with Ministry of Production Regional Boards to redistribute labour to ensure that the production of priority items for the invasion of France was not delayed.[23] While regional controllers carefully retained the broad support of the workforce through cooperating with unions and avoiding compulsion where possible, their authority over regional workforces was almost complete by the end of the war.

WALES

Ministry of Labour and National Service regional functions governing labour initially shared a similar approach to those within production. This meant that although its Cardiff-based Regional Controller managed 1,800 staff in 152 employment exchanges and other offices,[24] voluntarist approaches were prioritised. These initially worked well in Wales as recruiting a largely female workforce for the new ROFs proceeded smoothly throughout most of 1940. Two factors drove this success. One was the continuation of unemployment that still affected 79,709 people in May 1940.[25] The other was the ready availability of female labour. Married women had been generally excluded from the paid pre-war labour market, while unmarried women tended to work within domestic service and retail, often working long hours for poor pay. Yet the new munitions factories offered better pay and hours, and easily attracted female labour. Nevertheless, isolated labour shortages appeared. In August 1940 a lack of workers on airfield projects in Pembrokeshire was addressed by transferring labourers from Merthyr Tydfil.

But they soon claimed that delayed action bombs posed a risk, although the primary problem was low wages. They refused to work and returned home.[26] By November the Ministry of Labour and National Service reported difficulties in recruiting construction labourers for the explosives plant at Wrexham and warned that recruitment at Bridgend was becoming more difficult due to transport difficulties faced by workers commuting from Rhondda.[27]

Although production coordination remained embryonic, the Ministry of Labour and National Service regional function tightened its grip over the labour market as the growth in munitions production created thousands of vacancies. By late 1941 adverts in local newspapers throughout Wales were offering thousands of jobs in munitions factories. These included those declaring in November and December that 5,000 women were needed within weeks for factories in north Wales, with a similar number needed for the Auxiliary Territorial Service to carry out non-combat military activities.[28]

One tactic to drive recruitment was improving pay and conditions, apparent in the ROFs where management boosted wages, improved transport, enhanced welfare facilities such as nurseries, and provided hostels and housing to reduce commuting time.[29] These benefits formed an important element of recruitment efforts, such as an advert in the Caerphilly Journal in November 1941 offering 6,000 jobs for women involving 'light work on munitions' paying an average of '£3 per week' in locations where 'excess of [transport] fares over 3 shillings a week is paid, excellent hostels are available. Time for shopping can be arranged'.[30] Recruitment adverts were posted on hoardings and railway sites, a loudspeaker van toured Glamorgan and public meetings were held in a cinema. One worker at Bridgend recalled earning 'more than my father, a guard on the railways'.[31] Better pay and conditions within the ROFs meant that other employers paying less generous wages such as clothing manufacturers complained as to the difficulties of retaining their workforces.³² Male workers at Bridgend, Glascoed and Pembrey all earned more than coal miners, and while unskilled female workers in these factories were paid over a third less than their unskilled male equivalents,³³ these wages were still generally higher than in pre-war occupations. One female worker at the engineering ROF in Cardiff recalled that 'the wages were good ... they looked after us'.³⁴

The threat of compulsion remained an important recruitment tool and although relatively few workers were compelled, fear of sanctions prompted many to accept offers of work made by Ministry officials. By November 1941 Ministry officials had interviewed 53,246 women in Wales under the Registration of Employment Order, directing 13,404 to war work.³⁵ Local Interviewing Committees interviewed unoccupied women for industrial or service employment, while District Manpower Boards carried out similar responsibilities for those in employment. Their activities led to concern that workers would be sent to factories outside their localities, prompting Rhondda MP W. M. Mainwaring to explain the system to his constituents in mid-1942 in that successful appeals needed to prove that 'severe domestic hardship' would result from complying with instructions.³⁶

The Ministry also used Essential Work Orders to prohibit 358,218 workers in 1,604 undertakings throughout Wales from leaving their jobs without permission. While relatively few prosecutions were made, those convicted tended to be named in newspapers to ensure wider compliance. One example was two workers from Aberavon who were persistently between ten and forty minutes late for their shifts. They were each convicted and fined £2.³⁷

One female worker remembered how she 'had to register for work of national importance. They sent me out to [the] Glascoed' ROF.³⁸ Many were married women as registration exemptions gradually declined, as demonstrated in early 1942 when a Mass Observation study of Blaina and Nantyglo found that a 'large number' of the 600 female munitions workers from those areas were married and that the employment of large numbers of women was 'something quite new' for the area.[39] Other sources included disabled former tinplate workers and coal miners, many of whom were recruited by the Pembrey ROF.[40] Finally, factory inspectors could order firms to release employees and cancel vacancies, visiting 262 businesses throughout Wales in February 1941 to ensure that labour was not being hoarded.[41]

Meanwhile, industrial relations within munitions manufacture were generally calm, as reflected by low levels of unionisation and industrial action. Membership densities varied and although a union official argued in 1942 that 'women have started to see what trade unionism means ... it's easier now to recruit women to the union than men', less than a third of the Bridgend ROF workforce were members in that year.[42] An unorganised workforce unused to industrial work meant that new production techniques could be introduced with less risk of prompting disputes, enabling the official historian to argue that 'trade-union rules and customs of the trade had little time to solidify into a rigid system'.[43]

However, the primary cause of calm industrial relations was good pay and conditions, especially within state-run factories. Despite their scale, there were no strikes at Admiralty facilities from 1941 to 1945 and none at five of the ROFs; one Bridgend worker recalled that the factory was 'like a different world on its own, everything was well run, there were no strikes, or we never thought about it'.[44] Only seven strikes took place at the other two ROFs. All were unofficial and small in scale and were generally resolved in favour of the strikers. At the Pembrey explosives factory, forty-five plumbers went on strike for a day in 1941 over the refusal of one man to observe an overtime embargo; he promptly applied for a transfer. Strikes were more frequent at the Hirwaun ROF but a similar pattern was followed. The largest was in 1943 when 800 workers took strike action for a day after two absent workers were transferred to new jobs; management settled the strike by agreeing to set out their policies on absenteeism.[45]

Strikes were more frequent in privately operated factories, but industrial relations were again relatively calm. From 1940 to 1945, only fifty strikes occurred throughout Wales at privately operated engineering factories, the industry housing most munitions factories. Nevertheless, the size of the factories helped prompt a few large-scale strikes. One was in 1944 at an aircraft components factory in Llanberis where 1,352 workers went on strike for two days in 1944 over the management's resignation from the joint industrial council, before returning to work unconditionally on the advice of union officials.[46] Most were resolved quickly after a day or two of industrial action, and only three lasted more than a week. Others were often resolved by negotiations between unions and management, such as one in late 1942 over wages paid to female trainees transferred from south Wales to the Vickers-Armstrong aircraft factory at Broughton.[47] All this meant that disputes within engineering businesses accounted for only 3.4 per cent of all working days lost in Wales between 1940 and 1945, far fewer than other industries such as coal mining and tinplate (see Figure 1 in Appendix).

From 1942 munitions factories often featured Joint Production Committees, often known by other names including industrial councils. They were constituted along voluntary lines, and their effectiveness varied widely, although evidence in Wales is fragmentary. One example was recorded by Mass Observation in 1942. The process began when a union official at a south Wales munitions factory persuaded management to convene a committee. Management initially refused, with one manager saying that he would 'brook no interference from the men'. Nevertheless, they relented once shown the agreement between their employers' association and union representatives that mandated committee creation.[48] Although such agreements had been signed by May 1942, the Wales Regional Board recorded slow compliance throughout the rest of that year. Regional

Officers at the three supply ministries encouraged and supported their formation in contracting businesses,[49] but tended to adopt a more laissez-faire approach once committees began to operate.

By 1942 industrial conscription combined with the emerging preference system within production to enable the Ministry of Labour and National Service to recruit and direct labour to maximise production of designated items. Regional staff encouraged voluntary applications through advertising campaigns to encourage women to apply for munitions work and arranging bus services enabling commuting from isolated villages.[50] By mid-1942 over half of all war workers in Wales were female and they dominated many ammunition and engineering facilities.[51] One worker from Pembrokeshire remembers that she was asked to work at the Trecwn Admiralty depot. She initially refused given the recent death of her father, but:[52]

> I had to go to Morris Motors [in Llanelli]. It was war. I got called up ... I had to go to a tribunal ... two women interviewing me. And they were strict because they wanted everyone to go [to war work]. All my friends had gone off but me.

Finally, the Ministry could also identify 'mobile' staff for transfer. While few were compelled, with Mass Observation's study of Blaina and Nantyglo recording how its Labour Exchange Manager observed a 'great antagonism' amongst the workforce towards 'going away from the district', some 20,000 workers agreed to transfer from south Wales to England by the end of 1942.[53] Transfers declined by 1944, however, as labour supply throughout much of Wales became constrained. In January 1945 the Ministry of Labour and National Service told a Regional Board meeting that a Cardiff company, Machine Products, wanted to recruit 546 workers but that supply was unavailable. The minutes describe how the Chair promptly 'referred to official instructions and intimated that the demand must be met as the highest priority', and a further meeting was arranged to discuss how the demand could be met by releasing workers from other companies in Cardiff.[54] This and many other similar labour issues preoccupied ministry officials, but as the war ended they were dealing with the opposite problem of managing the transition to peacetime as munitions producers shed jobs and new peacetime manufacturing arrived.

CONCLUSION

The development of labour governance had some similarities with governance over production as both were protracted processes initially featuring voluntary approaches, later complemented with compulsion where needed. Yet developing labour governance was smoother. The Ministry of Labour and National Service was the undisputed lead on labour policy, meaning that there was no repeat of the intra-ministerial feuding that hampered coordination elsewhere. Moreover, the Ministry already possessed well-developed mechanisms that could be repurposed to suit wartime requirements. A regional structure helped it to understand and influence regional labour market dynamics, while its labour exchanges were ideally placed to monitor and direct local workforces. Both factors meant that national labour policies could be implemented locally by one ministry. Finally, Bevin was an authoritative figure whose political importance helped him remain in post throughout the lifespan of the coalition government, deploying his authority across government and the trade unions to achieve labour mobilisation. These factors meant that while Bevin was initially reluctant to resort to compulsion, his ministry soon began to construct a framework to marshal labour that blended voluntarism with the threat of compulsion. The resulting approach used existing structures but overlaid and controlled them with a coordinated national approach to enable a mobilisation that corralled the labour force throughout Britain to service the war industries.

The extent to which this approach succeeded was clear in Wales. Although the total workforce grew only marginally from 696,000 in 1939 to 699,000 in 1944, state intervention prompted radical structural change. The conscription of male workers reduced their number from 602,000 to 480,000; this reduction was largely offset by the increase of female workers from 94,000 to 219,000. The mass entry of women into the labour force was concentrated within munitions; their exclusion from the pre-war industrial labour market enabled their number in Wales to grow by 134 per cent, far more than the 30 per cent average across Britain. Meanwhile, the state minimised peacetime manufacturing to expand that of munitions. Workers in chemicals, engineering and vehicle construction were overwhelmingly producing munitions, and employment in these sectors grew from 22,000 in 1939 to 147,000 in 1944.[55] Although 38 per cent of chemicals, engineering and vehicle construction employees worked within state managed ROFs and Admiralty facilities, the balance was employed by private businesses contracted to one or more of the three supply ministries.

These structural changes combined to prompt the elimination of unemployment within a manufacturing labour market that remained dominated by businesses, operating within parameters set by the state that possessed comprehensive powers of direction but used them sparingly.

Notes

1 Parker, *Manpower*, p. 96.
2 Parker, *Manpower*, p. 123.
3 D. Jay, *Change and Fortune* (Hutchinson, 1980), p. 90.
4 M. Gowing, 'The Organisation of Manpower in Britain during the Second World War', *Journal of Contemporary History*, 7(1/2) (1972), 147–67 (154).
5 Parker, *Manpower*, pp. 210, 213.
6 Parker, *Manpower*, pp. 141, 145.

7. M. Williams, *A Forgotten Army: Female Munitions Workers of South Wales, 1939–1945* (University of Wales Press, 2002), p. 66.
8. Jay, *Change and Fortune*, p. 88.
9. Scott and Hughes, *The Administration of War Production*, p. 244.
10. Jay, *Change and Fortune*, p. 91.
11. *The Times*, 'Ordnance Factories', 6 August 1942.
12. E. A. G Robinson, 'The Overall Allocation of Resources', in D. N. Chester (ed.), *Lessons of the British War Economy* (Cambridge University Press, 1951), pp. 34–57 (p. 52).
13. A. Bullock, *The Life and Times of Ernest Bevin, II, Minister of Labour, 1940–1945* (Heinemann, 1967), p. 173.
14. Gowing, 'The Organisation of Manpower', 153.
15. TNA, CAB, 102/404, *Wages Policy in the United Kingdom in the Second World War*, 49.
16. Bullock, *The Life and Times of Ernest Bevin*, pp. 96–7.
17. Bullock, *The Life and Times of Ernest Bevin*, p. 95.
18. P. Inman, *Labour in the Munition Industries* (HMSO, 1957), p. 380.
19. Parker, *Manpower*, pp. 214, 216.
20. Parker, *Manpower*, pp. 296, 309–10; Gowing, 'The Organisation of Manpower', 162–3.
21. Scott and Hughes, *The Administration of War Production*, pp. 483–6.
22. TNA, LAB 12/137, *Note on the Regional Organisation of the Ministry of Labour and National Service with Particular Reference to the Arrangements Relating to Wales and Monmouthshire*, 1 April 1944.
23. TNA, 168/12, *Minutes of Regional Controllers Conference (Appendix)*, 8–9 March 1944, 1–2; 9–10 February 1944, 3.
24. TNA, LAB 12/137, *Note on the Regional Organisation of the Ministry of Labour and National Service*, April 1944, 2–3.
25. Williams, *DWHS, vol. 1*, p. 146.
26. TNA, LAB 12/82, *Ministry of Labour, Wales Division, Monthly Report*, 12 August 1940, 5; September 1940, 6; 14 October, 5.
27. TNA, LAB 12/82, *Ministry of Labour, Wales Division, Monthly Report*, 9 December 1940, 7.
28. *Rhos Herald*, 'Mother Finds a Way', 13 December 1941; *Flintshire County Herald*, '10,000 women can tip the scales for Hitler, or against', 5 December 1941.
29. TNA, LAB 102/129, *Housing and Hostels*, 1.
30. *Caerphilly Journal*, '£3 a Week Average Pay Offered to 6,000 Women in South Wales', 1 November 1941.
31. SWML, *Interviews Held by Mari A Williams with Twenty-two South Wales War Workers, 1991–93*, 23.
32. TNA, BT 64/3153, *Nuffield College Reconstruction Survey, South Wales Report*, 1941, 30.
33. TNA, POWE 20/62, *Royal Ordnance Factories, Typical Weekly Earnings; Estimated Average Earnings per Shift (Miners)*.

34 L. Verrill-Rhys and D. Beddoe (eds), *Parachutes and Petticoats* (Honno, 2003), p. 84.
35 TNA, LAB 12/82, *Ministry of Labour, Wales Division, Monthly Report*, 17 November 1941.
36 *Caerphilly Journal*, Letter from Mr W. H. Mainwaring, MP, 6 June 1942.
37 TNA, LAB 12/82, *Ministry of Labour, Wales Division, Monthly Report*, 17 November 1941; *Neath Guardian*, 'Late for Work Habit', 24 July 1942.
38 Interview with Linda Westerman cited in P. Carradice, *Wales at War* (Gomer Press, 2005), p. 79.
39 Mass Observation, *Mining Town–1942*, 1944, 88.
40 Inman, *Labour in the Munitions Industries*, p. 181.
41 TNA, LAB 12/82, *Ministry of Labour, Wales Division, Monthly Report*, 16 February 1941, 5.
42 Mass Observation, *Mining Town–1942*, 1944, 103; Williams, *A Forgotten Army*, p. 103.
43 Postan, *British War Production*, p. 431.
44 SWML, *Interviews held by Mari A Williams*, 20.
45 TNA, LAB 34/56, *Trade Disputes*, 1941; 34/58, *Trade Disputes*, 1943.
46 TNA, LAB 34/58, *Trade Disputes*, 1944.
47 *North Wales Weekly News*, 'Wages in Aircraft Factory', 12 November 1942.
48 Mass Observation, *Mining Town–1942*, 1944, 85–6.
49 TNA, BT 168/29, *Ministry of Production, Wales Regional Board*, 16 November 1942, 5; 23 November 1942, 1; 14 December 1942, 1.
50 TNA, LAB 102/877, *The Welfare of Industrial Workers*, 62.
51 *Western Mail*, 'More than Half War Workers in Wales Women', 23 March 1942.
52 Voices from the Factory Floor, *Elizabeth Mary Lewis*, http://www.factorywomensvoices.wales/uploads/VSW002.2.pdf, 3–4.
53 TNA, BT 168/2, *War Production in Dundee and South Wales, Production Executive*, 15 December 1942, 2; Mass Observation, *Mining Town–1942*, 1944, 38.
54 TNA, BT 170/215, *Regional Board Minutes*, 15 January 1945, 5.
55 B. Thomas, 'Post-war Expansion', in Thomas (ed.), *The Welsh Economy: Studies in Expansion*, pp. 30–1.

5

FACTORIES

THE MINISTRY OF SUPPLY

The most important of the three supply ministries in Wales after 1940 was initially the Ministry of Supply. While industrialists had been recently complaining about the lack of contracts, by December some 120 companies were under contract to the Ministry and many others held sub-contracts. Contracts divided broadly into those for two types of goods. One was for ammunition and weapons components, such as A. R. Adams and Son in Newport producing components for Lewis Gun mounts, Welsh Metal Industries in Caerphilly machining parts for artillery pieces, and Shepard and Sons in Bridgend producing mortar bombs. The other was common stores, such as William Thomas and Sons of Wrexham producing bedsteads and huts, the Royal Welsh Factory of Newtown manufacturing clothing, and Alf Jamon of Swansea producing tents.[1]

Most Ministry contracted factories were in south Wales, reflecting the activities of the Commissioner for Special Areas who had built the Treforest industrial estate and a few factories elsewhere including those at Merthyr Tydfil and Dowlais. Floorspace at Treforest doubled during the war while all but one or two factories were on war work by early 1941.[2] As mobilisation accelerated, factories expanded to fulfil ministry contacts. These included a former telephone factory in Merthyr Tydfil that expanded to employ 2,639 workers producing guns, fuses and cartridge cases for the Birmingham Small Arms company, a Metal

Box plant at Neath where 600 people made bomb components, and an Aberdare cable works producing shells and torpedoes.[3] Finally, the Polikoff factory in the Rhondda produced items including uniforms for Montgomery's North African Army and 'overcoats for Russia'; one worker remembered 'a huge, huge factory ... 2,500 people working'.[4]

By 1942 few factories remained available for requisition, forcing the Ministry of Supply and other ministries to requisition car and bus garages, market halls, former gaols and brickworks.[5] Meanwhile, firms displaced from Treforest migrated northwards to occupy disused colliery buildings, chapels and cinemas. Many such firms switched to wartime production once capacity problems arose elsewhere, with the Regional Board arguing that 'native firms' were 'little used' for war production until such pressure grew.[6] One example was Flex Fasteners that found alternative premises in Porth where it employed 300 people making helmet linings and anti-gas goggles.[7] Demand for industrial space meant that manufacturing spread throughout rural areas. Garages in Colwyn Bay assembled jeeps, while the ballroom of Gresford Lodge country house was used to manufacture fuses.[8] Most factories in less industrialised areas were small but there were exceptions, such as Cooke's Explosives near Porthmadog, a mining explosives factory where some 600 workers produced hand grenades.[9]

As well as contracting with private companies to produce munitions, the Ministry also constructed agency factories, operated by private companies who paid annual agency fees in lieu of rent. The main operator in Wales was ICI and arrangements were cost-effective, especially once annual fees were reduced in 1942 to 0.5 per cent of fixed capital invested by the government.[10] The company managed ammonia and methanol plants at Dowlais where some 600 people worked, and an ammonia plant at Pembrey.[11] Their most secret facility, however, was the Valley Works mustard gas factory at Rhydymwyn, Flintshire. By 1943 some 2,200 people were employed in a hundred buildings and a network of tunnels, eventually filling over four million munitions items including bombs, shells and mines. Hasty construction in a narrow valley prompted hazardous conditions symbolised by a waste incinerator shrouding surrounding buildings with toxic pollution.[12] The war prompted huge volumes of scientific innovation to develop new weaponry, but little took place in Wales. The exception was the Valley Works that hosted nuclear research as part of the government's 'Tube Alloys' project. In 1942 scientists began experimenting to enrich uranium for use in nuclear weapons although the factory's leading position was short-lived given the government's subsequent decision to pool research with the United States.

The most obvious Ministry of Supply focus was on ammunition and by early 1942 it managed seven ROFs in Wales employing 68,000 people, although the speed and scale of their expansion means that workforce data held in the archives is not always fully consistent. The filling factories at Bridgend and Glascoed constituted the first and largest type. The Bridgend factory employed 32,570 people by March 1942 with the speed of growth (see Figure 3 in Appendix) reflected by 1,272 men and 3,866 women joining its workforce in five weeks during March and April 1941. The demand of the armed forces for male conscripts meant that 59 per cent of the peak workforce at the Bridgend was female, as was 46 per cent at Glascoed (see Table 3 in Appendix).[13]

The scale of filling factories reflected the demand for munitions as well as the labour-intensive nature of production. Production began by filling projectile parts, usually with cordite. Charges, such as a cartridge case, were then loaded with high explosive before assembly to produce ammunition.[14] Factories incorporated hundreds of scattered buildings to minimise risk although working conditions could be poor; a worker at Bridgend recalled that 'nobody wanted to go' into one part of the factory handling explosives as their 'hair and skin would turn yellow'.[15] Between 1940 and 1945 the two factories produced many millions of munitions items. Those produced at ROF Bridgend were destined mostly for the army and included 9.3 million medium gun shells, 10 million trench mortar shells and 140 million detonators. Items produced by ROF Glascoed were spread more evenly across the services and included 4.5 million shells for the navy, 263,000 bombs for the air force, and 6 million smoke generators for the army.[16]

Explosives factories constituted the second type of ROFs. The largest was at Wrexham where two units were constructed with a combined weekly manufacturing capacity of 520 tons of cordite. Production began in late 1940 when some 500 workers were employed, although 6,000 workers were still constructing the second unit by May 1941. Nevertheless, both units were operating by November 1941 when 7,442 workers, 55 per cent female, were employed and 804 vacancies were being filled.[17] Employment peaked at 10,250 people in March 1942 (see Table 3 in Appendix).[18] The other explosives factory was at Pembrey that by June 1940 produced over two hundred tons of TNT weekly and was co-located with a smaller chemicals factory constructed by ICI The entire complex employed 2,174 people by the end of 1940 and 3,050 by April 1942.[19]

The third and final type of ROFs were the three engineering facilities. The first was in Cardiff and manufactured artillery pieces. While the scale of filling factories meant that construction was protracted, engineering ROFs were large sheds that could be built quickly. Construction of the 464,000 sq. ft factory began in March 1940, and the need to replace weapons lost in France meant that production commenced in August before the roof was complete.[20] Gun barrel forgings were delivered to the factory before being milled and finished by highly skilled operatives using machines often imported from the United States. Employment peaked at 4,020 people, 43 per cent female.[21] Unskilled labour was recruited from Cardiff and the valleys before being trained on site. Women played an important role; all wore uniform turbans to avoid accidents caused by hair entanglements, with supervisors recognisable by blue headgear. One female worker recalled that women 'could do anything a man could do with machinery ... I worked on Cincinnati lathes, they were big' while 'women worked the cranes ... over our heads'.[22] The factory was originally planned to produce 125 25-pounder guns a month, but average monthly output by July 1942 was 600, while total wartime output was 21,200.[23]

The second engineering ROF was a 233,000 sq. ft factory at Newport producing artillery and anti-aircraft guns. Construction began in March 1940 and production commenced in August.[24] Employment peaked at 2,440 people, 53 per cent female.[25] Its superintendent noted later that there was insufficient male labour to staff the factory and that the 'only alternative was the employment of girl labour'. He established a training school within the factory, after which the success of female labour was 'very surprising' to the managers of other engineering concerns who 'would not believe it until they actually visited the factory and saw the work being done'.[26] The final engineering ROF was at an isolated location near Hirwaun chosen because of labour availability. After its construction by 6,000 workers, the 519,000 sq. ft factory produced components for small arms ammunition from early 1942. Employment peaked at 8,600 workers in March 1944, of whom 54 per cent were female.[27]

As elsewhere, criticism of the improvised nature of production administration within ROFs increased after 1940. The Ministry of Supply responded by creating a filling factory regional structure in 1941, although explosives and engineering factories remained centrally managed. The Bridgend and Glascoed factories joined a Hereford facility to populate a 'Western Region' with a Regional Director, although his staff were restricted to supervising production and providing technical assistance.[28] Restrictions meant that day-to-day management authority remained decentralised as effective local control was a prerequisite to maximising production, and regional structures had little impact. The flexible nature of administration was further reflected in the choice of superintendents responsible for managing the Bridgend ROF. The first, Reg Edmonds, had spent his career at the Woolwich Arsenal before being transferred to establish the factory. He left in 1941 to become Assistant Director of the Western Region. His successor, Len Corbett, had managed a Fry's chocolate factory near Bristol with 5,000 employees and had no background in munitions.[29] Nevertheless, this appointment was pragmatic as Corbett had managed a large industrial workforce including many women, and worked in a paternalistic environment reflecting the Quaker origins of Fry's Chocolates. Both elements of his background were useful when managing Bridgend.

ROF governance was a conspicuous success as the factories were exceeding ammunition and explosive production targets by early 1941. Surpluses meant that overall employment at ROFs peaked in early 1942 and numbers at the four Welsh factories fell subsequently by 27 per cent from end 1941 to end 1943: from 51,300 to 37,561.[30] Some recruitment continued, such as miners and ex-servicemen certified as unfit in 1943, but the remarkable labour force mobilisation wound down. Employment then generally stabilised before the inevitable reductions towards the end of the war. In contrast, engineering ROFs were unaffected by ammunition surpluses and their employment levels remained stable.

THE MINISTRY OF AIRCRAFT PRODUCTION

Aircraft production after 1940 was driven by three forces. The first was how government intervention since the mid-1930s had built a privately managed industry although a large portion was guided, funded and housed by the state through the agency factory system. As a result, the Ministry of Aircraft Production was the only supply ministry without its own factories.[31] The second was dispersing production to reduce the impact of air raids in locations such as London, Birmingham and Coventry. The Ministry worked feverishly on dispersal and Wales emerged as a production location for components. Aircraft, however, were generally assembled in factories in regions with a track record in hosting large engineering concerns. The final force was the strategic bomber programme prompting more demand after 1942.[32] By 1943 almost 15 per cent of all certificates authorising factory construction throughout the UK issued by the Factory and Storage Control Function to the Ministry of Aircraft Production related to sites in Wales.[33]

The dispersal programme of 1940 identified low risk locations, but south Wales was relatively close to enemy bases in France while the Severn estuary was a prominent navigational marker for their bombers. These drawbacks prompted a wider search. One result was a factory in the unlikely surroundings of the Dinorwic slate quarry at Llanberis. It originated after bombing raids on 15 and 16 August 1940 damaged a Croydon factory operated by Rollaston Aircraft Services. Managers searched for a safer location and chose Llanberis on 30th August, where the plant was known as NECACO (North East Coast Aircraft Company) after a shell company used for administrative convenience. Equipment was moved from London and installed in a shed previously used for splitting and cutting slate. The factory, complemented by three smaller facilities in Caernarfon, produced bomber components. Fear of air raids prompted some machine tools to be installed in a tunnel lined with zinc sheets to prevent dripping water, although workers there were offered sun lamp sessions in winter. The factory operated continuously apart from Saturday afternoons, and employees worked twelve-hour shifts.[34]

NECACO was not the only relocation to northwest Wales. A seaplane maintenance facility employing 400 people was established on Anglesey by Saunders Roe in 1941 after its Isle of Wight operations were deemed unsafe.[35] By 1942 some 200 workers were adapting American seaplanes to meet RAF specifications. The company constructed hangars at Beaumaris but also used premises such as stables and garages. Finally, Daimler transferred production of aero-engine components to Bangor to employ around a thousand people after air raids on Coventry, as part of a dispersal programme to forty locations throughout the UK ranging from a skating rink to a deer park.[36] Employees worked in a factory constructed by the Ministry of Aircraft Production or in requisitioned bus garages,[37] while Penrhyn Castle became an administrative base. Meanwhile, dispersal overlapped with the Ministry's construction of factories. The largest in north Wales was built in Colwyn Bay for Ratcliffe Gauge and Tool Ltd, a London-based company with a small operation in Old Colwyn. Production began in late 1940, eighteen weeks after ground-breaking, when a thousand workers within a three-shift, twenty-four-hour system, seven-days-a-week operation produced aircraft spars and bomb release gear.[38]

Treforest Industrial Estate emerged as a key source of aircraft components in south Wales. Relocations included the British Overseas Aircraft Corporation, which moved from London to employ 1,650 people at the expense of twenty existing tenants, although the engine test beds had to be located elsewhere. Another seventeen factories were requisitioned for Helliwells, relocated from Walsall. By 1942, however, expansions at Treforest were being discouraged due to labour shortages, and industrialists were encouraged to consider Swansea and Llanelli.[39] Labour factors prompted the opening of factories in rural locations, such as one constructed from mid-1940 to produce tubular steel components in Newtown. Chosen for its rural location and female labour availability, it was managed by the West Midlands firm of Accles and Pollock. Employment peaked at some 3,000 people in 1944 with recruitment aided by childcare provision. The Ministry also established a smaller factory near Abergavenny in 1943 to produce engine radiators, while Prestigne hosted a Birmingham firm producing die castings.

As well as relocating production to Wales, by 1942 the Ministry also part-funded twenty-one companies expected to employ 24,445 people.[40] These included the Cwmbran factory built for the Birmingham firm of Joseph Lucas that employed 4,700 people manufacturing gun turrets for Lancaster bombers by 1942 when it planned to employ a further 2,800,[41] while in the subsequent year Morris Motors established a plant near Llanelli to produce items including Spitfire radiators. A nineteen-year-old female worker remembered catching the bus from Pontyberem to arrive at the Morris factory at six o'clock, working until five before arriving home just before seven o'clock; 'bath, food and bed ... didn't really have a life'.[42] Others included the Rotax factory in Merthyr Tydfil that switched from producing sewing machines to magnetos and starters, where the workforce grew from 35 in 1940 to 2,349 by 1943.[43] By 1945 seventeen companies manufacturing aircraft components and specialist metals operated in almost 3 million square feet of government-owned factories throughout Wales that had received over £8 million from the Ministry towards refurbishment and equipment. Twelve operated on 'commercial terms' where tenants paid rent, but the balance used 'agency terms' where the Ministry paid fees to the companies occupying each factory. Such fees were calculated using indicators such as capital invested by tenants and production volumes.[44]

The only airframe factory in Wales was the Vickers-Armstrong plant at Broughton that produced 5,540 Wellington bombers by October 1945, and 235 Lancaster bombers after mid-1944.[45] Employment peaked at 6,483 in November 1943.[46] Each aircraft was assembled in sixty hours using components sourced from just-in-time supply chains, reflecting the advanced nature of aircraft manufacturing. The focus on speed was illustrated by a requirement to divert Merlin engines from Wellingtons to Spitfires. Engineers adapted the airframe to fit alternative engines, producing remodelled aircraft within four months. The role of the private sector was clear as the plant was state-owned and depended on government orders but was managed by Vickers-Armstrong while all sub-contractors were private.

The factory gained a national profile in 1943 when the Ministry of Information filmed a successful attempt to assemble an aircraft in less than thirty hours. The footage was shown in cinemas to boost morale and demonstrated the importance of female workers – a voice-over declared 'here's Phyllis Evans, she was in service as a maid before the war' – as well their novelty, the film showing 'Grace Whalley and Hilda Dodd doing a man's job of work, assembling the bomber's cabin heater'.[47] Finally, the Welsh identity of the 'Chester Plant' was apparent in 1940 when employees and sub-contractors paid for one aircraft and decorated its fuselage with a red dragon and a Welsh-language inscription.

THE ADMIRALTY AND JOINT WORKING

The Admiralty was determined to maintain control over some production of naval munitions given its concern that material might be diverted to other services.[48] It developed and managed two munitions facilities in Wales. One was the Royal Navy Propellant Factory at Caerwent where 4,200 people produced cordite and other material.[49] The other was a factory at Milford Haven that was the UK's principal producer of naval mines.[50] It employed around a thousand people, and its products were stored nearby at the Admiralty's underground depot at Trecwn. Many of the themes apparent within ROF management appeared within Admiralty facilities, notably the need to recruit and retain a largely female workforce that prompted a focus on welfare; hostels were constructed to house 400 workers at Caerwent and 800 at Trecwn.[51]

While there were no Royal Dockyards or large private yards in Wales, the scale of the pre-war coal export shipping trade had prompted the manufacture of shipping items as well as ship repair. By early 1941 ninety-four companies in Wales were contracted to the Admiralty. While some were producing general stores, such as Oran and Ward in Cardiff sewing flags, and D.G. Hall and Co. in Newport manufacturing lifeboats, contracts were placed at twenty-six repair yards including those at Milford Haven, Cardiff, Barry, Newport and Swansea.[52] By the end of the war, some 9,800 people were employed in ship repair yards throughout south Wales.[53] Few vessels were built, although a yard at Chepstow produced sixty landing craft and facilities in north Wales included one in Bangor that produced twenty-eight motor launches.[54] Overall, however, the lack of a large-scale shipbuilding tradition meant that Admiralty procurement was often relatively small in scale, except for its facilities at Caerwent and Milford Haven. Throughout the war, the Admiralty obtained few 'nil certificates' in Wales from the Factory and Storage Control Function where its contractors were authorised to construct only 34,000 square feet of factory space.[55]

Finally, many companies held multiple contracts producing material for two or all the supply ministries, as well as other ministries such as the Mines Department, the Ministry of Food and the Ministry of Works and Buildings. The administrative difficulty of dealing with such companies across multiple ministries helped prompt greater coordination once capacity constraints emerged by 1942. Such companies provided a vast range of stores and equipment. Companies producing items for all three supply ministries included Crown Compositions of Swansea manufacturing paint, Elliot Equipment of Cardiff producing parachutes and ancillary equipment, while many others produced goods for two of the three ministries.[56] These included a factory at Landore near Swansea where over 1,500 workers produced cartridges for the Admiralty and Ministry of Supply, and a Chepstow wagon works whose production included oil tanks for airfields, ammunition wagons for the Ministry of Supply and steelwork for the Admiralty.[57]

One prominent example was Edward Curran, an engineering company with factories in Cardiff and Aberdare. It supplied the Ministry of Supply with millions of munition items such as incendiary bomb cases, the Admiralty with cartridge cases, all three ministries with engineered products including machine tools, and repaired aircraft for the Ministry of Aircraft Production. While most factories in Wales were 'branch plants' of larger companies headquartered elsewhere, Curran's autonomous management gave the company agency sufficient to control its expansion and diversification. Such diversification included repairing aircraft, converting Sherman tanks to minesweeping units, and producing machine tools including 600-ton presses. In other respects, however, Currans was like other plants. Wartime employment grew from 1,969 in mid-1939 to eventually peak at 12,800 people, almost 7,000 of whom were female.[58] Three thousand were drawn from outside Cardiff. Some early shift workers from the heads of the Valleys caught a 4.20 a.m. train to arrive by 6 a.m., and annoyance at lack of transport subsidy when compared with ROF workers prompted discontent, although an official tribunal into their complaints ruled subsequently against extending subsidy.[59] As elsewhere, the need to maintain morale prompted a welfare department that maintained a register of accommodation used by 600 employees in one twelve-month period, arranged treatment for ill employees, managed a benevolent scheme, and arranged sporting and social events.[60]

CONCLUSION

Britain-wide mobilisation to produce munitions focused initially on concentrations of secondary manufacturing outside Wales, given the common perception amongst officials and industrialists that its legacy of primary industries had prompted a workforce lacking sufficient skills within secondary manufacturing. Nevertheless, by the end of 1940 the Ministry of Supply was operating vast ROF's throughout Wales and had awarded contracts to many smaller businesses. The other supply ministries were less active although both were steadily increasing their contracting volume. Yet air raids and capacity shortages elsewhere prompted manufacturing businesses to relocate some production to Wales even as those already present supplanted their manufacture of peacetime goods with that of munitions.

Inflows to Wales continued after the air raid threat lessened because of its ongoing labour capacity, formed primarily from unoccupied females subject to industrial conscription as factories spread to rural areas unthinkable as industrial locations a few years previously. Meanwhile, manufacturing was gradually subjected to greater state direction, initially through the Factory and Storage Control Function, and subsequently through the Regional Board. The board assumed a vital role in mediating between the supply ministries and identifying suitable locations for factories operated by businesses whom they contracted. The dividing line between the state and private industry was further blurred by the dependence of many businesses on state support to construct and equip their new factories.

From 1942 activity declined at the Ministry of Supply's explosive and ammunition ROFs, but the impact of reducing employment was more than offset by the inflow of other manufacturing businesses. Many of the newly arrived factories were contracted to and often financially supported by the Ministry of Aircraft Production as it constructed a fleet of strategic bombers. Nevertheless, the legacy of dependence on primary industries remained visible as few aircraft were built in Wales where factories such as those on the Treforest Industrial Estate concentrated instead on components. A similar dynamic also impacted on naval procurement. Wales had never emerged as a major shipbuilding centre, meaning that the largest employer producing items for the Admiralty was its Caerwent plant. A few small vessels were built in yards including those in

Chepstow and Bangor, but the focus was on ship repairing and production of miscellaneous components. All this meant that by 1944 Regional Board Chair Thomas argued correctly that the war had 'brought a very great expansion and diversification of industry to the region'.[61]

Notes

1. TNA, BT 168/2, *Firms in Area Engaged on Government Contracts, or on War Production Sub-contracts, Wales Area Board*, 18 January 1941.
2. TNA, BT 168/5, *Report on Visit to South Wales*, April 1943, 3.
3. TNA, BT 168/5, *Letter from Wales Regional Board*, 20 July 1943, 3; Rowlands, *Something Must Be Done*, p. 166.
4. Voices from the Factory Floor, Margaret Chislett, *http://www.factorywomensvoices.wales/uploads/VSE012.2.pdf*, 3-4; C. Baber and D. Thomas, 'The Glamorgan Economy, 1914–1945', in John and Williams, *Glamorgan County History, Volume V*, p. 564.
5. TNA, BT 170/215, *Regional Board Minutes*, 9 April 1945.
6. TNA, BT 168/1, *Review of War Production Position in Wales*, February 1942, 2.
7. TNA, LAB 12/82, *Ministry of Labour, Wales Division, Monthly Report*, 14 July 1941, 2.
8. A. G. Veysey, *Clwyd at War* (Hawarden: Clwyd Record Office, 1989), p. 45.
9. Voices from the Factory Floor, Susan Jones, *http://www.factorywomensvoices.wales/uploads/VN016.2.pdf*, 7.
10. Ashworth, *Contracts and Finance*, p. 156.
11. Rowlands, *Something Must be Done*, pp. 153, 164; GLA, D377/82, *No. 12 Unit Ammonia and Ethanol Plants*, 1.
12. TNA, AVIVA 22/3337, Rhydymwyn, 8; N. J. McCamley, *Disasters Underground* (Pen and Sword, 2004), pp. 148–50; Edgerton, *Britain's War Machine*, p. 202.
13. TNA, LAB 12/82, *Ministry of Labour Monthly Reports*, 21 April 1941, 6; CAB 102/272, *Females Employed in Royal Ordnance Factories*.
14. Hornby, *Factories and Plant*, p. 93.
15. NLW, MS 23071E, *Women in World War 2: Manuscript Accounts: Interview with Mair Davies*.
16. TNA, CAB 102/76, *History of the Filling Factories: Wartime Outputs*.
17. TNA, CAB 102/625, *The Histories of 22 Royal Ordnance Factories 1881–1944: Wrexham*, 1-2; TNA, LAB 12/82, *Ministry of Labour Monthly Reports*, 12 May 1941, 3; 17 November 1941, 8.
18. TNA, CAB 102/272, *Females Employed in Royal Ordnance Factories*.
19. TNA, CAB 102/625, *The Histories of 22 Royal Ordnance Factories 1881–1944: Pembrey*, 3; TNA, LAB 12/82, *Ministry of Labour Monthly Reports*, 9 December 1940, 7; CAB 102/272, *Females Employed in Royal Ordnance Factories*.

20 TNA, CAB 102/270, *ROF Floorspace*; M. Christensen, 'Royal Ordnance Factory, Llanishen, Part 1', *Quarterly Journal for British Industrial and Transport History*, 33 (2002), 33, 35.
21 TNA, CAB 102/272, *Females Employed in Royal Ordnance Factories*.
22 NLW, MS 23071E, *Women in World War 2: Manuscript Accounts: Interview with Edna Gorshkov*.
23 Christensen, M. 'Royal Ordnance Factory, Llanishen, Part 2', *Quarterly Journal for British Industrial and Transport History*, 34 (2002), 25.
24 TNA, CAB 102/270, *ROFs Projected, October 1939–May 1940*; *ROF Floorspace*.
25 TNA, CAB 102/272, *Females Employed in Royal Ordnance Factories*.
26 TNA, CAB 102/629, *General Notes on Procedure at ROF Newport*, 1, 2.
27 TNA, BT 64/3105, *Nuffield College Regional Reconstruction Survey, West Wales Report*, 50; CAB 102/270, *ROF Floorspace*; CAB 102/272, *Females Employed in Royal Ordnance Factories*.
28 TNA, CAB 102/630, *The Filling Factory Organisation*, 33; CAB 102/272, *Regional Administration of Filling Factories*.
29 Clubb, *The Welsh Arsenal*, pp. 83–6.
30 TNA, CAB 102/272, *Employment at ROFs 1939–1943*.
31 Ashworth, *Contracts and Finance*, p. 220.
32 *Statistical Digest of the War*, p. 152.
33 TNA, BT 131/28, *The Control of Factory and Storage Space*, annexes.
34 R. Chambers, *Bless 'Em All* (Bridge Books, 1995), pp. 52–4.
35 TNA, BT 64/3135, *Comments on Nuffield College Reconstruction Survey, North Wales Report*, 1942; TNA, LAB 12/82, *Ministry of Labour, Wales Division, Monthly Report*, 16 February 1941, 2.
36 Lord Montagu and D. Burgess-Wise, *Daimler Century* (Haynes Publishing, 1995), p. 243.
37 TNA, LAB 12/82, *Ministry of Labour, Wales Division, Monthly Report*, 16 June 1941, 2.
38 A. Hughes, *The Second World War in the Borough of Conwy* (Conwy Town Council; 2019), pp. 10–11.
39 TNA, BT 168/29, *Ministry of Production, Wales Regional Board*, 2 November 1942, 2; Rowlands, *Something Must be Done*, p. 157.
40 TNA, BT 168/1, *List of Capital Projects in South Wales*, 28 February 1942.
41 TNA, BT 106/10, *Memorandum on Joseph Lucas, Cwmbran*, 1942.
42 Voices from the Factory Floor, *Gwen Eira Evans*, http://www.factorywomensvoices. wales/uploads/VSW014.2.pdf, 2.
43 TNA, BT 168/5, *Letter from Wales Regional Board*, 20 July 1943, 3.
44 TNA, CAB 102/274, *Government Owned Factories Operated by Contractors on Agency/ Commercial Terms*, 1945.
45 Smith, *Hawarden*, pp. 33, 35.
46 TNA, CAB 102/275, *Employment by Airframe Firms*.
47 Ministry of Information, *Worker's Weekend*, 1943 (online). Available at https://www.youtube.com/watch?v=zlVLZ23OiFs (Grace Whalley and Hilda Dodd at 2:16; Phyllis Evans at 4:38).

48 Hornby, *Factories and Plant*, p. 60.
49 TNA, BT 64/3395, *List of Factories in Metal Engineering and Chemical Industries*, Chepstow and Severn Area, 1943.
50 J. D. Davies, *Britannia's Dragon: A Naval History of Wales* (The History Press, 2013), p. 223.
51 TNA, CAB 102/129, *Housing and Hostels*, 29, 31.
52 TNA, BT 168/2, *Firms in Area Engaged on Government Contracts, or on War Production Sub-contracts*, Wales Area Board, 18 January 1941.
53 *Wales and Monmouthshire: A Summary of Government Action 1st August 1945–31st July 1946*, 18.
54 Davies, *Britannia's Dragon*, p. 230; GA D2054/4, *Messrs Fairfield-Mabey Ltd, Private Journal*.
55 TNA, BT 131/28, *The Control of Factory and Storage Space*, annexes.
56 TNA, BT 168/2, *Firms in Area Engaged on Government Contracts, or on War Production Sub-contracts*, Wales Area Board, 18 January 1941.
57 TNA, BT 63/3105, *Nuffield College Reconstruction Survey, Report on West Wales*, May 1942, 39; GA, D2025/5, *Chepstow Wagon and Construction Works, Private Journal*.
58 *The War Effort at the Curran Works*, pp. 18–19; TNA, BT 64/3153, *Nuffield College Reconstruction Survey, South Wales Reports*, 1941, 54.
59 TNA, CAB 102/877, *Welfare of Industrial Workers*, 89.
60 *The War Effort at the Curran Works*, p. 16.
61 *Western Mail*, 'Bright Prospects for Welsh Industry', 19 September 1944.

PART THREE

WARTIME NATURAL RESOURCE
INDUSTRIES, 1940–1945

6

COAL MINING

GOVERNING THE UNITED KINGDOM'S COAL INDUSTRY

Coal was vital to the war economy as it fuelled electricity, railways and industry. Yet annual production fell continually and by 1945 annual output throughout Britain was over a fifth lower than in 1940. Although falling production was linked initially to a workforce that declined from 749,000 in 1940 to 698,000 in 1941, it then stabilised at around 710,000 but output continued falling (see Figure 4 in Appendix).[1] Declining output was prompted instead by falling productivity. This problem dominated governance while the industry accounted for around half of strikes and working days lost across all industries from 1940 to 1944.[2]

The military crisis of mid-1940 prompted the TUC to accept a Conditions of Employment National Arbitration Order that outlawed strikes and lockouts, introducing compulsory arbitration. Yet proscription struggled to prevent unofficial strikes. Crucially, Bevin saw prosecutions as inflammatory and counter-productive; an attempted mass prosecution in Kent later in the war only succeeded in proving the impracticability of disciplining large and determined bodies of workers.[3] All this meant that governance throughout the war was contested between government, coal owners and unions.

Ironically given later trends, the government's chief concern in June 1940 was a coal surplus. An export drive to gain revenue had been mounted earlier in the year while miners were stopped from leaving the industry without permission from their local labour exchange. Within a few weeks, however, the disappearance of continental markets prompted mounting unemployment as mines closed or reduced output. The Mines Department disposed of excess stocks by requisitioning coal mostly for sale in the UK, although some was exported to Egypt and South America.[4] Meanwhile, the government addressed surplus labour by relaxing controls to enable miners to enlist or accept jobs in the munitions industries.[5] Many promptly escaped unemployment or poor working conditions and the workforce fell by over 10 per cent from June 1940 to Spring 1941.[6] Leavers tended to be young and the industry was damaged greatly by their absence.

While governance experiments proliferated elsewhere, the coalition government was unwilling to provoke the hostility of mine owners or miners and preferred inaction. Pre-existing production and development cartels were left largely untouched, although a War Emergency Assistance Scheme was administered by the Central Council of Colliery Owners from late 1940. It used the pre-war legislative framework to deploy a levy on coal to compensate less efficient collieries impacted by wartime conditions. The advisory Coal Production Council met only once from November 1940 to March 1941 while many District and Pit Production Committees lapsed amongst the confusion of mid-1940.[7] Overall, complacency reigned as falling exports meant that production seemed adequate.

Yet demand increased and shortages loomed by mid-1941, a prospect *The Economist* described as 'truly extraordinary'.[8] Characteristically, the government's reaction was voluntarist. Representatives of government, mine owners and unions agreed at a production conference in March 1941 to use structures such as Pit Production Committees to strive towards national production targets, with committees given target figures weekly by the Mines Department.[9] Production and employment, however, continued to fall and by early 1941 the national shortage of miners was estimated at 50,000. Initial attempts to bolster the workforce again relied on voluntary approaches. Bevin appealed via radio for ex-miners to return while the Ministry of Aircraft Production asked its sub-contractors to release labour but few volunteered, prompting compulsion. In May 1941 the government used an Essential Work Order to stop miners leaving the industry and granted extensive authority over the workforce to National Service Officers at the Ministry of Labour and National Service, as well as Local Appeal Boards.[10] From July ex-miners were obliged to register at employment exchanges and asked to return to the industry. Although many factories were reluctant to release workers, 41,331 ex-miners were transferred over the subsequent twelve months while the Army and RAF released 9,088.[11]

These measures stabilised workforce numbers and, although strikes in 1940 and 1941 caused manageable output losses, problems escalated from early 1942. A pre-war profit-sharing system enabling wages to rise in step with living costs continued to operate, but growth in non-wage costs reduced profits and owners' ability to fund wage increases. From 1941 miners' average weekly earnings were ranked fifty-ninth out of almost a hundred industrial occupations, behind those in engineering, shipbuilding, metal manufacture and government-run munitions factories.[12] Other sources of discontent included poor welfare facilities and the continuing ability of coal owners to pay shareholder dividends. Fractious industrial relations drove absenteeism and poor discipline. The Essential Work Order meant that miners could not be dismissed except for gross misconduct, and management lost a harsh but effective means of enforcing discipline. Mine managers were instructed instead to report persistent absentees to Pit Production Committees that interviewed absentees and could report them to National Service Officers for prosecution. Enforcement became the committees' primary activity, prompting unpopularity that harmed their ability to discuss and agree on productivity improvements.

By 1942 the government was being dragged towards intervention. Labour MP and President of the Board of Trade Hugh Dalton argued in May that 'unless we get the coal, we cannot get the arms. Unless we get the arms we cannot win the war'.[13] Dalton's proposals to 'get the coal' had two elements. One was reducing demand by rationing following a plan prepared by William Beveridge. Rationing, however, became a proxy for Conservative backbench discontent as to Labour influence within the coalition and was dropped.[14] The other was to requisition the industry but the government resisted, preferring instead to appoint a Ministerial Committee charged with drafting proposals to secure 'such practical control over the workings of the mines as is necessary to increase … war-time efficiency'.[15]

Meanwhile, the coal industry was subsumed into the 'production crisis'. By April 1942 *The Economist* was arguing that 'no other industry of equal importance has abandoned so little of its peacetime methods' and that mines should be integrated by district within a state-led approach that 'comes very close to temporary socialisation', warning its readers against being 'frightened of such words'.[16] In the last week of May 88,608 working days were lost to industrial action as were 90,000 tons of output while the industry descended in what a later wages inquiry described as a 'volcanic' condition.[17] By June Secretary for Mines David Grenfell had accepted compromise, telegraphing all stopped collieries to 'insist on [an] immediate return to work, wages claims will be considered nationally'.[18]

Attempts to resolve the crisis prompted an unwieldy compromise between both political wings of the coalition government and their supporters. The government's June 1942 White Paper set out a cumbersome 'dual control' system where colliery companies and their managers retained responsibility over day-to-day production, but overall responsibility lay with state-appointed Regional Controllers under a new Ministry of

Fuel and Power headed by Gwilym Lloyd George, Liberal MP for Pembrokeshire.[19]

New governance arrangements involved each colliery nominating one person to carry out the Controller's instructions, but his authority was conditional as only management could issue work orders. Meanwhile, pit production committees lost their role controlling absenteeism to Ministry of Labour and National Service Regional Investigation Officers who could recommend prosecution if miners 'impeded' operations.[20] The advisory and ineffective Coal Production Council was supplanted by a National Coal Board that was also constituted as an advisory body. Finally, the industry-run financial stabilisation systems were remodelled into a government-run Coal Charges Account. This system divided the industry by district, and if sale proceeds in any were below production costs, deficiencies were offset by a levy on all coal sold in the UK. The net result was to transfer funds from efficient to less efficient districts: a potentially unsustainable system but one that was unavoidable given the impossibility of transferring labour.[21] Yet the compromise embodied by dual control was prompted by a desire to avoid offending mine owners or miners. This impetus meant that governance structures were poorly defined. The Ministry never issued Regional Controllers with general instructions as to how they were to discharge their functions, leaving them instead to find their own methods of operation.[22]

But miners' discontent was driven primarily by their poor pay compared to other industries, not industrial governance. The White Paper recommended the creation of a board to investigate miners' pay; the government promptly created one chaired by Lord Greene. Miners' Federation Secretary Ebby Edwards told the board that 'there is revolution in the coalfields, and there is revolution within the miners' families because of the great disparity between miners' wages and ... those employed in munition and other war factories'. In response, Sir Evan Williams, President of the Mining Association of Great Britain and Chair of the Monmouthshire and South Wales Coal Owners' Association accepted that disparity existed but argued that there was no automatic link between wage increases and greater productivity. Claiming that there was a 'spirit abroad throughout the industry ... of a very dangerous nature',[23] he instead proposed output and attendance bonuses. The Greene Board reported within nine days, recommending a minimum wage, an industry-wide flat rate wage increase, output bonuses, and the creation of national negotiation machinery that would help both sides to agree on employment terms and conditions.[24] The government implemented these and although output bonuses proved unworkable in practice, the average pay of miners relative to workers elsewhere rose dramatically from fifty-ninth out of almost a hundred industrial occupations to twenty-third.[25]

Two other elements completed the jigsaw of government initiatives. One was concentration. Less productive collieries were to be closed and their labour transferred to more productive coalfields. Yet miners and mine owners opposed transference, the government shied away from compulsion and concentration foundered. The other was mechanisation, but this was compromised by a shortage of machinery and skilled labour, while poor industrial relations hampered the introduction of new working patterns needed within mechanised collieries. Meanwhile, pay and governance reforms were complemented by efforts to raise production by exhortation. In August 1942 Churchill addressed a mass meeting in London of three thousand miners, managers and owners. He compared miners to soldiers and merchant seamen in terms of their importance to the war although, significantly, the press was excluded, in part because of concerns about potential interruptions from disgruntled miners.[26] Union representatives joined these attempts. In the same month Edwards claimed that there was a 'mentality amongst some miners that reflects an unconcern for the dangers which the country is faced with' and that all workers should 'co-operate wholeheartedly to immediately increase the production of coal'.[27]

One year after dual control was introduced, Gwilym Lloyd George could only tell the War Cabinet that its main achievement was preventing an even worse situation.[28] Yet raising pay, reforming governance and exhortation had achieved little and production fell from 205 million tons in 1942 to 199 million in the following year. Difficulties in sourcing labour finally forced the government to resort to industrial conscription in late 1943. Conscripts to the services were chosen by lottery for diversion to the mines and were known as 'Bevin Boys' after the Minister for Labour and National Service. Many struggled to adapt, and their avoidable coal face absenteeism was over double that of other miners.[29] Continued poor performance prompted the Minister for Fuel and Power to propose nationalisation in October 1943. However, the government was reluctant to act as it feared that the mine owners would mobilise backbench support, while even discussing nationalisation might prompt strikes to force action. Churchill famously rejected nationalisation in a stormy House of Commons debate where he argued that their position was 'everything for the war, whether controversial or not, and nothing controversial that is bona fide not needed for this war'.[30]

Directionless governance was symbolised by a generous pay award prompting industrial crisis. The Greene Board recommendations included a National Reference Tribunal to adjudicate wage demands that had re-emerged as increased earnings elsewhere reduced miners' relative pay. The tribunal was chaired by Lord Porter and in January 1944 it awarded a minimum wage to miners amongst the highest of any industries. Yet it worsened the relative positioning of the highest paid miners within the workforce; these earned more due to differences in work and responsibilities but differentials between their wages and those of other miners now decreased or disappeared. Unions and mine owners began district negotiations over piece rates and allowances to minimise differentials, but the government refused to adjust coal prices to finance pay rises.

The inevitable result in early 1944 was widespread strikes, prompting Bevin to denounce coal mining furiously and publicly as a 'black spot'. He told the miners to stop creating 'anarchy' through 'wrecking your leaders and industrial agreements' before warning them that industrial unrest was endangering his policy of relying on joint industrial cooperation to regulate industrial relations and that 'other steps' might become necessary as 'we are not going to lose this war, whether it is apprentices or miners or anybody else'.[31] The unavoidable outcome of the government's failures, described diplomatically by the official historian as displaying 'traces of confusion [and] a failure to keep pace with events', was retreat to avoid disruption during the preparations for D-Day.[32] Its efforts to keep wages negotiations at arm's length collapsed as Bevin intervened, promptly ignoring the mine owners by negotiating an agreement favourable to the Miners' Federation of Great Britain.

Although miners' weekly earnings were now fourteenth out of one hundred industries, with higher earnings elsewhere generally attributable to munitions factories with substantial overtime hours,[33] mining production and productivity continued to decline. As war ended, both sides rehashed old arguments. While an unwilling government had been dragged towards ever greater involvement, it was unable to overcome industrial and labour interest groups to resolve industrial problems. Meanwhile, the workforce was determined to reinforce wartime gains in peacetime by securing nationalisation, prompting the January 1945 reorganisation of the Miners' Federation of Great Britain into a National Union of Mineworkers.

GOVERNING THE WELSH COALFIELDS

UK-wide problems were concentrated in Wales where average output per head across both coalfields fell by over a quarter in four years, and production by over a third (see Figure 5 in

Appendix). In 1940, the two Welsh coalfields employed 137,164 men producing 34.7 million tons, of which over 93 per cent of employment and production was in the south. By 1945, employment in north Wales had increased by 2 per cent, but total production had fallen by 21 per cent. In south Wales, employment declined by 14 per cent and output by 37 per cent.[34]

Efficiency fell against a backdrop of 817 unofficial strikes from the third quarter of 1939 to the second quarter of 1945. Over half ended after miners obtained concessions or the promise of investigation, otherwise work resumed unconditionally. Although they were generally short, with 93 per cent lasting five days or fewer and half lasting a day or less, their frequency meant that over a million days were lost. Turbulent industrial relations meant that the industry accounted for 61 per cent of strikes and 74 per cent of days lost throughout Wales between 1940 and 1945 (see Figure 2 in Appendix).[35]

Both coalfields struggled but circumstances and characteristics combined to have particularly negative impacts in south Wales whose coalfield contained 322 collieries in 1943, of which 214 employed more than fifty miners and accounted for over 98 per cent of its output.[36] Within days of the military eclipse of 1940, coal piled up at docksides and ships en route to France were recalled although anthracite shipments to Canada continued.[37] By August most steam coal collieries were on short time with five employing 2,000 men suspending operations indefinitely. The north Wales coalfield was less affected and full-time working continued.[38] While industrial relations were calmer than usual, underlying tensions were symbolised by the determination of Neath Valley miners to retain their customary day holiday to visit the Neath Fair. Their managers disagreed but lost a court case and the miners holidayed in September.[39]

By November 1940 the collapse of the south Wales export trade meant that 21.6 per cent of insured miners throughout Wales were either suspended or unemployed.[40] Over the winter of 1940 some 21,000 unemployed miners were placed in other industries including those in England. Many transfers, however, were temporary such as the forty miners from the Ammanford area who were sent to Northampton.[41] The South Wales Miners' Federation resisted permanent transfers given their resemblance to pre-war transference as well as the risks to production posed by what Horner described as denuding districts 'of their youth'.[42] One example was its response to a proposal to transfer 3,000 miners to Somerset by demanding higher wages in that coalfield,[43] prompting government to retreat quickly.

The appointment of Cabinet Ministers drawn from the Labour Party dismayed mine owners but incentivised their co-operation with the Federation to reduce the risk of intervention; in mid-1940 Coal Owners' Association Chair Williams told his members that the new government might intervene if prolonged disputes broke out and that any such intervention would most likely remain in force after the war had ended.[44] Meanwhile, Horner simultaneously urged cooperation while defending members' interests. In 1940 he told the Federation annual conference that he wanted to 'maintain complete independence' by avoiding 'unhealthy collaborations which ignores class relations'.[45] The endemic mistrust between both sides of industry was recorded by the verbatim minutes of the joint committee established in 1940 to discuss production. One example was in mid-1941 when Coal Owners' Association Chair Williams told Horner that 'I've been attempting for years to prove to you on your side, so that you could prove to the men, that we are working for you even more than you are working for us', to which Horner replied drily that 'there are no facts to substantiate your explanation'.[46]

Deadlock meant that the government's initial actions in Wales were voluntarist and unsuccessful. In June 1940, for example, Secretary for Mines Dai Grenfell addressed a conference in south Wales where he called for extra effort from miners.[47] Although the advisory Coal Production Council was occasionally active, such as when it advised the Department of Mines on the cessation of financial support to a failed colliery in Glanamman whose men could be absorbed by surrounding mines,[48] it had little influence. Pit Production Committees demonstrated how the government's reluctance to intervene created confusion. Miners wanted to discuss production topics such as poor management and equipment, but managers preferred to discuss absenteeism and disciplinary measures. The result was that both sides tended to talk past each other and achieve little.

Miners' resentment of coal owners surged, prompting one to complain in November 1940 that 'sacrifices are always one-sided'. Nevertheless, the South Wales Miners' Federation worked to defuse tension and drive greater production despite some elements opposing an 'imperialist war' until the entry of the Soviet Union in 1941.[49] Efforts included a meeting of the South Wales Joint Production Committee of the Coal Production Council of June 1940, when worker and employer representatives discussed proposals for boosting production.[50] By March 1941 most south Wales collieries had resumed full production. While officials and mine managers had recently been preoccupied with labour surpluses, they now faced the opposite problem as unemployment amongst insured miners was 5.6 per cent and vacancies in south Wales were hard to fill. In north Wales, the industry needed a further 500 miners by April when the Ministry reported that it 'may be necessary to recall some of the miners transferred to other industries'.[51]

Poor wages inevitably harmed recruitment. Alternative industrial employment was once scarce in the coalfields, especially south Wales, but munitions industries now offered better pay.[52] Skilled men could earn between £6 13s. and £7 19s. per week at the Bridgend, Glascoed and Pembrey ROFs but miners over the age of 21 earned substantially lower salaries of £4 6s. in south Wales, and £4 8s. in north Wales.[53] Munitions shifts were longer than mining, which, combined with the need to commute to distant factories, meant that some workers in Blaina left their homes before 6 a.m. and did not return until 8 p.m. Yet mining coal was far more strenuous and dangerous than producing munitions, with 172 miners killed in work accidents throughout Wales in 1941.[54] One was at Blaenclydach drift colliery where a tram derailed killing six and injuring a further seventy.[55] Relative wages were also poor for surface trades. In mid-1940 fitters at Ffaldau colliery resigned after realising that their weekly wage of 67 shillings were far less than the 83 shillings that they could earn at a ROF construction site.[56] In 1942 a workers' representative on a Pit Production Committee summed up dissatisfaction as follows:[57]

> There's no division of opinion on the adequacy of wages. They are ridiculously low ... in relation to the standard of living and ... in comparison to wages paid for other trades.

Anger was stoked by the influx of women into the munitions factories prompting a common perception that female munitions workers earned more than men, although 'semi-skilled' women (women were not listed officially as 'skilled') at Bridgend and Glascoed ROFs earned a weekly average of £3 12s., more than a quarter less than miners. Nevertheless, the ability of women to earn industrial salaries was interpreted by some men as challenging their breadwinner status.

Grievances heightened the salience of two problems. One was recruitment. By July 1941 all ex-miners had to register with employment exchanges and were asked to return but, of the 22,000 ex-miners in Wales asked, 17,000 refused. Thirteen thousand were interviewed in August and asked to reconsider, but only 1,350 agreed to return. Meanwhile, colliery management delayed the process by insisting on individually interviewing men who wanted to return while munitions plants were often reluctant to release skilled ex-miners. Problems persisted throughout both coalfields and although workforces were eventually stabilised, the Ministry of Labour and National Service observed that the 'predominant feature [in Wales] is not so much labour shortage as the frequent complaint of low output per man-hour'.[58] The other problem was the poisonous working atmosphere in many collieries prompting unofficial strikes.[59] Anger at wages disparities became a central issue, symbolised by the Blaenavon section of the South Wales Miners' Federation writing to the Minister of Labour and National Service to declare 'give us a square deal and we'll produce the coal'.[60] Absenteeism rose while productivity in both coalfields fell. Crucially, anger was sharpened by the legacy of the depression that spurred a deep mistrust of government and coal owners.

Owners did little to dispel negative perceptions and were often reluctant to engage with workers' representatives. Reluctance extended to their clerical staff whose union complained as to pay and conditions at four south Wales companies. Such disputes would normally be arbitrated by a Ministry of Labour and National Service tribunal where the Coal Owners' Association represented owners. However, the association refused to recognise the clerical union or represent its members, forcing the union to appeal each case to the Ministry. The Ministry referred the cases to the National Arbitration Tribunal that ordered at least one of the companies to amend their practice but made no ruling on recognition.[61]

Underlying discontent remained a powerful motivating factor. The Mass Observation study of Blaina and Nantyglo conducted in March and April 1942 observed that miners and their families exhibited 'uncertainty ... viewed through consciousness of wrongs suffered and a demand for the rectification of particular grievances'.[62] All this meant that in the second quarter of 1942 strikes reached their highest level since 1939.[63] While less disrupted than south Wales, disputes in north Wales included those at Gresham, Black Park, Bersham and Hafod collieries.[64] One notable dispute was the continuation of a long struggle at the Point of Ayr pit between a company backed union and the independent union representing miners in north Wales. It was eventually addressed in a manner demonstrating both the government's desire to avoid confrontation and the drawbacks of this approach. The state appointed a committee of inquiry that brokered an agreement enabling both unions to operate, but the agreement contained many compromises and was described later by the committee chair as 'not perhaps a perfect instrument'.[65]

Industrial relations for apprentices were especially turbulent. The reasons were not hard to identify as they worked from the age of fourteen, were paid less than adult miners and were more likely to suffer accidents. Wage disparities meant that the Ministry of Labour and National Service Regional Industrial Relations Officer noted that their 'sweethearts and sisters receive bigger wages than they do'.[66] The predicable result was widespread strikes after 800 Rhondda apprentices produced a 'Pit Boy's Charter' calling for better wages and conditions.[67] Federation conciliation failed, its officials were shouted down in mass meetings and 10,000 went on strike in mid-1942.

The government's June 1942 answer to governance, productivity and output problems was dual control and pay rises. Yet Ebbw Vale MP Aneurin Bevan recognised correctly that dual control resulted from its inability to overcome industrial interest groups and thus had poor prospects, arguing that the parliamentary debate was conducted in a 'tepid atmosphere because all the various interests have been squared beforehand'.[68] Many managers were enraged by the confusion, claiming that they had been 'stripped of every vestige of authority', while Llanelli MP Jim Griffiths observed how they had been placed in an 'invidious' position given their need to serve 'two masters', arguing perceptively that 'this is the place where the elaborate machinery [of governance] might break down'.[69] Nevertheless, one important innovation was the Regional Controllers. While other production structures generally treated Wales as one unit, coal mining governance instead reflected separate coalfields and east–west economic linkages. South Wales was combined with the Forest of Dean and Somerset, and northeast Wales was joined to Lancashire and Cheshire as part of the North Western Region. Controllers also benefited from Regional Advisory Boards under the auspices of the National Coal Board.

Regional Controllers were expected to assist Gwilym Lloyd George's plan to rejuvenate the industry through pay increases, concentration and mechanisation. Pay in both coalfields rose throughout 1942 and 1943, and in mid-1943 calmer industrial relations prompted a relieved Federation to cable General Montgomery to congratulate his army on its success in Sicily, stating that 'we undertake to do all within our power to produce the coal to sustain this new offensive'. However, the boost to relative wages lessened over time and the General's reply of 'please give my best wishes to all south Wales miners and tell them that if they will produce the coal we will finish the job here on the battlefront' coincided instead with renewed strikes including one at Penrhiwceiber that was sparked by changes to wages calculations prompting the earnings of a few men to dip temporarily below the minimum wage.[70] Attempts by the local lodge, the Regional Controller and Federation leadership to broker a settlement failed and 1,100 miners stopped work, followed by those in surrounding collieries.[71] As was often the case, the strength of workforce feeling and the need to reopen pits meant that mine owners were forced to retreat. Both sides agreed to be bound by arbitration carried out by the Regional Controller, who found in favour of the miners.

Meanwhile a tense atmosphere prevailed in north Wales where the Point of Ayr owners refused to comply with all the findings of the committee of inquiry into worker representation. The Regional Controller investigated and exposed a series of petty provocations. Managers refused to allow independent union members to attend meetings held to discuss soup rations, and although they erected a hut allowing the union to collect subscriptions, they sited it in front of their office windows so that they could observe who had joined the union.[72] The Regional Controller condemned management's behaviour as 'provocative and well-nigh unbearable' and the mine was, unusually, nationalised.[73]

If little progress was made in boosting productivity through increasing pay, even less was made with mechanisation or concentration. While the amount of coal in north Wales cut by mechanical means increased after 1940, progress in south Wales was limited. Lack of success had many causes including difficult geology, the difficulty of imposing new working practices, and the tendency of owners to favour pneumatic picks that were cheaper than the more productive but expensive coal-cutting machines.[74] The government opened new opencast workings including a site above Blaenavon worked by Canadian Army units but, while the new workings were productive as 810 men produced 390,000 tons in 1944, all such workings accounted for less than 2 per cent of coal production in south Wales.[75]

Concentration also foundered. The Ministry of Fuel and Power noted that only 6.3 per cent of miners in south Wales and 5.4 per cent in northeast Wales were employed on highly productive work, far less than those in geologically favourable coalfields such as South Derbyshire.[76] Such discrepancies offered obvious potential for concentration and transfer. Yet the Ministry knew that miners would be opposed and its officials recommended that 'Scotsmen are transferred first, rather than Welshmen'.[77] Nervousness was justified. In 1942 the Regional Controller attempted to transfer twenty-five miners from south Wales to the northwest of England and six to the Midlands. The proposal met with a storm of protest from chapels as well as union branches representing miners, teachers and railwaymen, and was dropped.[78] By April 1943 the Controller reported that only one pit in south Wales had been closed as other schemes had not proceeded due to fears of industrial unrest.[79] The few schemes thereafter were known as 'internal concentration' as they closed less productive faces within individual mines and avoided intra-regional transfers. Similar dynamics existed in north Wales where a typical scheme was one at Gresford Colliery that raised output by only twelve tons a week.[80]

One high-profile cause of low productivity was absenteeism. Between September 1942 and May 1943 absenteeism in south Wales ran at between 13 and 16.8 per cent, although these proportions included 'unavoidable' absences such as those caused by sickness.[81] A survey of coal-face absenteeism in mid-1943 found rates varying from 5.86 at Glynogwr to 22.01 at Aberaman, with average time lost throughout south Wales doubling between Fridays and Saturdays.[82] While care should be taken with comparisons, a UK-wide survey of munitions factories carried out for the War Cabinet found that 'avoidable' absenteeism was generally lower. In February 1943 shifts lost were 8.5 per cent for male workers.[83] Systems for dealing with absent workers were strengthened in 1942 but managers were often reluctant to launch prosecutions out of fear of further inflaming the workforce; the Regional Controller argued that absent or undisciplined miners were 'often defiant and will not respond to any remedy'.[84] Finally, younger miners were especially disgruntled and absenteeism among face-workers in south Wales under 31 was twice that of those over 40.[85] Miners could be prosecuted under the Essential Work Order for refusing orders to work but these were used sparingly given their lack of impact. A typical example in June 1943 involved two miners at Seven Sisters Colliery. When interviewed by officials, one argued that he 'was not going to be driven by any man' and the other that 'he did not want any boss on my back'. Both were fined £2 by magistrates but refused to pay, preferring the alternative of 25 days in gaol.[86]

In sum, relations remained unsalvageable when the owners retained operational and financial control, miners resisted attempts to link productivity to wages, and employment terms and conditions remained poor. On the management side, many mine owners were uncooperative, while the financial support obtained through the Coal Charges Account had little impact on their behaviour even though both coalfields were amongst the largest recipients in the UK.[87] On the worker side, the South Wales Miners' Federation strongly supported the war effort on anti-fascist grounds but also as an opportunity for greater state intervention, arguing that 'once this [war] is done, we can ... go forward unitedly to conquer new fields of social advance, increasing the rate of development towards socialism'.[88] Yet while miners shared their union's determination to win the war, they would not suspend their generalised dissatisfaction to focus solely on production. This dynamic was well illustrated by the Mass Observation study of Blaina. It found that although most residents thought that their communities would be ignored and sidelined after the war, some argued that they 'would not be hoodwinked again as they were in the 1918 election', while others declared that they needed to gain 'sufficient power to force a change'. One miner's wife summarised local feelings by observing how the 'living dread of black times again' permeated the area.[89]

Mutual distrust was apparent within Pit Production Committees, broadly supported by senior figures within the Federation but distrusted by many miners and managers. Distrust helped prompt poor outcomes: the Ministry of Labour and National Service admitted in August 1942 that most committees in Wales 'have never functioned satisfactorily'.[90] The Fed supported the committees but struggled to convince their members of their worth.[91] Mistrust helped prompt one committee, at Penallta, to collapse in March 1943 after the manager claimed that he had been 'grossly insulted' by a worker representative who accused him of dishonesty. Wider views were reflected by a worker on the Abergorki Committee commenting on a government poster promoting the contribution of each ton of coal to the war: 'the ton of coal is the thing, but the miner is still the bottom dog'.[92] In the same year South Wales Association of Colliery Managers President David Jeffreys cited a 'complete lack of discipline now existing in the mines' and threatened to withdraw his members from committees.⁹³ The nine committees in north Wales addressed issues ranging from safety to transport,⁹⁴ but their success also depended on voluntary cooperation that was often impossible to achieve.

The failure of dual control in Wales was clear by mid-1943 where acute labour problems in the southern coalfield led to the curious involvement of Lord Victor Rothschild, head of MI5's counter-sabotage section who was concerned as to 'unrest amongst workers during the past year in coalfields' throughout Britain. Rothschild read a *Western Mail* article alleging sabotage in south Wales but, after a prolonged correspondence with police and civil authorities, incidents where equipment had been harmed were eventually resolved as 'malicious damage' by dissatisfied youths as opposed to deliberate 'sabotage' aimed at impeding the war effort.⁹⁵ Miners were disgruntled but were not saboteurs.

In June 1943 the Ministry of Fuel and Power asked Regional Controllers for their views as to falling production. While North West Regional Controller Gordon MacDonald was relatively sanguine about industrial relations,⁹⁶ sentiment within the north Wales coalfield was poor as reflected by the Point of Ayr Pit Production Committee rejecting his idea for servicemen to deliver motivational targets as 'it would be difficult to get men to stay' to listen.⁹⁷ Similar problems throughout the coalfield prompted the Controller to tell the committees that he was a 'little disturbed' as to their failure to meet targets, but he did little other than suggest a meeting that 'may help in bringing about a most desirable improvement in output'.⁹⁸

The situation in south Wales was, however, far worse. Regional Controller William Jones detailed how problems had combined to create a 'general unsettled feeling' where 'very slight cases are sufficient to cause strikes'. Absenteeism was increasing but he was reluctant to enforce compulsory Sunday night shifts as 'we should fail if any defence was put up'. Discontent was stoked by production arrangements lacking the 'rapid change and improvisation' of munitions. A lack of nutritious food and pithead baths produced fatigue, while disputes over piece rates and allowances remained common. Meanwhile, the failure of many managers to adjust to wartime conditions prompted 'frayed nerves' while Pit Production Committees were consumed by 'bickering and arguments' and achieved little.[99]

Yet the government had no intention of intervening. Instead, it watched as the Porter award prompted widespread strikes by ignoring the impact of pay rises on differentials. The problem was so obvious that mine owners and unions in Wales worked quickly to offset impacts by raising piece rates,[100] only to be stymied by the government's refusal to increase the price of coal to pay for wage adjustments. Ten thousand men went on strike initially and within a few days the strike was almost complete, with Horner warning that if the strike persisted, munitions factories would 'be in a serious position within a fortnight' given their dependence on coal.[101] Federation leaders worried that the strike would rebound to the detriment of the miners. Horner argued later that the miners should have 'refused to resort to strike action', criticising some of his own members, especially younger miners, who lacked an understanding of the fragility of union power.[102] Such misgivings prompted the Federation to persuade its members to return after a confusing week when 500,000 tons of production was lost amidst what its Executive Committee heard was 'complete chaos … men going in and coming out like a concertina'.[103]

The fiasco enraged the government. It condemned mine owners for negotiating with unions, while the Ministry of Labour and National Service's Regional Industrial Relations Officer angrily compared the 'mental condition' of south Wales miners to a 'sick patient [during] a long and troublesome illness [who] displays restlessness, querulous and a general unreasonableness'.[104] Yet government backtracked and addressing 'certain other matter concerning allowances peculiar to south Wales' formed part of its announcement resolving the dispute.[105] Even the government's defeat did not quell disputes or prompt it to grip the industry. In south Wales, the Powell Duffryn benefit society refused to admit union members to its pension schemes, and dispute flared when workers at Tower Colliery at Hirwaun were expelled after joining the Clerical and Administrative Union. The government meekly refused to become involved, merely asking the unions in late 1944 to pressure the employers and refrain from 'precipitate' action.[106]

Industrial relations were equally poor in north Wales where recruitment remained difficult. In September 1943 North West Controller McDonald held a press conference at Gresford Colliery to announce an 'urgent' need to recruit 700 to 800 miners throughout the coalfield, stating 'any men who were physically fit up to the age of 41 would be welcome'.[107] By September 1944 the Point of Ayr Pit Production Committee observed frequent absenteeism, some caused by men preferring other work: one miner had a medical certificate for lumbago but was seen driving tractors. Problems were especially apparent with 'Bevin Boys' who were characterised as often 'quite disinterested and look[ing] forward to the end of the war'.[108] McDonald noted in 1944 that 'it is commonly agreed that the side on which Pit Production Committees most need strengthening is in their relations with the rest of the workmen and officials in the colliery'. However, his suggestions to boost cooperation became increasingly desperate, such as suggestion boxes with participation incentivised by prizes.[109]

By 1945 average earnings per shift in south Wales were almost double those of 1938.[110] Yet productivity continued falling amidst unrest that included forty-three strikes in the last quarter of 1944. One example was in September when 159 'Bevin Boys' undergoing training demanded paid holidays. Their anger faced management with what civil servants termed euphemistically 'a little difficulty', forcing the Ministry of Labour and National Service to intervene. Turbulent industrial relations continued into the subsequent week when 1,800 miners at three collieries went on strike to support thirty apprentices dissatisfied as to their pay.[111] In December 1944 the south Wales Regional Controller made yet another appeal for more production, but to little effect. Meanwhile, miners remained sceptical as to Pit Production Committees, while in March 1945 the Powell Duffryn Federation lodges representing 45,000 miners argued that there was a 'total lack of co-ordination' between committees, managers, and Regional Controllers.[112] All this meant that the coalfields ended the war in a parlous and exhausted state as both sides of industry viewed each other with hostility, watched by a hesitant and frustrated government.

CONCLUSION

American experts who surveyed the industry throughout the UK in mid-1944 reported incredulously that 'there does not exist in the minds of coal owners, management, labour leaders and the individual miners an adequate willingness to subordinate all considerations to the military necessity of increasing production'.[113] Problems were concentrated in Wales where coal owners and miners were locked in conflict.[114] The former were determined to retain managerial control, while the latter were equally determined to reinforce their wartime gains by securing state control of the industry. Relations were worsened by the scars left from the inter-war depression, but the government was unable to decisively address industrial problems. This reluctance stemmed partly from a desire to avoid a repeat of its experience during and after the First World War but mostly from how both parties within the coalition government sought to advance the interests of their supporters within the industry: the Conservatives for the mine owners, and Labour for the unions. Shifts in relative power enabled regional unions to achieve their industrial relations goals of national bargaining machinery and higher wages, although not state ownership.

Nevertheless, the government's imposition of dual control and pay rises was just sufficient to avoid threatening the war economy. Falling production was offset by the state's success at controlling distribution and consumption, activities lacking well-organised interest groups. The state minimised exports and drove more efficient industrial usage through a programming system that monitored demands and matched them to supply, while domestic consumption was reduced by restricting supply and campaigning for less consumption. Gwilym Lloyd George's 1943 arguments to the War Cabinet as to intervention preventing an even worse outcome were demonstrated clearly in Wales. The government's steady compromises prevented a complete breakdown in production although regional controllers had little impact. In sum, interest groups and their political supporters were stalemated. No changes were possible under the coalition government unless a full-blown crisis emerged, although miners' leaders and Labour politicians were planning for when political circumstances might change. In April 1945 Dalton diarised bitterly that Coal Owners' Association Chair Williams 'deserves nothing from this community [south Wales] apart from a tombstone.'[115]

Notes

1. *Statistical Digest of the War*, pp. 75, 81. Parts of this chapter draw on material within Gooberman, '"Revolution in the Coalfields": Industrial Relations in Wartime South Wales, 1939–45', *Labor History*, 63/1 (2022), 55–72.
2. A. Clegg, *History of British Trade Unions, Volume 3* (Clarendon Press, 1994), p. 239.
3. Bullock, *The Life and Times of Ernest Bevin, Volume III*, pp. 267–8.
4. TNA, POWE 26/406, *Brief for Secretary of State (The Export Trade)*, 5 September 1940.
5. Court, *Coal*, pp. 134–7.
6. Supple, *History of the British Coal Industry*, p. 504.
7. Supple, *History of the British Coal Industry*, pp. 517–18; Court, *Coal*, p. 318.
8. *Economist*, 'The Coal Shortage', 19 July 1941.
9. Glamorgan Archives, *SWMF Executive Council Annual Report, 1941–42*, 21.

10 J. McIlroy and A. Campbell, 'Beyond Betteshanger: Order 1305 in the Scottish Coalfields during the Second World War, Part 1: Politics, Prosecutions and Protest', *Historical Studies in Industrial Relations*, 15 (2003), 27–72 (37–8).
11 TNA, LAB 8/1473, *History of Labour Supply from May 1940*, 7–8.
12 TNA, POWE 20/62, *Average Weekly Earnings in coal mining and other industries*, July 1941.
13 Hansard (Commons), 17 March 1942, vol. 378, col. 1444.
14 Jeffreys, *The Churchill Coalition*, pp. 96–7.
15 Cited in Supple, *History of the British Coal Industry*, p. 522.
16 *The Economist*, 'Shortage of Coal', 11 April 1942; 'Plan for Coal', 18 April 1942.
17 TNA, POWE 20/62, *Report of the Board of Investigation, Part 7, Time Lost Through Disputes*.
18 *Western Mail*, 'Resume Work in all Pits at Once', 3 June 1942, 4.
19 Court, *Coal*, p. 204.
20 TNA, CAB 71/13, *Progress Report on Operation of the White Paper Scheme by the Minister of Fuel and Power*, 17 June 1942, 3.
21 Ashcroft, *Contracts and Finance*, pp. 167–8.
22 TNA, POWE 28/83, *Memorandum Dealing with the Operation of the Coal Control*, 1 January 1944.
23 TNA, POWE 20/62, *Board of Investigation into Miners' Claims, First day*, 9 June 1942, 5, 13.
24 TNA, POWE 20/62, *Report of the Board of Investigation*, 15 March 1942.
25 Court, *Coal*, p. 266.
26 Supple, *History of the British Coal Industry*, p. 560.
27 *Caerphilly Journal*, 'Cilfynydd News', 29 August 1942.
28 TNA, CAB 71/13, *Progress Report on Operation of the White Paper Scheme by the Minister of Fuel and Power*, 17 June 1943, 5.
29 TNA, POWE 26/441, *Ministry of Fuel and Power to National Conciliation Board*, 30 January 1945.
30 Hansard (Commons), 13 October 1943, vol. 392, col. 921.
31 *The Times*, 'Gravity of Strikes', 5 April 1944, 4.
32 Court, *Coal*, p. 257.
33 Court, *Coal*, p. 266.
34 Williams, *DWHS, vol. 1*, pp. 299–300; Supple, *History of the British Coal Industry*, p. 539.
35 L. Gooberman, 'Revolution in the Coalfields', 59.
36 *Regional Report on the South Wales Coalfield* (HMSO, 1946), p. 59.
37 TNA, LAB, 12/82, *Ministry of Labour Monthly Report, Wales*, 17 June 1940, 2.
38 TNA, LAB 12/82, *Ministry of Labour Monthly Report, Wales*, 12 August 1940, 2.
39 K. Howells, 'A View from Below: Tradition, Experience and Nationalization in the South Wales Coalfield, 1937–1957' (unpublished doctoral dissertation, University of Warwick), 225–7.
40 TNA, LAB 12/82, *Ministry of Labour Monthly Report, Wales*, 11 November 1940, 3.
41 TNA, LAB 8/1473, *History of Labour Supply from May 1940*, 6.

42 NLW, BT 4/9/1, *Joint Production Committee Minutes*, 18 November 1940, 22–3.
43 TNA, LAB 12/82, *Ministry of Labour Monthly Report, Wales*, September 1940, 3.
44 NLW, *MSWCOA General Meeting Minutes*, 8 July 1940.
45 SWML, *President's Address to SWMF Annual Conference*, 1940.
46 NLW, BT 4/9/1, *Joint Production Committee Minutes*, 7 April 1941.
47 Francis and Smith, *The Fed*, p. 396.
48 TNA, POWE 20/47, *Mines Department to SWMF*, 20 March 1942.
49 Francis and Smith, *The Fed*, p. 400.
50 *Western Mail*, 'Plans to Increase South Wales Coal Production', 5 June 1940.
51 TNA, LAB 12/82, *Ministry of Labour Monthly Report, Wales*, 17 March 1941, 8; 21 April 1941, 8–9.
52 Jay, *Change and Fortune*, p. 89.
53 TNA, POWE 20/62, *Royal Ordnance Factories, Typical Weekly Earnings*; *Estimated Average earnings per shift (miners)*.
54 Williams, *DWHS, vol. 1*, p. 333; Mass Observation, *Mining Town–1942*, 78.
55 GLA, *SWMF Executive Council Annual Report*, 1941–2, 40.
56 TNA, LAB 10/366, *Ministry of Labour Industrial Relations Officer, Wales Region, Weekly Report*, 27 April 1940, 1.
57 Mass Observation, *Mining Town–1942*, 43.
58 TNA, LAB 12/82, *Ministry of Labour Monthly Report, Wales*, 11 August 1941, 7; 29 August 1942, 2.
59 *Western Mail*, 'The Miners' New Agitation', 9 April 1941; 'Welsh Miners who are not Playing the Game', 18 September 1941.
60 *Western Mail*, 'Miners' Protest to Mr Bevin', 21 July 1941.
61 TNA, POWE 20/59, *Industrial Relations Department (Cardiff) to Headquarters*, 1 April 1942; *National Arbitration Tribunal; Award no 242*, 28 August 1942, 3.
62 Mass Observation, *Mining Town–1942*, 55.
63 TNA, LAB 34/57, *Trade Disputes*, 1942.
64 *Western Mail*, 'Another Gresford Strike', 9 May 1942, 3, 'Hafod Strikers Still Out', 19 May 1942, 3.
65 TNA, POWE 20/60, *Chair of Tribunal to Minister of Labour*, 11 May 1942; TNA, POWE 20/66, *Report on Point of Ayr Colliery Dispute*, 2.
66 TNA, LAB 10/368, *Ministry of Labour Industrial Relations Officer, Wales Region, Weekly Report*, 30 May 1942.
67 S. Broomfield, 'The apprentice boys strikes of the second world war', *Llafur*, 3/2 (1981), 53–67.
68 Hansard (Commons), 11 June 1942, vol. 380, col. 1293.
69 *Western Mail*, 'Pit Managers Losing Authority', 11 October 1943, 6; *Neath Guardian*, 'Welsh MPs on the Coal Plan', 19 June 1943.
70 *Western Mail*, '*Remember?*', 9 March 1944.
71 Francis and Smith, *The Fed*, pp. 406–7.
72 TNA, POWE 20/66, *Report on Point of Ayr Colliery Dispute*, 3, 5.
73 K. Gildart, 'Coal strikes on the home front: miners' militancy and socialist politics in the second world war', *Twentieth Century British History*, 20/2 (2009), 121–51 (134). Hansard (Commons), 13 May 1943, vol. 389, col. 904.

74 Howells, *A View from Below*, pp. 293–6.
75 Williams, *DWHS*, vol. *1*, p. 311.
76 TNA, POWE 22/150, *Productivity of Individual Pits*, 3.
77 TNA, POWE 22/150, *Concentration Prospects*, 11 February 1943, 3.
78 TNA, LAB 8/1473/6, *History of Labour Supply from May 1940*, 6.
79 TNA, POWE 22/150, *Notes for a Meeting of the Concentration Committee*, 12 April 1943, 3.
80 TNA, POWE 22/150, *Statistical Report on Concentration*, June 1943, 5.
81 TNA, POWE 20/78, *Figures of Absenteeism amongst Coal Face Workers*.
82 TNA, POWE 20/78, *Memorandum by the Regional Controller, Wales*, 5 June 1943, Appendix B.
83 TNA, CAB 71/13, *Absenteeism in Industry*, 19 August 1943, 1–2.
84 TNA, POWE 20/78, *Memorandum by the Regional Controller, Wales*, 5 June 1943, 8.
85 Supple, *History of the British Coal Industry*, p. 566.
86 *Neath Guardian*, 'Valley Colliers Disobeyed Orders', 11 June 1943.
87 Supple, *History of the British Coal Industry*, p. 585.
88 Francis and Smith, *The Fed*, p. 404.
89 Mass Observation, *Mining Town–1942*, 69, 206.
90 TNA, LAB 12/82, *Ministry of Labour Monthly Report, Wales*, August 1942, 2.
91 NLW, BT 4/9/1, *Joint Production Committee Minutes*, 2 February 1942, 31.
92 NLW, BT 3/5/9, *Penallta Pit Production Committee Minutes*, 1943; *Abergorki Pit Production Committee Minutes*, 1 November 1943.
93 Gildart, *Coal Strikes on the Home Front*, 134.
94 TNA, COAL 77/5931, *Northwest Bulletin of the Ministry of Fuel and Power*, January 1945, 1, 4.
95 *Western Mail*, 'Coal Output Impeded by Wilful Acts of Damage', 17 November 1942; POWE, 26/ 424, *Letter from Lord Rothschild*, 6 September 1943.
96 TNA, POWE 28/78, *Memorandum by the Regional Controller, North West*, 4 June 1943.
97 TNA, COAL 77/5931, *Point of Ayr Pit Production Committee*, 1 December 1943.
98 TNA, COAL 77/5931, *Memorandum from Regional Controller, North Western Region*, 30 November 1943.
99 TNA, POWE 20/78, *Memorandum by the Regional Controller, Wales*, 5 June 1943, 1–10.
100 NLW, A1/22, *MSWCOA General Meeting Minutes*, 28 February 1944.
101 TNA, LAB 10/446, *Ministry of Labour Industrial Relations Officer, Wales Region, Weekly Reports*, 10 March 1944; *Merthyr Express*, 'The Coal Crisis', 11 March 1944.
102 SWML, *President's Address to SWMF Annual Conference*, 1944, 4–5.
103 Francis and Smith, *The Fed*, p. 412.
104 TNA, LAB 10/446, *Ministry of Labour Industrial Relations Officer, Wales Region, Weekly Report*, 31 March 1944.
105 *Western Mail*, 'Minister's Pledge to Discuss Welsh Coalfield Aims', 9 March 1944, 1.
106 TNA, POWE 20/88, *Note on Clerical Workers at Powell Dyffryn*, 11 October 1944.

107 *Rhos Herald*, 'North Wales Needs 700 to 800 More Coal Miners', 18 September 1943.
108 TNA COAL 77/5931, *Point of Ayr Pit Production Committee*, 1 November 1944, 15 November 1944.
109 TNA, COAL 77/5391, *North West Regional Controller to Pit Production Committees*, 29 September 1944.
110 Williams, *DWHS, vol. 1*, p. 175.
111 TNA, LAB 10/446, *Ministry of Labour Industrial Relations Officer, Wales Region, Weekly Report*, 8 September 1944; 15 September 1944.
112 *Pontypridd Observer*, 'Combine's Pertinent Questions', 24 February 1945.
113 *United States Coal Commission: Report on UK Coal Industry*, June/July 1944, cited in Gildart, *Coal Strikes on the Home Front*, p. 128.
114 Gooberman, 'Revolution in the Coalfields'.
115 LSE Digital Library, DL1HD01, *Diary of Hugh Dalton*, 21 April 1945.

7

METAL MANUFACTURING

GOVERNING METAL MANUFACTURING, UNITED KINGDOM

Metal manufacturing was central to the war effort as iron and steel were used across munitions production, aluminium was vital within aircraft production, while other metals such as lead, magnesium, zinc and tin were used commonly throughout all types of manufacturing. Their importance meant that metal manufacturing was enveloped within a complex but effective UK-wide governing structure. Yet processes were fluid, prompting Ministry of Supply Permanent Secretary Oliver Franks to characterise the operations of the committee leading their governance as an 'argumentative process' where each ministry had to make its case against those of others.

Franks also argued that 'after planning came the problem of control'.[1] The apex of control was a cross-departmental Materials Committee allocating raw materials to ministries sponsoring munitions and civilian users. The next level was formed from multiple Raw Materials Controls with comprehensive powers over the supply and demand of designated metals. They were usually managed by the Ministry of Supply, although from August 1940 the functions that became the Light Metals Control sat within the Ministry of Aircraft Production.[2] Controls developed their own supervisory approaches, acted autonomously and were often formed from pre-war industry bodies repurposed as government agents.

Their autonomy prompted the official wartime history to argue that the Controls treated their ministerial superiors 'more like as benevolent neutral or loyal ally than as a supreme overlord'.[3] They were organised generally on a UK-wide basis, although occasional regional offices reflected geographic industrial concentrations. Finally, their work was aided by the Board of Trade's suppression of peacetime manufacturing.

The most prominent metal manufacturing activity was iron and steel. While the UK's coal output fell, annual steel production remained relatively static at around 13 million tons from 1940 to 1943, before declining.[4] Meanwhile, the almost complete cessation of exports after 1941 combined with import availability to enable deliveries to rise from 13.9 million tons in 1940 to their 1943 peak of 16.1 million tons (see Figure 6 in Appendix for indexed figures).[5]

By mid-1940 the Materials Committee oversaw a Steel Distribution Scheme, described euphemistically by the Iron and Steel Trade Confederation union as 'somewhat complicated' and dependent on 'the willing co-operation of steel users'.[6] The administrative process began when ministries submitted quarterly estimates of their requirements. The committee then compared these requirements against the Iron and Steel Control's weekly estimates of available steel before authorising tonnages to each Ministry. Finally, ministries determined firm level steel usage by issuing 'M' forms to their contractors that enabled their acquisition of a fixed quantity of steel. Contractors then issued further 'M' forms to their sub-contractors to acquire steel within this fixed amount. By 1943, the Materials Committee was allocating 79.1 per cent of all steel deliveries to the three supply ministries and the system continued with limited adjustments, although in 1942 the government transferred responsibility for the Committee from the Ministry of Supply to that of Production.[7]

The Iron and Steel Control had two tasks. One was to secure raw materials, as although domestically mined ore accounted for two-thirds of consumption, its poor quality meant that imported ore provided half of all metallic content.[8] This task was given greater urgency from mid-1940 as German advances stopped imports from Sweden, Norway and French North Africa.[9] In response, imports were obtained from other countries such as Brazil, while ore mining in the UK was intensified. Nevertheless, the poor quality of domestic ore prompted pig iron production to fall, necessitating greater use of scrap. The other task was production supervision. While the Control could issue orders to control the supply and distribution of raw materials, and direct firm-level activity, it preferred informal coordination albeit within its overall programmes overseeing imports, production and distribution.[10] Informality was prompted by the Control's trade association origins. Most staff were either sourced from the pre-war British Iron and Steel Federation or were industrial secondees, prompting the Select Committee on National Expenditure to describe it in 1943 as the 'personnel of the Iron and Steel Federation in government uniform'.[11]

Many other raw materials controls operated but the most relevant to metal manufacturing were Non-Ferrous Metals, and Light Metals. By mid-1940 the Non-Ferrous Metal Control was responsible for the supply and demand of copper, zinc and lead, while other metals such as tin were added later.[12] Seventeen control orders set out its powers but these formed a framework within which it developed autonomously, prompting Director A. G. Charles to describe an evolutionary process as it 'expanded and developed as the changing situation appeared to direct'. Administrative equilibrium was reached by 1943 when 270 people were employed as its activity peaked, before declining as ammunition production reduced. It managed supply through securing imports and controlling demand, reduced demand through licensing users including scrap and identifying alternative materials to replace metal within manufacturing. Such activities reduced civilian demand for copper to around 10 per cent of pre-war totals, and overall consumption of tin by 50 per cent, assisted by Board of Trade orders controlling consumer goods production.

Demand was further managed through production licences. While the Iron and Steel Control controlled distribution through supervising end users, the Non-Ferrous Metal Control did the opposite as once civilian uses had been reduced, supply was adequate to meet approved demand. The Control thus regulated consumption by issuing licences and allocating ore to metal manufacturers who had to provide a schedule of all end user firms contracted to purchase the metal produced; some 150 licence applications were received daily detailing up to 10,000 end users.[13] Finally, the Light Metal Control focused on aluminium, silicon and magnesium. It was the sole buyer and seller of all domestically produced or imported metals within these categories,[14] and tightly controlled the production of individual companies.

The Iron and Steel Control was organised on a UK-wide level given the integrated nature of the industry, even after bomb damage to its London headquarters in late 1940 prompted 500 staff to relocate to a country house near Leamington Spa. Nevertheless, specialist outposts operated in a few locations while district liaison officers helped companies source steel. Industrial geography, however, meant that south Wales was subsumed into a south Wales and southwest area and north Wales into a northwestern area. District officers were generally sourced from the industry. The south Wales and southwest England Area Officer was Edgar Rees, a scrap importer who was prominent within trade associations.[15] The Non-Ferrous Metal Control had its headquarters in Rugby, Warwickshire but two regional offices including one in Swansea managed local relationships.[16] Finally, the Light Metals Control was based in Banbury, although subsidiary functions overseeing sub-sectors existed in Birmingham and Buckinghamshire.[17] Yet regional officers within any of the Controls did not sit on the cross-departmental Area or Regional Boards overseen by the Ministry of Production and its predecessors. They were represented instead by regional officers from the Ministry of Supply, or, in the case of Light Metals, the Ministry of Aircraft Production.

Controls' activity was supported by government intervention in labour and prices. Metal manufacturing businesses often struggled to recruit and retain labour given the demands of the armed forces and the availability of lighter and often equally well-paid work in the munitions industries. In mid-1940 the Ministry of Supply told firms asking for additional labour that their requests 'were one among many' and might not be 'met immediately', before providing the names of its Regional Officers who could take up their case with the Ministry of Labour and National Service.[18] In February 1941 Bevin met with unions and employers to stress his preference for voluntary agreements but the need to preserve workforce levels meant that greater intervention was inevitable.[19]

In May 1941 Bevin instructed the Non-Ferrous Metals Control to conclude a guaranteed weekly wage agreement with unions,[20] before announcing a Ring Fence Scheme in August. It prevented workers within most metal manufacturing business from leaving the industry and was designed to be more comprehensive than the Essential Work Orders, which applied to individual firms only.[21] Meanwhile, regional committees formed from both sides of industry, as well as government representatives including those from the Ministry of Labour and National Service, and the Controls, controlled labour movements between firms.[22] Finally, although blast furnace operators, for example, were the eighth highest paid of almost one hundred industrial occupations in mid-1941,[23] the Ministry of Labour and National Service pressed firms to increase wages elsewhere by refusing to direct labour into companies unless their wages rose. Pressures within the iron and steel industry culminated in mid-1942 when it was forced to accept weekly minimum earnings for all employees.[24] Nevertheless, wages were generally sufficient to maintain the wartime labour force.

In terms of pricing, control orders fixed metal prices to avoid inflationary pressures although such orders often operated in tandem with other initiatives to preserve the viability of metal manufacturing businesses. By 1941 some steelmakers were unable to break even. The government responded by adapting an existing industry-run levy on steel purchases that was designed to avoid price distortions by subsidising firms importing raw material and machinery. The levy was repurposed to subsidise high-cost firms subject to profitability caps. The system was later dependent on government subsidy and was effective but complex. One result of what the official history described as the 'extremely intricate' and 'extraordinary' system was to conceal plant-level production costs, prompting investigations from often baffled MPs; the Select Committee on National Expenditure noted in 1943 that the price control system within iron and steel was the most 'extensive and elaborate' system within the wartime economy.[25]

Finally, the modern nature of much of the industry helped the control marshal activity. Controller Sir Charles Wright argued in 1940 that the industry had 'more steel capacity than could be supplied with raw materials' and that there was 'no reason whatever' to construct a completely new steelworks.[26] Much of the industry remained largely unchanged throughout the war and no new plants were constructed. However, expansions were common, such as within alloy steel furnace units whose combined capacity doubled between 1940 and 1943.[27] Other schemes were smaller and funded through a mixture of private and state capital, including a few blast and open hearth furnaces. Nevertheless, the war effort required more aluminium than could be produced or imported, and the government worked to build capacity.

Modernisation and higher wages helped prompt relatively benign industrial relations, as wages grew strongly between 1939 and early 1944.[28] Relative industrial peace helped both sides of industry to agree on longer working hours, continuous production at weekends, as well as the wartime suspension of the sliding scales linking wages to prices and their replacement with a tonnage bonus and a cost-of-living element. Unions also cooperated generally with the assimilation of unskilled labour, including women. Yet women were less commonly employed in metal manufacturing than the munitions industries. In June 1942 only 13.5 per cent of the workforce were female, prompting the Iron and Steel Control to issue an eighteen-page list of occupations where women were already employed within the industry and advise employers as to the 'urgent need for the employment of women wherever possible'.[29]

While most metal manufacturing industries experienced stability or growth during the war, there were two exceptions. These were sheet steel and tinplate, where many businesses operated small, unmodernised factories and were already under pressure from larger facilities opened before the war. War worsened their competitive positioning given the loss of export markets and the curtailing of domestic demand for products such as tobacco tins. The result was surplus capacity that in the case of sheet steel prompted a concentration scheme supervised by the Board of Trade to release labour, materials and factory space.[30] Meanwhile, the tinplate industry, concentrated in south Wales, was affected by the loss of its export markets and many plants became idle.

GOVERNING METAL MANUFACTURING, WALES

The experiences of wartime metal manufacturing in Wales can be summarised as falling into three categories. The first were those characterised by relative stability, the second were where production grew, and the final category were those in decline.

The first category comprising relative stability was formed primarily from the larger and more modernised steelworks that worked at full capacity throughout the war. These included plants at Ebbw Vale, Port Talbot/Margam, Cardiff and Shotton. Shotton, for example, employed some 6,000 people and always operated at full capacity. Constant production necessitated the use of metal sheets to black out the buildings at night, producing conditions described by one employee as 'hot as hell and as black as hades' but enabling war production to exceed three million tons of ingots and two million tons of steel sheets.[31] Although steel production in south Wales declined by 14.5 per cent between 1940 and 1945 (see Figure 7 in Appendix), most of this decline was between 1940 and 1941, after which production was more stable as munitions production headed towards its 1944 peak. Meanwhile, employment also dropped by 15 per cent, from 72,900 people in 1939 to 62,300 in 1945, while the percentage of females within the workforce grew from 4.4 per cent to 18.5 per cent.[32]

Demand for steel shadowed the growing production of munitions and, by September 1940, Brymbo was at full capacity with staff working weekend shifts, while the Shotton strip mill was operating a daily pattern of three eight-hour shifts.[33] By the end of the year, the Ministry of Supply had contracted eighty-two companies throughout Wales to produce raw materials, most for metals. These included prominent firms such as Baldwins whose plants at Swansea, Gowerton, Neath and Panteg produced castings and steel sheets, and Brown Lenox and Company whose Pontypridd plant produced bombs casing, anchors, steel chains and castings. Yet demand was such that many smaller firms were also under contract. These included Britannia Foundry at Porthmadog for structural steelwork and Neath Steel Sheet for roofing sheet.[34]

Although the Iron and Steel Control was disinterested in building new plants, it drove efficiency by supporting the modernisation and expansion of existing facilities. In May 1940, for example, a blast furnace at Brymbo restarted, rolling mills reopened at Neath and Pontardawe, and three steel furnaces entered production at Llanelli.[35] Guest Keen and Nettlefolds

(GKN) Chair Samuel Beale argued that 'war meant control – control of supplies, control of production, control of the destination of products and of the prices at which they were to be sold'.[36] Overall, the Iron and Steel Control tended to benefit larger firms prompting their general acceptance of its governance, a dynamic illustrated by the intertwined activities in south Wales of the GKN and Guest Keen Baldwins (GKB) companies.

GKN's Cwmbran plant was contracted by the Ministry of Supply and the Admiralty to produce goods including machine parts, screws and nails, while its Castle Works in Cardiff produced goods including nuts, spikes and wire for the Ministry of Supply, the Admiralty and Ministry of Aircraft Production.[37] In November 1942 the Control asked GKN to increase its weekly output at Cardiff by 300 tons, encouraging agreement by providing half of the cost of acquiring and installing new machinery. The Control also provided financial support when GKN needed to replace its nail machines in Cardiff in 1944 given their prolonged use by three shifts daily.[38] Nail production duly increased from 24,570 tons in 1944 to 29,423 tons in 1945. Nevertheless, the lack of large-scale capacity expansions meant that there were no dramatic overall production increases. Combined steel output from the three mills onsite was 209,490 tons in 1940, growing by some 15 per cent to peak at 241,209 tons in 1943 before falling back to 229,600 tons in 1945.[39]

Similar dynamics were apparent within GKB's Margam/Port Talbot complex where 3,600 people were employed by 1944 producing 12,300 tons of steel ingots, rails, sections and plates weekly. Few new blast furnaces were built in the UK during the war,[40] but one was at Port Talbot/Margam. By 1940 the plant's two blast furnaces had operated at full capacity for two years, prompting both to be reconstructed and supplemented with a new furnace. Other modernisations included expanding the ore bunker capacity by almost one-third and installing new gas cleaning and water pumping systems. Meanwhile, new open-hearth furnaces were installed at GKB's Briton Ferry and Cardiff plants.[41] Expansion elsewhere was generally limited, although a foundry to produce bomb castings at Baldwin's Landore plant was among those funded by the government in 1942 as part of a larger scheme to offset shortages.[42]

As well as encouraging modernisation, the Iron and Steel Control also drove improved efficiency by encouraging cooperation between producers. Some cooperation was vertical within supply chains and was usually conducted with at least tacit approval from the Control. GKN, for example, purchased shares in the Somerset Wire Company to obtain its commitment to purchase wire rod from its Castle Works, followed by similar activities in relation to other engineering and wholesale suppliers.[43] Other cooperation was horizontal across producers. In May 1942 the Control 'suggested' that GKB should cease some light bar mill operations in south Wales, enabling them to be concentrated at an underused GKN facility at Cwmbran. As part of this approach, GKN agreed to pay GKB £4,000 a year in compensation for loss of business until the end of the war, after which payments would cease and GKB would be free to re-enter the market.

The wartime experiences of GKN's Cwmbran facility, formed from brickworks, a colliery, foundries and bolt works, reflected broader trends. Its metal manufacturing and engineering facilities once depended on producing railway goods. Most of their export trade was suspended during the war but supplanted by munitions such as trench mortar bomb cases and metal bolts for the Ministry of Supply, and bomb cases for the Admiralty. Despite such orders, two of the three foundries had 'little work' or were 'idle' in May 1942, prompting intervention from the Iron and Steel Control followed by a large Ministry of Supply order for bomb components. Meanwhile, capital investment continued although managers fretted as to the time needed to obtain official consent. In April 1941, for example, the company succeeded in gaining verbal authorisation to reconstruct part of their foundry operations but were left waiting 'some weeks' for written authorisation, noting that 'it seems very difficult to get the business hurried through to its final stages'.[44]

Steel producers were constrained, however, by their inability to sustain pre-war levels of ore imports. Imports to south Wales fell by some two-thirds, declining from 994,723 tons in 1940 to 321,595 in 1942.[45] In response, the Control prioritised domestic iron ore mining but reserves were often worked out. Output, mostly from one mine at Llanharry in south Wales employing 300 miners, peaked at 232,500 tons in 1940, before falling to 119,700 tons by 1945.[46] Meanwhile, industrial relations within ore mining had more in common with the coal industry than iron and steel, while ore miners were represented by the South Wales Miners' Federation. In late 1940 the Ministry of Supply official managing home ore attempted to resolve problems at the Llanharry mine through a voluntary approach. He asked the mine manager to read out a letter to a workforce mass meeting stating that he 'cannot help wondering whether the miners fully appreciate the fundamental national importance' of their work, before arguing that Bevin would be 'seriously perturbed ... if the facts of this case was brought to his notice'. However, disputes continued and the miners' complaints after the 1944 Porter Award that their wages compared poorly with coal mining reached the national arbitration board.[47]

One factor driving metals manufacturing efficiency was that pay was relatively attractive when compared to other industries. In July 1941 average weekly earnings of adult males in the occupational categories of Iron Puddling, Blast Furnace work, and Iron and Steel Tubes were all within the upper quartile of industries throughout Britain.[48] Yet isolated wage disparities prompted reluctance to transfer into the industry during the early years of the war, such as in August 1941 when 400 men released from tinplate works in west Wales refused to transfer voluntarily to drop forging and brass foundry plants in England, as better paid jobs were available in local ROFs. The Ministry of Supply wanted to force transfer, but local Ministry of Labour and National Service officers advised caution as magistrates might be reluctant to punish workers refusing to move hundreds of miles and accept reduced weekly earnings.[49] Recruitment problems, however, eased as wages increased and more workers were mobilised. One example was the John Summers plant at Shotton where, although almost one-third of its 6,000 staff enlisted for service, many of their posts were filled by female workers registered and directed by local Ministry of Labour and National Service officers.[50] Although many women gained employment, much of the industry remained overwhelmingly male. At John Summers, women were concentrated in laboratories, packing and transport, not the strip mill, foundries or furnaces.[51]

The second category of metals manufacturing was where capacity expanded. While the Iron and Steel Control discounted the need for new steelworks, it and other controls had to react to demand for aluminium and specialist steels such as alloys and armour plate exceeding domestic production capacity. Alloy production was concentrated in Sheffield and the need to disperse such activity in case of air raids led to south Wales plants doubling their proportion of the UK's output of electric furnace ingot between 1939 and 1946 from 3 to 7 per cent. Electric furnaces were generally installed in existing steelworks to reduce the need for new ancillary equipment such as those installed at Brymbo near Wrexham and Panteg in south Wales.[52] Light alloys and aluminium were particularly important as the construction of a strategic bomber force from 1942 prompted what the Light Metals Control described as a 'tremendous expansion' in orders.[53]

Expansion prompted the Ministry of Aircraft Production to cooperate with the Light Metal Control and the Non-Ferrous Metal Controls to develop capacity in Wales. Capacity was developed through financially supporting businesses producing specialist metals. By the peak of the war effort, seven factories totalling 1.3 million square feet received financial support. The largest was Northern Aluminium at Rogerstone near Newport whose plant covered three quarters of a million square feet and employed over 5,000 workers, but there was also a concentration around Swansea featuring factories operated by ICI Metals, the British Aluminium Company, Robert Byness, and the Magnesium Metal Corporation.[54] Moreover, two smaller factories in Cardiff produced aluminium forgings and powder as part of a broader concentration of munitions manufacture,[55] while an aluminium smelting plant operated at Dolgarrog in north Wales. Finally, scrap metals were identified and used, such as those produced as manufacturing by-products or obtained from bomb sites or wrecked aircraft; the Non-Ferrous Metal Control, for example, arranged for an ore dressing plant at a disused mine at Halkyn in Flintshire to process waste produced by brass mills.[56]

Meanwhile, the controls monitored factory performance. In late 1941, for example, the Light Metal Control noted that it was giving 'close attention' to a 'disappointing' plant in Cardiff managed by International Alloys Ltd that was producing only 1,350 tons of magnesium out of a 2,000-ton capacity. It gave 'every possible assistance' to raise production through sourcing additional labour and machinery before production finally reached capacity in mid-1942.[57] A similar pattern occurred when a brass foundry at the Orb works in Newport was closed, reconstituted and reopened in late 1941 after the union agreed new working practices to enable greater productivity.[58] Finally, efforts were made to boost the production of domestic non-ferrous ore. The Benallt mine on the Llŷn peninsula reopened to produce 60,000 tons of manganese ore needed for high strength steel alloys for uses including propellers and armour plate. Nevertheless, explorations elsewhere such as those for manganese in Caernarfonshire and Merioneth, and zinc in Ceredigion, failed to find viable reserves.[59]

The combination of relatively high wages and state investment helped prompt stable industrial relations throughout metal manufacturing, except for tinplate. By 1942 Joint Production Committees were increasingly common although the Iron and Steel Confederation union warned its members not to expect too much from such advisory bodies.[60] The relatively few disputes that took place were often resolved through arbitration. One example was in 1942 when the Confederation obtained greater Sunday overtime payments for its members at the Port Talbot and Margam works. Stability was reflected by Board of Trade data showing that, although there were seventy-nine strikes in metal manufacturing excluding tinplate from 1940 to 1945, these were generally short lived. Meanwhile, the union punished strikers when their behaviour was seen as harmful to its interests or to war production in general. One example was in December 1940, when it investigated a dispute in Llanelli and fined strikers who had left their workplace without removing furnace charges.[61]

The overall volume of disputes peaked in 1944 as the union attempted to resolve eight disputes in south Wales in the first quarter. Such disputes proceeded against a backdrop of widespread uncertainty as munitions production throughout the UK began to fall amidst debates as to post-war prospects: the largest was 5,200 workers at Richard Thomas & Co. in Ebbw Vale striking for three days in 1944 over the behaviour of on-site police officers before work resumed pending negotiations. Nevertheless, after mid-1940 only ten strikes lasted a week or more and these generally affected fewer workers in smaller plants. The only such strikes at larger facilities were 634 workers striking for twenty-one days in late 1940 over the dismissal of an electrician at the Richard Thomas Plant at Ebbw Vale until what the Board of Trade called an 'amicable agreement' was reached, and sixteen workers striking for eight days at GKN Newport in early 1945. All this meant that total days lost to industrial disputes for metal manufacturing excluding tinplate between 1940 and 1945 was only 4.1 per cent of those throughout Wales (see Figure 2 in Appendix).[62]

The final category of metal manufacturing was where activity reduced, encompassing sheet steel and tinplate. Sheet steel had experienced a brief boom prompted by demands for air raid shelters, but this was short-lived as such demand was met. Moreover, the large mills at Ebbw Vale and Shotton could meet demand by mid-1940, and by 1941 the latter's weekly production was enough for 50,000 Morrison shelters.[63] By May works at Pontardawe, Neath and Llanelli were idle while the J. Lysaught plant at Newport had temporarily laid off 1,500 workers.[64] In mid-1941 the Ministry of Labour reported 'further slackness', stoppages and short-time working,[65] as the government considered options to shrink the industry to release floorspace for other uses.

The Iron and Steel Control instructed the UK-wide trade association, the Sheetmakers Conference, to identify the firms to continue in production and those to close. Of the seventeen steel sheet plants in Wales employing 13,746 people in 1941, six were to close releasing 1,486 workers for transfer to other industries. Although the affected plants were mainly small, while some had already ceased production, the process reflected the extent to which governance had been sub-contracted to private interests. The management of one factory in Pontypool to be closed argued that it was fully occupied on war work and claimed with some justification that the programme had been guided by larger members of the trade association to assist their post-war prospects, such as John Summers and its Shotton plant.[66]

The industry most affected by reducing demand was the fragmented, labour intensive and outmoded 'hand rolling' tinplate industry, formed from eighty works of varying sizes and ownership concentrated around Llanelli and Swansea.[67] Employment fell as a result of the loss of export markets and, by August 1940, the Ministry of Labour observed that the position within Welsh tinplate was 'bad' as the industry was working 'at little more than half capacity' and 21 per cent of its insured workers were unemployed. Christmas holidays were extended and, by February, representatives of the midlands drop forging industry arrived in Llanelli to select men for transfer. Of the 24,180 workers forming the south Wales tinplate workforce in July 1940, a total 2,170 had been released by June 1941, such as a works at Gorseinon releasing 444 workers of whom all but twenty-nine were placed in ROFs or metal manufacturing elsewhere.[68] The Non-Ferrous Metals Control also transferred some workers to the West Midlands but only a few hundred were affected.[69] Meanwhile, the Regional Factory and Storage Control Function began to requisition redundant or underused works, taking thirty-five by November 1941.[70]

In early 1941 the government appointed the Essendon Committee to report on concentrating and rationalising the industry. It appointed a sub-committee under H. Leighton Davies of Baldwins to investigate combining a redundancy plan with releasing plant for wartime uses.[71] The findings appeared in October 1941, proposing that underutilised or surplus plants could be made available for other uses. But instead of a centrally administered concentration scheme, it reflected industry interests by proposing industry cooperation to identify surplus capacity, even discussing how to assist the post-war resumption of the export trade on which the industry once depended.[72] The Committee, however, had neglected to ask the Factory and Storage Control Function to provide evidence. Its controller, Cecil Weir, promptly visited Wales to consult with his regional officials before objecting to the committee's conclusions given its proposed maintenance of surplus floorspace, arguing that such a policy was a 'luxury that cannot be afforded in these times'.[73]

The President of the Board of Trade agreed with the Essendon Committee's rejection of a formal concentration scheme in favour of waiting for the industry to agree. Yet the Board did not need a scheme, given the state of the industry, announcing instead that it would 'requisition ... as many tinplate works as can be spared without prejudice to war-time production'.[74] However, requisitioning was occasionally fraught as tinplate companies and their surrounding communities were strongly opposed to such losses, while administrative dysfunction was often apparent. One example was two plants in Pontypool proposed for closure and the transfer of their premises to the Ministry of Aircraft Production. This proposal prompted furious local opposition and Weir noted that he was being 'bombarded' with 'letters and telegrams of protest'.[75] Embarrassingly, the production and premises officers of the Ministry had misunderstood each other. Production officers eventually visited the factories only to announce that they were unsuitable for their requirements, prompting Weir to demand that all requests for space be coordinated within supply ministries before being submitted.[76]

Further difficulties were prompted by most of the requisitioned plants being used for storage, not production, meaning that jobs lost were not replaced. These included one in Llangennech used by the Admiralty as well as those in Llanelli taken for uses including tobacco storage after Liverpool was bombed. Meanwhile, opposition to the loss of jobs mounted. With the support of Llanelli MP Jim Griffith, the Production Executive's Wales Regional Board argued that factories emptied by concentration should be used for production not storage, arguing that 'the feeling on the matter is very strong indeed', and that all labour should be retained locally.[77] Despite such appeals, the Factory and Storage Control Function refused to allocate empty works to production, prompting the Regional Board to plaintively respond that it was 'entitled to know the reason for this state of affairs'.[78] In response, the Board of Trade argued that there was insufficient electricity in southwest Wales to host new production, a claim denied furiously by the Regional Board.

Frustration prompted Swansea Town Council to organise a meeting in December 1941 where industrialists, MPs and officials including those from the Wales Regional Board, met to discuss how to attract more production into Wales, including into works vacated by tinplate concentration. Industrialists and politicians raged at the lack of production, only to be told bluntly by Factory and Storage Control Function Regional Controller Walters that they were 'very largely to blame' as 'you cannot expect the government to wave a magic wand ... you must go and tell government supply departments what you can produce'.[79] Nevertheless, the Ministry of Supply wearied of 'constant' reports and deputations, and dismissed ideas such as using vacant premises for tank production on the grounds of practicality. In January 1942 Walters simply informed one company after a long correspondence that he could not 'consent to any factory in my region working short time ... making fractional use of available space'.[80] By the following month, the Board of Trade was refusing to respond to complaints from the West Wales Advisory Panel of the Production Executive's Wales Regional Board.[81] Finally, the industry had been further harmed by the loss of refined tin imports from Malaya after its occupation by Japanese forces as, although the industry in south Wales relied on imports from Bolivia and West Africa, global tin supply was pooled with the United States.[82]

By 1943 the tinplate workforce throughout Britain stood at only 10,000, compared to 26,670 in July 1939.[83] The concentration of the industry in southwest Wales meant that by 1943 dramatic regional declines prompted another meeting of MPs and industrialists at Swansea to discuss what the *Western Mail* described as a 'Welsh tin-plate crisis'. In mid-1940 the industry employed 11,262 people in the Swansea region but this fell by over a third to 6,516 by mid-1943.[84] Closures combined with pre-existing factors to prompt tinplate production throughout the UK to almost halve from 977,000 tons in 1940 to 512,000 tons in 1945.[85] Meanwhile, industry-wide negotiations as to concentration were delayed by disagreements as to which plants should close. A scheme was finally agreed in 1944 only for the Board of Trade to argue that it underestimated the level of concentration necessary during wartime and refused to accept the proposals,[86] although the primary reason was its desire to use its ability to reject the scheme as leverage to steer post-war industrial reconstruction.

Despite the relatively small size of the industry, it accounted for 6.8 per cent of all days lost to strikes in Wales between 1940 and 1945, behind only coal in the industrial ranking of days lost between 1940 and 1945 (see Figure 2 in Appendix). Days lost in tinplate were almost treble those lost in engineering and five times greater than iron and steel, although both employed far more workers. There were twenty-one strikes, for example, in 1942. One involved 252 workers at the Elba Mill in Swansea striking for three days over wages, before returning to work having obtained concessions from management.[87] While the Board of Trade recorded the immediate cause of most disputes as wages, the speed at which the industry shrank helped prompt turbulent industrial relations and political argument.

CONCLUSION

The government prioritised ensuring the production of enough metals to sustain munitions production. The need to provide sufficient metals prompted a requirement to match raw materials to production demand, to expand or contact production where it was needed, and ensure that metal manufacturing industries operated at maximum capacity and efficiency. The integrated nature of much of the metal manufacturing industry prompted a UK-wide approach divided between industries that each had separate controls. There were no nationwide regional structures, while regional representation was largely absent. There were no equivalents of the Wales only, or south Wales only, governance structures of other industries.

Once the materials committee took control of economy-wide allocation, in mid-1940, Controls could focus on guiding and marshalling the industries for which they were responsible. They combined formal orders with more informal methods, drawing on the extent to which they were based on pre-war trade associations, and continued to source key staff from industry secondees. Different metal manufacturing industries had radically varying experiences, based on the extent to which their output types and levels matched the requirements of the munitions industries. In sum, a system emerged that lacked systematic regional governance but was responsive, flexible and pragmatic. Franks described the structures governing raw materials as 'always imperfect, and always learning'.[88]

State interventions varied from removing excess capacity through concentration schemes, through to encouraging vertical and horizontal businesses amalgamation, to funding expanded and new facilities. By mid-1941 the Iron and Steel Controller declared that the UK 'could meet all our demands for raw steel'.[89] The influence of leading industry figures within the controls was subject to criticism as to potential conflicts between their commercial and governance interests, but the modernisation of the 1930s helped governance systems operate effectively. When this was combined with the availability of large-scale imports of ore and metals, mainly from north America, large-scale difficulties in supplying the metal needs of the munitions industries were avoided.

Notes

1 Franks, *Central Planning and Control*, pp. 12–13.
2 TNA, AVIA 10/298, *Organization and General Functions of Control*, 28 September 1943, 1.
3 Hurstfield, *The Control of Raw Materials*, p. 409.
4 *Statistical Digest of the Second World War*, p. 105.
5 Keeling and Wright, *The Development of the Modern British Steel Industry*, p. 60; Burn, *The Steel Industry, 1939–1959*, p. 9.
6 Glamorgan Archives, DITSC/24, *Iron and Steel Trade Confederation Reports*, 30 June 1940, 125.
7 BT 131/28, *Priority and Allocation*, 27–8; Howlett 'Resource Allocation in Wartime Britain: The Case of Steel, 1939–45', 538; Hurstfield, *The Control of Raw Materials*, p. 418.
8 Hurstfield, *The Control of Raw Materials*, p. 334.

9   Keeling and Wright, *The Development of the Modern British Steel Industry*, p. 12.
10 Burn, *The Steel Industry, 1939–1959*, pp. 5–6.
11 House of Commons, *14th Report of the Select Committee on National Expenditure, 1942–1943*, 68.
12 TNA, AVIA 22/3087, *Statutory Rules and Orders, Raw Materials (Tin)*, 1941; AVIA 12/85, *History of the Non-Ferrous Metal Control*, 1947, 3.
13 TNA, AVIA 12/85, *History of the Non-Ferrous Metal Control*, 1947, 17, 18–19, 22–24, 47,.
14 TNA, 10/298, *Light Metals Control Organization*, 28 September 1943, 1.
15 TNA, AVIA 22/61, *District Liason Officers*; *Western Mail*, 'Iron Merchants' New President', 24 April 1942.
16 TNA, AVIA 12/85, *History of the Non-Ferrous Metal Control*, 1947, 15.
17 TNA, 10/298, *Light Metals Control Organization*, 28 September 1943, 2–3.
18 Glamorgan Archives, D561/1/8/2/33, *Labour Requirements*, June 1940.
19 Glamorgan Archives, DITSC/25, *Iron and Steel Trade Confederation Reports*, 31 March 1941, 29.
20 TNA, AVIA 12/85, *History of the Non-Ferrous Metal Control*, 1947, 38.
21 Keeling and Wright, *The Development of the Modern British Steel Industry*, pp. 58–9.
22 Parker, *Manpower*, p. 222.
23 TNA, POWE 20/62, *Average Weekly Earnings in Coal Mining and Other Industries*, July 1941.
24 Inman, *Labour in the Munition Industries*, pp. 157, 164.
25 Ashworth, *Contracts and Finance*, pp. 163–5; House of Commons, *14th Report of the Select Committee on National Expenditure, 1942–1943*, 67.
26 Hurstfield, *The Control of Raw Materials*, p. 341.
27 BT 131/88, *Iron and Steel Narrative*, 1952, 128.
28 BT 131/88, *Iron and Steel Narrative*, 1952, 191.
29 Glamorgan Archives, D561/1/8/2/33, *Wartime Employment of Women in the Iron and Steel Industry*, 5 June 1942.
30 TNA, BT 131/24, *Concentration of Production, Explanatory Memorandum* (Cmd 6528) (HMSO, 1941), 2; TNA, BT 131/2, *Memorandum on the Functions of the Board of Trade*, October 1941, 7.
31 Redhead and Goodie, *The Summers of Shotton*, pp. 139, 143.
32 Williams, *DWHS, vol. 1*, pp. 135, 355.
33 Glamorgan Archives, DITSC/24, *Iron and Steel Trade Confederation Reports*, 30 September 1940, 191.
34 TNA, BT 168/2, *Firms in Area engaged on Government Contracts, or on War Production Sub-contracts, Wales Area Board*, 18 January 1941.
35 TNA, LAB 12/82, *Ministry of Labour Monthly Report, Wales*, 20 May 1940, 2.
36 Lorenz, *GKN: The Making of a Business*, p. 80.
37 TNA, BT 168/2, *Firms in Area Engaged on Government Contracts, or on War Production Sub-contracts, Wales Area Board*, 18 January 1941.
38 E. Jones, *A History of GKN, Volume 2, 1918–1945* (Macmillan, 1990), pp. 304–5, 312.
39 Jones, *A History of GKN, Volume 2, 1918–1945*, p. 131.

40 Burn, *The Steel Industry, 1939–1959*, pp. 13–14; Parry, *History of the Steel Industry in the Port Talbot Area*, pp. 113–14.
41 Burn, *The Steel Industry, 1939–1959*, p. 14.
42 TNA, BT 131/88, *Iron and Steel Narrative*, 1952, 144.
43 Jones, *A History of GKN, Volume 2, 1918–1945*, p. 305.
44 Gwent Archives, D409/2, *GKN Cwmbran, General Managers Report*, 2 May 1942; 26 April 1941; 29 August 1942; 27 September 1941, 10.
45 Parry, *History of the Steel Industry in the Port Talbot Area*, p. 285.
46 Williams, *DWHS*, vol. 2, p. 351; Glamorgan Archives, D561/1/9/1/29, *Statement of the Employers' Case*, 6.
47 Glamorgan Archives, D561/1/8/2/33, *Director of Home Ore Control to S. Martin, 9 September 1940;* D561/1/9/1/29, *Statement of the Employers' Case*, 2–3.
48 TNA, POWE 20/62, *Average Weekly Earnings in Coal Mining and Other Industries*, July 1941.
49 Inman, *Labour in the Munition Industries*, p. 164.
50 Smith, *A Century of Shotton Steel*, p. 32.
51 Redhead and Goodie, *The Summers of Shotton*, p. 139.
52 Burn, *The Steel Industry, 1939–1959*, pp. 16–17.
53 TNA, 46/433, *Memorandum on the Provision of Fabricated Materials for Aircraft Construction*, 27 April 1942, 1.
54 TNA, BT 64/3392, *Estimates of Post War Unemployment*; CAB 102/274, *Government Owned Factories Operated by Contractors on Agency/Commercial Terms*, 1945.
55 Baber and Thomas, 'The Glamorgan Economy, 1914–1945', in John and Williams (eds), *Glamorgan County History, Volume V*, p. 565.
56 TNA, AVIA 12/85, *History of the Non-Ferrous Metal Control*, 1947, 27.
57 TNA, AVIA 46/433, *Light Metal Control Report*, November 1941, 2; December 1941, 2; July 1942, 4.
58 Glamorgan Archives, DITSC/25, *Iron and Steel Trade Confederation Reports*, 31 December 1941, 210.
59 BT 131/88, *Iron and Steel Narrative*, 1952, 65; J. Macve, 'The search for Zinc Blende in Mid Cardiganshire during World War 2', *Ceredigion*, XI, 3 (1992), 271–88.
60 Gwent Archives, D3417/1/16, *Man and Metal*, March 1942, 1.
61 Glamorgan Archives, DITSC/25, *Iron and Steel Trade Confederation Reports*, 31 March 1941, 26.
62 TNA, LAB 34/55, *Trade Disputes*, 1940; LAB 34/56, *Trade Disputes*, LAB 34/60, *Trade Disputes*, 1945.
63 D. A. Thomas, 'War and the Economy: The South Wales Experience', in Baber and Williams (eds), *Modern South Wales: Essays in Economic History*, pp. 251–77 (p. 257); Smith, *A Century of Shotton Steel*, p. 32.
64 TNA, LAB 12/82, *Ministry of Labour Monthly Report, Wales*, 20 May 1940, 3.
65 TNA, LAB 12/82, *Ministry of Labour Monthly Report, Wales*, 14 July 1941, 5; 17 November 1941, 5.

66 TNA, BT 131/108, *Committee Concentrating Production, Steel Sheet Industry*, 10 October 1941; *Concentration of Sheet Steel Industry*, September 1941.
67 P. Jenkins, *Twenty by Fourteen: A History of the South Wales Tinplate Industry, 1700–1961* (Gomer, 1995), pp. 222–6.
68 TNA, LAB 12/82, *Ministry of Labour Monthly Report, Wales*, 10 August 1940, 3; 10 February 1941, 7; 15 June 1941, 7.
69 TNA, AVIA 12/85, *History of the Non-Ferrous Metal Control*, 1947, 38.
70 TNA, BT 106/10, *Note by the Storage Controller on the Storage Position in South Wales Relating to Tinplate Works*, 17 November 1941.
71 Minchanton, *The British Tinplate Industry*, p. 234.
72 TNA, BT 106/10, *Report of the Essendon Committee*, 29 October 1941, 3, 13.
73 TNA, BT 106/10, *Note by the Storage Controller on the Storage Position in South Wales Relating to Tinplate Works*, 17 November 1941; *Remarks on Essendon Report by P. A. Water, Storage Controller*, November 1941.
74 TNA, BT 106/10, *President of the Board of Trade to Lord Essendon*, 5 December 1941.
75 TNA, BT 106/10, *Sir Cecil Weir to Wales Regional Controller of Factory and Storage Function*, 18 March 1942.
76 TNA, BT 106/10, *Note from Controller of the Factory and Storage Control to President of the Board of Trade*, 22 January 1942.
77 *Western Mail*, 'Llanelly MP asks, Who is holding things up?', 22 September 1941; TNA, BT 168/2, *Wales Regional Board to Production Executive*, 27 February 1942.
78 TNA, BT 168/32, *Summary of Regional Board Matters for the Consideration of Mr Bevin*, 24 October 1941.
79 TNA, BT 168/2, *Closing of Tinplate and Other Works and Industries in south Wales, Meeting held in Swansea, 21 November 1941*, 9.
80 TNA, BT 106/10, *R. Waters to G. Latham, Richard Thomas Ltd*, 3 January 1942.
81 TNA, BT 168/2, *Board of Trade to Production Executive*, 23 February 1942.
82 TNA, BT 131/88, *Iron and Steel Narrative*, 1952, 178.
83 Minchanton, *The British Tinplate Industry*, p. 233.
84 *Western Mail*, 'Welsh Tin-Plate Crisis', 19 April 1943; TNA, 64/3105, *Nuffield College, Social Reconstruction Survey, Swansea Industrial Region*, 3.
85 Williams, *DWHS, vol. 1*, p. 356.
86 *Western Mail*, 'Future of the Tinplate Industry', 3 October 1944.
87 TNA, LAB 34/57, *Trade Disputes*, 1942.
88 Franks, *Central Planning and Control*, p. 15.
89 *Western Mail*, 'New Plans under Essential Work Order', 7 August 1941.

8

AGRICULTURE

GOVERNING THE UK INDUSTRY

Thorough pre-war preparations and an absence of clashing ministries meant that agricultural governance was stable throughout the war. While other Ministries jostled for position against a backdrop of administrative uncertainty, authority over agriculture and its products was divided clearly between two ministries: Food and Agriculture. The Ministry of Food was evacuated to requisitioned hotels in Colwyn Bay in June 1940 where 5,000 civil servants supervised UK-wide import programmes as well as the sale and distribution of most agricultural products.[1] Meanwhile, the Ministry of Agriculture acted as a food production department by controlling farming throughout England and Wales. There was some administrative friction between both ministries, but this was addressed by mid-1941 when they agreed a concordat clarifying a division of responsibilities.[2]

The primary goal of the Ministry of Agriculture was to reduce import dependence, given carriage on ships being vulnerable to enemy U-boats. Shipping losses increased after the fall of France prompting Minister of Agriculture Robert Hudson to make a UK-wide radio broadcast in November 1940 when he declared that:[3]

> You have seen the in the papers the number of ships we have lost to enemy attack. We have lost not only the cargoes they

are carrying but also the cargoes they would have carried on future voyages ... our job is to try and make that loss good.

The problem was obvious as imports under Ministry of Food programmes decreased from 19.3 million tonnes in 1940 to 11 million in 1944,[4] although most of this decline was bulky feeding stuffs such as wheat, barley and maize. These were substituted with home-produced goods where possible, or with less bulky imports when not. For example, although wheat imports almost halved from 5.8 million tons in 1940 to 2.8 million tons in 1944, ensuing problems were managed by encouraging the public to consume potatoes instead of bread. Meanwhile, imports of meat and some dairy products rose. Tinned meat imports increased from 123,300 tons in 1940 to 213,500 in 1944, milk powder more than quadrupled from 15,800 tons to 83,000 tons, while pork increased fivefold from 68,600 tons to 389,400. Even live animal imports continued as 560,300 cattle mainly from Ireland were brought to the UK in 1940 and 401,600 in 1944.[5]

While import substitution was effective, the food strategy would have failed without more agricultural production. Although total acreage farmed throughout Britain after 1940 remained steady at 30 million acres, the government's 'ploughing up' campaign converted 5 million acres from grassland to arable, changes that combined with declines in livestock farming to produce dramatic results. From 1940 to 1944 the tonnage of wheat produced throughout Britain grew by 93 per cent, barley by 60 per cent and potatoes by 49 per cent, although ploughing up prompted declines in most animal husbandry types. The number of cattle grew marginally by 3 per cent over the period but those of sheep fell by 24 per cent, pigs by 55 per cent and poultry by 38 per cent (see Table 4 in Appendix). A key measure of output was calories available for human consumption. These have been estimated as having doubled during the war although such calculations are beset with methodological difficulties.[6] Overall, the government succeeded in its most important aim of ensuring that the population could obtain enough food to fulfil their basic needs, although increasing domestic production formed part of a broader programme to secure supplies.

The war granted vital strategic importance to agriculture as the government launched modernisation and investment programmes to incentivise production by removing commercial risk and increasing returns. The number of tractors in Britain trebled, while farms were enveloped by subsidies, guaranteed markets and fixed prices paid by the Ministry of Food. Even though land yields per acre increased, there was no transformation in productivity. Instead, the war prompted a structural realignment and modernisation that aimed to maximise the output of arable crops,[7] which, when combined with higher prices, helped real net farm income to treble between 1938–9 and 1941–2.[8]

A vast bureaucratic machine emerged as the Ministry of Agriculture directed policies to reduce import dependence but delegated their implementation to the County War Agriculture Executive Committees (CWAECs). Thorough pre-war planning meant that the government did not need to refashion the CWAECs during wartime, although their grip over the industry was tightened from 1940. In this context, the Minister explained in his November 1940 broadcast how their authority extended to farms seen as underperforming:[9]

> There remain the farms that are badly farmed and farms where the land is inherently poor or bad. They present a real problem ... No single remedy applies to them all. We shall have to afford them many different kinds of help.

The Ministry of Agriculture appointed CWAEC members to deliver its county level 'ploughing up' and acreage crop production targets. Crop production targets were extended to include potatoes in 1941, sugar beet in 1942, and wheat in 1943.[10] The CWAECs issued cultivation orders instructing individual farmers to grow specified crops in specified fields.

Refusal to obey could be met with court-ordered fines and, in extreme cases, dispossession. Many other tasks lay beneath these activities. The CWAECs gathered detailed survey data on every farm, marshalled agricultural labour, administered credit and subsidy schemes, rationed goods such as feedstuffs, advised on production methods, administered land seized for disobeying cultivation orders, and deployed their own stocks of agricultural machinery and labour.

The breadth and depth of the CWAEC responsibilities gave them almost complete control over agriculture, while their decentralised nature ensured that government policies could be implemented in the smallest farms in the most remote locations. Although compulsion was rare, the threat was always present and acted as a powerful incentive to cooperate. In 1942 the government issued a 'green book' to every farmer in the UK that detailed its policies and determination, reflected by an earlier statement from the Minister for Agriculture that:[11]

> Committees should spare no pains to safeguard their good relationship with the general body of farmers [but] I have delegated to the Committees wide powers, and I wish them to use these to the full extent where the ignorance, the apathy or the opposition of an individual makes this necessary in the interests of the national food campaign.

GOVERNANCE STRUCTURES IN WALES

While intra-governmental disputes were largely absent, governance structures throughout England and Wales were complex. Five layers of governance (see Figure 8 in Appendix) enabled Whitehall to extend its control over farms in Wales.

The five layers were divided into two sets. One lay within the Ministry of Agriculture and contained two layers. The first was Ministry functions where executive power was centralised and deployed through issuing circulars to the CWAECs setting out policies to be implemented locally. Over 1,900 circulars were issued throughout the war on some three hundred topics with the most common being finance and accounts, machinery, feeding stuffs, labour, tractors, and reservation from military service.[12] Although CWAECs were given autonomy to flex approaches to suit local circumstances, they had to meet ploughing-up and production targets while absorbing a relentless flow of ministry circulars: the Cardiganshire CWAEC received twelve in one week in March 1943 on topics including Colorado beetles, disposing of cats, and permits for rubber boats. No action was taken on Colorado beetles while the others were referred to sub-committees.[13]

The second layer within the Ministry was regional functions. While officials in Scotland and Northern Ireland used their administrative autonomy to create more centralised governance approaches, this was impossible in Wales where governance was subsumed within the England and Wales structure of the Ministry of Agriculture. In July 1940 the Minister for Agriculture, after visiting CWAECs throughout England and Wales, appointed liaison officers to strengthen linkages between his Ministry and the CWAECs. These officers gathered in London to be told by the Minister that their role was to help deliver 'more drive and less hesitation to enforce where necessary a higher standard of cultivation in the light of the critical situation'.[14] Each was allocated four or five counties where he attended CWAEC meetings and reported difficulties to London. They also met as a group monthly, along with the Minister and Permanent Secretary.[15]

These posts enhanced the influence of the Welsh Department of the Ministry of Agriculture, created in Aberystwyth as part of a pre-war regional structure across England and Wales. Three officers were appointed in Wales. One was Cadwaladr Bryner Jones. He was already Secretary of the Welsh Department, and his influence grew steadily. Counties throughout mid and south

Wales were overseen by Bryner Jones, or his colleague J. Morgan Jones. Meanwhile, the staff of agricultural colleges emerged as important influences, and Professor White of the University College of North Wales was appointed as the liaison officer for north Wales counties.[16] Morgan Jones succeeded Bryner Jones as Welsh Secretary in 1944, by when he was already Chair of the Cardiganshire CWEAC while Bryner Jones chaired the Montgomery CWAEC.

The second set of governance in Wales was formed from three layers within the thirteen CWAECs. The first and most important was the CWAEC Executive Committee comprised of between eight and twelve volunteer members appointed by the Ministry. The second was District Committees, comprised of between four and seven volunteers who generally elected their chair. In some districts, these committees possessed extensive powers devolved from executive committees, but in others they tended to monitor farmers to ensure that executive committee instructions were obeyed. By April 1944 eighty-six district committees existed with a combined total of 828 members. The third and final layer was specialist sub-committees, usually at a county level, to cover a vast range of topics from land drainage, labour supply and fertiliser supply, to machinery. There were 151 of these, with a combined total of 1,323 members.[17]

These layers combined to create large and complex governance structures. One such structure was in Montgomeryshire where by 1944 there were twenty-one committees with a combined membership of 150. The Executive Committee had eight members and the seven district committees had between six and eight. Finally, fourteen technical committees focused on issues ranging from milk production to pest control. The smallest was an agricultural requisites committee allocating grants with two members but the largest was a livestock, milk, and rationing committee with fifteen. Meanwhile, most sub-committees deployed technical and support staff, with each district sub-committee controlling a district officer and assistants.[18]

Executive committee members were appointed by the Ministry and, although the Women's Land Army and labour interests each had one representative, members were appointed as individuals and not as representatives or nominees of organisations such as the National Farmers Union (NFU).[19] Moreover, they were inevitably drawn from those who wielded rural influence. The thirteen executive committee chairs in Wales were all men: seven were aldermen while others were justices of the peace or estate managers. One example was Monmouth where chair Sir L. Foster Stedman was also a Justice of the Peace, a Conservative councillor, a council member of the Royal Agricultural Society of England (reflecting the unclear administrative status of the county of Monmouth) and previously an agent for the Tredegar Estate. Most Chairs also sat on, or chaired, specialist sub-committees; Stedman sat on ten and chaired eight.[20]

While the aristocratic element of society was less prominent in Welsh rural society than in England, there were exceptions. One was Lord Anglesey who used CWAEC labour and machinery to plough up his golf course and cricket ground, before the Committee assessed one of his tenants as having left his land in a 'semi-derelict' condition. The tenant was promptly dispossessed and his land taken under the management of Lord Anglesey, who subsequently joined the CWAEC executive committee.[21] Nevertheless, the nature of the work carried out by the district committees meant that local knowledge was vital, and their members were usually local farmers. There was generally little difficulty in recruiting members given the attractiveness of wielding authority in the national interest, although the volume of work caused occasional problems. One example was the Letterston District Committee in Pembrokeshire that lacked three members in 1942 and unsuccessfully resisted one member's attempt to resign as 'his place would be difficult to fill'.[22]

As the CWAECs extended their control over agriculture, each built administrative capacity. They employed cultivation officers to set quotas on farms, labour officers to marshal seasonal labour, machinery officers to control CWAEC stocks, estate staff to manage seized farms, as well as advisory and clerical staff. As examples, in late 1940 the Pembrokeshire CWAEC wanted a machinery officer to manage its stocks, the Cardiganshire CWAEC sought a feeding stuffs officer to manage rationing, while the Glamorgan CWAEC wanted 'skilled vermin destroyers' including 'rat catchers, mole catchers and rabbit catchers'.[23] By early 1941 Caernarfonshire CWAEC employed fifteen cultivation officers and had decided to move to larger offices.[24] Finally, CWAEC staffing was supplemented by agricultural colleges. The government's desire to modernise the industry was reflected in its June 1940 decision to close these colleges and divert their staff to the CWAECs to provide technical assistance. Staff diverted in Wales included those from the University College of Wales Aberystwyth's Department of Agriculture, while those that remained at the University's Plant Breeding Station were used as advisers. In mid-1941, for example, the Welsh Department of the Ministry of Agriculture asked CWAECs clearing upland bracken to seek assistance from specialists at the Plant Breeding Station.[25]

THE INDUSTRY IN WALES

As throughout the UK, the most important CWAEC activity in Wales was prompting farmers to grow more foodstuffs by enforcing ploughing-up and cultivation orders. As well as allocating farm level ploughing-up quotas, CWAECs also issued cultivation orders that by 1944 covered potatoes, sugar beet, wheat and flax. Farmers were asked each June to submit schedules of their proposed cropping activities within each field. A cultivation order usually followed, ordering them to harvest specified acreages of crops, accompanied by ordnance survey reference numbers for the fields to be seeded.

The mammoth task of issuing thousands of orders was carried out by cultivation officers, responsible for localities within districts where they visited farms to set targets and monitor progress.[26] As the war progressed and the need to replace imported foodstuffs increased, the annual countywide quotas increased and CWAECs' attitude to enforcement tightened. Their ultimate sanction was the dispossession and eviction of farmers, after which land was requisitioned for the duration of the war and the subsequent five years. Resistance was almost pointless as the process was under CWAEC jurisdiction and there was no legal right of appeal, although ministerial agreement was needed for evictions. Yet seizure was controversial and protracted, and most CWAECs preferred to avoid it. Moreover, CWAECs were required to compensate the owners of seized land, often through paying them rents discounted for remediation costs. In 1941 Montgomery CWAEC, for example, took possession of one vacated and isolated upland sheep farm only after attempts to find new tenants failed, prompting extensive discussions within district and executive committees as to the least disruptive course of action.[27] Meanwhile, throughout the war, Radnorshire CWAEC prosecuted only thirty cases of cultivation order breaches.[28]

Nevertheless, the discretion given to committees as to how they governed meant that some gained a reputation for zealousness. One was the Cardiganshire CWAEC whose district committees by July 1940 had each identified at least one farm where enforcement action should be taken, potentially including the dispossession of those unwilling or unable to comply with orders.[29] By September, the CWAEC was receiving letters from local individuals as to 'badly neglected' fields, prompting visits from its officers, the chair was inspecting farms with a 'view to taking possession', while one in a 'deplorable' state was to be supervised 'with a view to forcing the owner to sell'. Other farmers were instructed to destroy weeds and trim hedges in specified fields.[30] By 1942 its district committees were monitoring many 'problem' farms but seizing them was nevertheless reserved for the worst offenders, with thirty-five, covering 2,752 acres, taken during the war.[31]

Few appeals against cultivation orders in such counties were successful. In Cardiganshire 172 appeals were made in December 1940 but only around one-fifth resulted in reduced quotas.[32] Most farmers cooperated but some were taken to court and fined for non-compliance, with 116 cases recorded in Cardiganshire and Carmarthenshire between 1940 and 1944.[33] The staff complement of the Cardiganshire CWAEC grew to resemble a large estate, with a chief finance officer, an estate manager and three farm overseers recruited in May 1942.[34] Elsewhere, the Pembrokeshire CWEAC advertised for a farm superintendent to manage 1,000 acres in October 1940, and by late 1941 Carmarthenshire CWAEC was offering journalists tours of rejuvenated farms it had seized on the grounds of their 'semi-derelict' status.[35]

Other CWAECs were more lenient, reflecting differing local conditions and the personalities of committee chairs. In general, most CWAECs preferred to use peer pressure from neighbours and visits from their executive officers to persuade reluctant farmers to obey. This dynamic meant that of the forty-seven farmers in Caernarfonshire who appealed their cultivation orders in October 1941, almost half were granted reductions. Meanwhile, the same CWAEC was reluctant to refer non-compliance cases to the Ministry for prosecution and farm monitoring was lenient. These differences in approaches meant that only six farms, covering 992 acres, were seized throughout the county,[36] some owned by an industrial concern at Dolgarrog where land was required for a drainage and cultivation scheme. One common tactic was prosecuting a few particularly obstructive farmers to encourage wider compliance. One farmer in Montgomeryshire, for example, ignored an order for 1944 to plant half an acre of potatoes and one acre of root crops. While little output was lost, the committee decided to prosecute, arguing that if it 'issued orders and these were disobeyed and they took no steps to bring the culprit to book, this would undoubtedly encourage defaulters'. The case was heard by magistrates who levied a fine of five pounds plus costs.[37] Overall, relatively few farms throughout Wales had been seized by 1946: 212 holdings covering 27,000 acres. Moreover, few farmers were evicted even when they lost their land and the total seized included 2,833 acres of common land requisitioned for upland clearance.[38]

One important element of 'ploughing up' was upland clearance. Newly cultivated land was needed not only to increase production, but also to offset the loss of farmland to military training areas such as Castlemartin in Pembrokeshire and Eppynt in Breconshire, which formed part of the 10 per cent of the surface area of Wales held by the War Office by 1945.[39] Yet, many schemes reflected the limits of centralised planning as they were ambitious but expensive and impractical. The most prominent example was in Montgomeryshire. Pre-war research at University College Aberystwyth had established the feasibility of converting uplands to pasture. This approach was adopted enthusiastically by Montgomery CWAEC in one of the UK's largest reclamation schemes that cleared 6,000 acres of rough grazing land above a thousand feet for potato crops. Clearance began in the summer of 1940 and continued for two years. The Ministry of Agriculture provided machinery imported from the United States, including 'prairie buster' ploughs. Potatoes were then planted, some in farrows a mile and a half long.[40] The project was publicised to help boost morale as producing enough potatoes to feed Manchester, while the Minister praised the scheme as an 'amazingly good show that other counties should emulate'. However, officials began to query the cost of deploying large amounts of machinery requiring labour, maintenance and fuel. Their concerns escalated and were one factor in the CWAEC being eventually disbanded due to friction between the chair and the NFU, before being reconstituted in late 1944 under new leadership.⁴¹

As well as upland reclamation, marshes were drained to create arable land. One project was a 4,000-acre marsh at Malltraeth in Anglesey.⁴² The CWAEC began reclamation in 1941 after urging from the Ministry of Agriculture in London, but the scheme was beset with difficulties and eventually cost twice its original estimate despite the use of Italian prisoners of war. Local opinion saw the project as overambitious as the coastal marsh was exposed to tidal floods that destroyed arable crops, farmers were reluctant to maintain the drainage ditches that they believed were pointless, while the CWAEC resented what it saw as the imposition of an unrealistic scheme and was reluctant to take enforcement action. Even the Ministry of Agriculture's Welsh Division was cynical, arguing in December 1943 that Malltraeth was 'one of those delectable schemes that is pulled out of the drawer for examination when there is an emergency' even though the chances of the scheme 'being economically possible' were minimal. An inspection in 1944 exposed a 'depressing prospect ... a shabby expanse of rushes, weeds and scrub ... well over half the marsh is in various stages of dereliction'.⁴³ Arable crops struggled, and the scheme achieved little before reverting to rough pasture. Other schemes were, however, more successful. A similar but more realistic scheme to improve some 1,000 acres at Borth Bog in Cardiganshire from 1942 involved the CWAEC reconstructing seven miles of sea embankments and improving drainage channels. While local farmers were dubious and some land proved unusable, much was used for agriculture.⁴⁴ Meanwhile, Denbighshire and Flintshire CWAEC organised schemes including draining ninety acres in the Conwy valley.⁴⁵

Aside from supervising ploughing-up and cultivation orders, CWAECs in Wales busied themselves with a vast range of other activities. One was gathering data, reflecting how the war effort throughout the economy was often characterised by 'scientific' approaches. These extended to agriculture where the Ministry was eager to obtain more data to inform planning decisions than those available through the sample-based farm management survey in place since the mid-1930s. In June 1940 the Ministry instructed each CWAEC to gather detailed information on all farms in their counties to 'assist in the immediate task of food production'.[46] Data were to include the condition in which farms were kept and their soil type and crop acreage, with Bryner Jones informing each CWAEC that although classifying each farm on an 'A' (farmed well) 'B' (farmed moderately) and 'C' (farmed badly) basis was 'difficult', data were 'essential as a basis for future policy'.[47]

Although CWAECs were still building administrative capacity and needed to prioritise increasing food production, thousands of forms were distributed and some farms were inspected, but the information was far from complete given the chaotic circumstances of mid-1940. One example was in Caernarfonshire where the CWAEC quickly sent 3,106 forms to farmers, of which 1,250 were returned enabling a report to be drafted.[48] While county-level findings were far from complete and were often inconsistent, Breconshire CWAEC grading 30.8 per cent of all farms as 'C', compared to 6.9 per cent in Pembrokeshire and 1.8 per cent in Denbighshire,[49] they were useful in informing CWAEC activity. In 1941 the Ministry decided to carry out a new National Farm Survey, observing that it could form a 'permanent Doomsday [*sic*] book record' and assist 'physical post-war planning'.[50]

The Ministry issued detailed instructions to CWAECs as to the thirty-two data points expected on each farm,[51] and district committee members and executive officers set out to visit and survey every holding of more than five acres. Some committees such as Montgomery were understandably reluctant to take on such a large task. It proposed a postal survey, but was rebuffed.[52] Controversially, the process of surveyors grading farmers as to their ability remained, a process considered more scientific than the generalised approach of the 1940 survey. Farmers judged as achieving more than 80 per cent of the potential output of their land were graded as 'A', those achieving between 60 and 80 per cent were 'B' and those achieving less than 60 per cent were 'C' and could expect greater scrutiny.[53] In 1942 the Ministry supplied CWAEC liaison officers with sample letters to be sent to farmers in each category, and those for 'C' farmers observed that CWAECs 'possessed extensive powers to secure the improvement of badly managed farms', including 'taking possession of land … it is incumbent on you forthwith to make every effort to raise the standard of your operations, and periodical inspections of your farm will be made to see that this is being done'.[54]

Yet a 'scientific' survey of this scale had pitfalls. The subjective nature of grading prompted inconsistency, while there were no official channels for contesting grading decisions.[55] Some counties were harsh, but others were generous and graded high proportions of their farmers as 'A' in part to avoid having to carry out any further inspections to track progress. The choice of approach often changed over time. When the need to produce food was at its greatest, district committees such as Llanfyllin in Montgomeryshire appointed groups of farmers to support and advise 'C' farms in their areas. However, as the war progressed and the need for more food became less urgent, CWAECs were more ready to reassess 'C' farms, with one example being Flintshire where many 'C' farms were regraded to 'B' in 1944.[56]

The scale of the survey also caused problems. The first iteration was supposed to be completed by March 1942 but CWAECs struggled to complete their work. The executive committee of the Flintshire CWAEC observed in September 1941 that the task was progressing very slowly and impacting their ability to calculate ploughing quotas.[57] Most Welsh CWAECs had not completed fieldwork by September 1942, while collating national datasets became what the Ministry described euphemistically as a 'major operation' as the task of checking survey results before entering a sample of 40,000 farms throughout Britain to punch cards for analysis by electrical calculating machines was 'a slow, monotonous job'.[58] Yet Ministry economists had ambitious plans to collect data on the performance of a sample of farms. These were to include granular details such as crop yields even if used as livestock feed, until agricultural economists at the University College of Wales Aberystwyth tactfully reminded the ministry that 'evidence here is largely verbal. Very few records are kept in Wales'.[59] All these drawbacks meant that while data helped CWAECs control agriculture, the survey had little impact on UK-wide planning, analyses above county level did not emerge until June 1945,[60] and the official history is noticeably silent on its achievements.

Yet issuing instructions and gathering data could only go so far if farmers were to produce more arable crops, as they needed help to source sufficient labour. CWAEC Labour Officers recommended individuals for deferral from military call-up while the age at which agricultural workers were automatically reserved from conscription was raised to twenty-five from March 1941.[61] Younger workers, however, could apply for temporary or permanent deferment. They applied to the CWAECs, which assessed each case and sent recommendations to the Ministry of Labour and National Service's district manpower boards. The Caernarfonshire labour sub-committee received 459 applications in June 1941 and recommended deferrals for 80 per cent.[62] By end 1943 all CWAECs employed mobile labour gangs to deploy on schemes including drainage and reclamation, although lowland areas tended to feature larger gangs. As examples, Caernarfonshire employed fewer than fifty labourers in 1941 while Denbighshire employed 101 'outdoor workers' in 1943.[63]

Overall, CWAECs assembled and deployed a remarkably varied labour force to ensure that quotas were met. Arable crops needed a large-scale seasonal workforce that was assembled by labour officers using a mix of voluntary and formally directed labour. Much experimentation took place. One example in April 1941 was Flintshire CWAEC asking local religious ministers to appeal for harvest volunteers during their sermons.[64] A more effective approach was, however, liaising with schools and universities to organise harvest camps. These included those in Monmouthshire where 470 children were housed in village and church halls.[65] Some CWAECs attempted to source labour from locally stationed army and RAF units, although commanding officers were often reluctant to release servicemen.[66] Holidaymakers were another important source of labour; the 1943 Pembrokeshire potato harvest was collected with the aid of 1,250 volunteers from cities including those in the West Midlands. Holidaymakers harvested in return for food, pay, lodging at Broadhaven and Newgale, while their relatively short thirty-hour week enabled leisure time.[67]

Other sources included prisoners of war, initially Italians captured in North Africa. By 1945 over three and a half thousand prisoners were employed by CWAECs throughout Wales, some billeted in farmhouses and others in small camps scattered throughout the countryside,[68] where they worked six-and-a-half days a week and were paid a basic wage. Women were also important. Although the Women's Land Army had its own county-based governance system, Welsh CWAECs employed 2,427 by 1944 while their Labour Officers helped find accommodation and identify farms where labour was needed.[69] Finally, CWAECs also marshalled workers from Ireland, such as those employed to reclaim Borth bog.[70] All this meant that CWAECs directed large labour forces in localities throughout Wales; in July 1944 a Pembrokeshire district committee noted that '18 land girls, 33 Irishmen, 53 Italian prisoners and 70 holiday campers' were working locally.[71]

The CWAEC-driven modernisation involved wholesale mechanisation, especially the replacement of horses with tractors, although machinery shortages meant that initial progress was slow. Flintshire CWAEC observed a tractor shortage in January

1941 when it could allocate only to the 'most urgent cases'.[72] Nevertheless, imports from north America reduced shortages and enabled CWAECs to build up their stocks as many farmers sold their horses and bought tractors. The CWAECs rented machines to other farmers, and to contractors who although independent could be directed to farms or projects. The Caernarfonshire committee, for example, advertised in 1942 that it was 'desirous' to rent its seed dusting machines to farmers for a daily rate of 5 shillings.[73] In some counties, including Carmarthenshire and Pembrokeshire, the CWAECs sponsored parish networks where farmers hired machinery to their neighbours or carried out mechanised work on neighbouring farms.[74]

By 1944 the CWAECs throughout Wales had been supplied with some 11,000 machines, including 2,000 tractors, 900 potato diggers and 400 threshers.[75] The trajectory of mechanisation can be illustrated by Caernarfonshire. While the CWAEC could order only three tractors in October 1940, it was placing large-scale orders by the end of 1941 and was short of storage space.[76] By October 1942 it held hundreds of items including ninety-four tractors and in the following January it complained of a shortage of tractor ploughs as so many tractors were now being used, while by June it held over a thousand items including 113 tractors, 137 ploughs and 112 potato diggers.[77] The extent of mechanisation was such that some farmers were provided with hydroelectric devices to mechanise milking.[78] By the following year, the number of tractors in Wales reached 11,305, from 1,932 in 1937.[79]

Reductions in the import of bulky items meant dramatic falls in the import of feeding stuffs, and from February 1941 CWAECs operated coupon-based rationing systems that were later extended to include fertilisers, steel, timber and wire.[80] The committees also managed government financial support schemes. They had provided some finance since February 1940, but this was expanded in September 1941 by the Goods and Services scheme that enabled them to issue loans to farmers for agricultural improvements if they could not obtain credit from banks or suppliers. CWAECs appointed sub-committees to process applications, while flexible repayment terms were offered including the ability to repay in goods or services, or through deductions from ploughing-up subsidies.[81] Many other support schemes were partly or wholly administered by CWAEC sub-committees, such as the Hill Sheep Subsidy Scheme from 1941 and the Hill Cattle Scheme from 1943. By 1944 the Ministry for Agriculture credited these schemes as having lifted upland farmers in Wales 'from acute economic need to a reasonable level of prosperity'.[82] Meanwhile, an agricultural requisites scheme provided funds to purchase items including lime and seed oats, while other schemes included subsidies for clearing bracken,[83] draining land, or accessing water sources. Thousands of farmers benefited from such support with, for example, 128 farm drainage schemes approved in Pembrokeshire by 1941 including one that drained 676 acres around Freshwater West.[84]

The relentless expansion of CWAEC influence even extended to pest control. By July 1943 the Caernarfonshire CWAEC employed thirteen people, including seven from the Women's Land Army, to kill rats and was considering employing more. Their activity combined with that of farmers and authorised trappers exempted from conscription to kill vast numbers of wildlife. Trapping on eighty-three farms between August 1942 and March 1943 killed 18,890 rabbit couples that were sold as food, realising a profit for the CWAEC. Finally, the CWAECs contributed towards bounties for foxes and organised shooting parties to target pigeons, often inviting army officers stationed locally.[85] CWAECs also forced farmers to control infestations. Resistance was as futile as attempting to avoid other directions. By September 1940 Cardiganshire CWAEC was ordering farmers to kill rabbits, while in July 1941 the owner of the Nanteos Estate near Aberystwyth claimed not to have received a letter from the CWAEC ordering her to destroy rabbits. She instructed her solicitor to query if the letter had been sent. This infuriated the CWAEC, and it promptly ordered her to destroy the rabbits within ten days or it would organise trapping and charge full costs afterwards. Although estate staff began trapping, the Committee warned the owner as to the consequences of not obeying instructions and it later ordered a Pest Officer to submit a 'full report' on progress to ensure compliance.[86]

The CWAECs and their sponsoring Ministry were determined to not only overhaul the industry, but also to modernise attitudes towards farm management and technology. This impulse prompted an interest in education and most committees established technical development or demonstration sub-committees. Many of these arranged 'fireside chats' where neighbours were invited to a farmhouse to hear experts discuss efficiency and output, or public meetings such as one in Llanfyllin in May 1942 when an adviser from the University College of Wales Aberystwyth spoke on 'how to make your farm self-sufficient'.[87] Other sessions involved more specialist audiences such as one given by a beekeepers association in Monmouthshire in 1944.[88] Other efforts were larger, such as the four events in Caernarfonshire in 1943 on new approaches attended by two thousand farmers. In the following year, the CWAEC worked with the Ministry of Information to arrange a mobile film van to show 'agricultural films of an education value'. Over two thousand people attended screenings, including five hundred attendees each in Sarn and Penygroes.[89]

All this frenetic activity impacted the working lives of all farmers. One Radnorshire hill farmer, George Lewis, recalled how 'officialdom moved with surprising speed, issuing instructions as to how many acres we should plough and what we should plant in these areas'. His ploughed acreage was doubled but appeals against cultivation orders were 'largely useless'. One of his fields illustrates the extent to which farmers were enveloped by CWAEC authority, as well as the practical difficulties of controlling agriculture.[90] Lewis was instructed to grow a specified acreage of potatoes. The choice of field was important because planting an area smaller than the order specified could prompt enforcement action, while planting a larger area would not attract a larger payment. Lewis chose an irregularly shaped field that he judged was the correct size to fulfil the order. Nevertheless, he expected the irregular shape to reduce the size of headlands at the end of each row when compared to ploughing a rectangular field, meaning that he was planning to plough a greater proportion of his field than was normal.

Yet the CWAEC used standard assessments based on ordnance survey maps and disagreed with Lewis's calculations. A cultivation officer arrived at the farm with a tape measure to assess the size of the field, but the tape was too short to measure its full length. The inspector asked Lewis to hold one end of the tape before walking down the field until it ran out. Lewis then walked to the spot where the tape ended, and the cultivation officer walked on. But controlling one end of the measure while the officer's back was turned enabled Lewis to 'return the goal posts to their proper place. Quota fulfilled! Cheating? Not in my book'. Lewis may have derived some satisfaction, but the episode demonstrated how the CWAECs enabled the authority of the Ministry of Agriculture to be implemented throughout the country, farmers knew that all but the most minor disobedience was pointless and that CWAEC activity often benefited them as the field in question was drained by pipes part-funded by the Committee.

CONCLUSION

Transformation formed the central theme of 'Land at War', the government's mass market account of the wartime industry written by novelist Laurie Lee. Published in 1945, it condemned pre-war agriculture as featuring 'neglect and deterioration … not a happy story' while in 1939 'the land lay listening, waiting for something to happen'. However, by 1945 government intervention had 'profit[ed] the land by proper employment and change, giving us new crops, new ways, new farms'.[91] Although this account has to be qualified as the impact of modernisation on crop yields was relatively limited, with most output growth driven instead by increased arable acreage,[92] greater demand for home-produced food combined with effective state intervention and higher prices paid to farmers to prompt sudden and unaccustomed prosperity.

The extent of the transformation was clear in Wales. Rural areas were rejuvenated and given a new sense of purpose as farm incomes increased dramatically, much of which was reinvested. Nevertheless, the amount of cultivated land fell by 64,000 acres because of those taken for army training even though reclamation schemes offset some of the acreage lost. Yet land use changed dramatically. Within the 2.5 million acres under cultivation, grassland fell by 500,000 acres and was replaced by arable. The acreage of potatoes almost trebled, while that of barley and wheat almost doubled. While the use of often marginal land meant that production of some crops such as potatoes often grew by less than their acreage change suggests, changes were even more dramatic than the UK averages given the pre-war focus on livestock in most of Wales. From 1940 to 1944, wheat output increased by 270 per cent, barley by 135 per cent and potatoes by 183 per cent, although offset by decreases in the number of most animals given the need to focus on arable production. The number of sheep fell by 13 per cent, and pigs by 47 per cent, although those of cattle was relatively stable, growing by 11 per cent over the period (see Table 5 in Appendix).

Transformation and modernisation were by-products of the need to procure greater self-sufficiency, but three factors enabled such changes to take place. The first was the level of resources made available, whether channelled directly through CWAECs or indirectly by fixing prices paid to farmers and guaranteeing markets. The war facilitated an ambitious and generously funded modernisation programme that prompted a pragmatic if resigned acceptance of the onerous controls implemented by the CWAECs. The second was that these controls enabled CWAECs to grip and direct the industry. The final factor was how extensive pre-war preparations created flexible yet workable governance structures that enabled rapid and total mobilisation. Structures drew on existing power dynamics, while CWAECs were decentralised and autonomous. Nevertheless, CWAECs had their critics. Some were accused of favouring larger farms, while others were heavily criticised for their inflexibility in imposing unrealistic cultivation orders and their enthusiasm for seizing land. Despite such criticism and their occasionally bewildering administrative complexity, the CWAECs stand out as one of the most consistent and successful wartime governance structures in Wales.

Notes

1 C. Lowe, *Colwyn Bay Accredited, The Wartime Experience* (Bridge Books, 2010), p. 84.
2 Murray, *Agriculture*, p. 312.
3 TNA, MAF 232/10, *Minister of Agriculture's Broadcast*, 26 November 1940.
4 *Statistical Digest of the War*, p. 184.
5 *Statistical Digest of the War*, p. 167.
6 Martin, *The Development of Modern Agriculture*, pp. 53–4.
7 J. Martin, 'The structural transformation of British agriculture: the resurgence of progressive high-input arable farming', in Short, Watkins and Martin (eds), *The Front Line of Freedom: British Farming in the Second World War*, pp. 34–5.
8 J. K. Bowers, 'British Agricultural Policy Since the Second World War', *The Agricultural History Review*, 33/1 (1985), 66–76. (66).
9 TNA, MAF 232/10, *Minister of Agriculture's Broadcast*, 26 November 1940.
10 Murray, *Agriculture*, p. 301.
11 Murray, *Agriculture*, p. 369.
12 Murray, *Agriculture*, p. 337.
13 TNA, MAF 80/3724, *Cardiganshire CWAEC minutes*, 5 March 1943, 10.
14 TNA, MAF 232/10, *Second Conference of Liaison Officers*, 4 July 1940.
15 Murray, *Agriculture*, p. 328.

16 Welsh Secretary of the Ministry of Agriculture, *Nature* 153 (1944), 18–19; *North Wales Weekly News*, Public Appointment, 30 December 1943.
17 TNA, MAF 112/195, *Personnel of Committees in Wales and Monmouthshire*, 18 April 1944.
18 TNA, MAF 112/198, *Montgomeryshire War Agricultural Executive Committee, Committees*, 1944.
19 G Cox, P. Lowe and M. Winter, 'From State Direction to Self-regulation: The Historical Development of Corporatism in British Agriculture', *Policy & Politics*, 14/4 (1986), 475–90 (479).
20 Short, *The Battle of the Fields*, p. 112.
21 Chambers, *Bless 'Em All*, p. 43.
22 TNA, MAF 80/5001, *Minutes, Letterston District Committee*, 29 June 1942.
23 *Western Mail*, 'Public Notices', 18 November 1940; 16 December 1940.
24 TNA, MAF 80/3717, *Minutes, Caernarfonshire CWAEC*, 7 February 1941, 2; 18 March 1941, 1.
25 TNA, MAF 80/3843, *Minutes, Flintshire CWAEC*, 23 June 1941, 4.
26 *North Wales Weekly News*, 'War Agricultural Committee', 1 February 1940.
27 TNA, MAF 112/91, *Report by Land Commissioner on Bacheidden and Bryndau Farms*, 21 January 1941, 1.
28 *Western Mail*, 'War Record of "Little" County', 27 September 1946.
29 TNA, MAF 80/3723, *Minutes, Cardiganshire CWAEC*, 19 July 1940, 3.
30 TNA, MAF 80/3723, *Minutes, Cardiganshire CWAEC*, 20 September 1940, 2; 27 September 1940, 1.
31 Moore-Colyer, *Farming in Wales, 1936–2011*, p. 52.
32 TNA, MAF 80/3723, *Minutes, Cardiganshire CWAEC*, 20 December 1940, 1–9.
33 Moore-Colyer, *County War Agricultural Executive Committees in Wales*, 574.
34 TNA, MAF 80/3724, *Minutes, Cardiganshire CWAEC*, 6 May 1942, 4.
35 *Western Mail*, 'Fine Farms that used to be Derelict' 11 November 41, 3; 'Public Appointments', 1 October 1940, 4.
36 Moore-Colyer, *County War Agricultural Executive Committees in Wales*, 579; TNA, MAF 80/3718, *Minutes, Carnarvonshire CWAEC*, 29 October 1941.
37 TNA, MAF 112/195, *Note: Welsh Department Ministry of Agriculture*, 30 August 1944; *Return of Proceedings Before Magistrates*, 7 November 1944.
38 Moore-Colyer, *County War Agricultural Executive Committees in Wales*, 579; TNA, MAF 112/91, *Commons Requisitioned in Wales and Monmouthshire*.
39 Davies, *A History of Wales*, p. 603.
40 *Western Mail*, 'Potatoes Now Where Bracken Grew', 25 August 1941, 3; Short, *Battle of the Fields*, 243.
41 *Times*, 'Montgomery Agricultural Committee', 22 October 1944.
42 TNA, MAF 70/25, *Malltraeth Marsh Drainage Scheme*, 3 September 1945, 1.
43 TNA, MAF 70/25, *Minutes Relating to Malltreath*, 10 December 1943; 3 August 1944.
44 TNA, MAF 80/3732, *Minutes, Cardiganshire CWAEC*, 6 May 1942, 1; MAF 112/195, *Borth Bog, No. 2 Scheme*, April 1943.
45 *North Wales Weekly News*, 'A North Wales Conference', 31 December 1942.

46 TNA, MAF 38/213, *Circular to CWAECS*, 5 May 1941.
47 TNA, MAF 80/3718, *Minutes, Caernarfonshire CWAEC*, 21 June 1940.
48 TNA, MAF 80/3718, *Minutes, Caernarfonshire CWAEC*, 12 July 1940, 2 August 1940.
49 TNA, MAF 38/209, *Summary of Preliminary Reports by WAECs on the Farm Survey*, 1940, 10.
50 TNA, MAF 38/209, *Farm Survey Progress Report*, July 1943, 1.
51 TNA, MAF 38/209, *Farm Survey, Instructions for the Completion of the Primary Record*, May 1941.
52 Short, *The Battle of the Fields*, p. 123.
53 Moore-Colyer, *Farming in Wales*, p. 49.
54 TNA, MAF 232/10, *Conference of Liaison Officers*, 19 June 1942.
55 Martin, *The Development of Modern Agriculture*, 46.
56 TNA, MAF 80/4090, *Minutes, Flintshire CWAEC*, 11 January 1944; MAF 80/5001, *Minutes, Llanfyllin District Committee*, 12 March 1942.
57 TNA, MAF 80/3843, *Minutes, Flintshire CWAEC*, 1 September 1941, 1.
58 TNA, MAF 38/209, *Farm Survey Progress Report*, July 1943, 2, 4, 5.
59 TNA, MAF 38/467, *Memorandum of Character of Records for National Farm Management Survey*, 22 December 1944, 2.
60 TNA, MAF 38/473, *War-Time Farm Survey of England and Wales, Summary Report*, June 1945.
61 Murray, *Agriculture*, p. 123.
62 TNA, MAF 80/3718, *Minutes, Caernarfonshire CWAEC*, 19 June 1941.
63 TNA, MAF 80/3718, *Minutes, Caernarfonshire CWAEC*, 27 June 1941; MAF 58/57, *Denbighshire CWEAC Review of Machinery Operations*, 20 September 1943, 1.
64 TNA, MAF 80/3843, *Minutes, Flintshire CWAEC*, 7 April 1941.
65 *South Wales Gazette*, 'Abertillery and Blaina Students Helping Farmers', 24 August 1942.
66 TNA, MAF 80/3843, *Minutes, Flintshire CWAEC*, 29 July 1941, 1.
67 *Western Mail*, 'Voluntary Harvest Workers' Triumph', 27 September 1943, 4.
68 Hughes, *The Second World War in the Borough of Conwy*, p. 28; Williams, *DWHS*, vol. *1*, p. 255.
69 Williams, *DWHS*, vol. *1*, p. 255; TNA, MAF 80/3843, *Minutes, Flintshire CWAEC*, 22 December 1941.
70 TNA, MAF 80/3732, *Minutes, Cardiganshire CWAEC*, 5 March 1943, 2.
71 TNA, MAF 80/5001, *Minutes, Letterston District Committee*, 29 July 1944.
72 TNA, MAF 80/3843, *Minutes, Flintshire CWAEC*, 27 January 1942, 4.
73 *North Wales Weekly News*, 'Seed Dusting Machines', 19 March 1942.
74 Short, *Battle of the Fields*, pp. 79–80.
75 TNA, MAF 112/195, *Ministers' Brief for Welsh Debate*, 17 October 1944, 3
76 TNA, MAF 80/3717, *Minutes, Caernarfonshire CWAEC*, 28 October 1940; 11 July 1941, 4–5.
77 TNA, MAF 80/3718, *Minutes, Caernarfonshire CWAEC*, 24 June 1943, 5–7.
78 Chambers, *Bless 'Em All*, p. 48.
79 Williams, *DWHS*, vol. *1*, p. 286.

80 Murray, *Agriculture*, p. 330.
81 Murray, *Agriculture*, pp. 169–70, 293, 330.
82 TNA, MAF 112/195, *Ministers' Brief for Welsh Debate*, 17 October 1944, 5.
83 *North Wales Weekly News*, 'Grants for the Eradication of Bracken', 14 May 1942.
84 TNA, MAF 80/4123, *Minutes, Pembrokeshire CWAEC*, 28 May 1941.
85 TNA, MAF 80/3718, *Caernarfonshire CWAEC Minutes*, 26 March 1943, 4; 30 July 1943, 2.
86 TNA, MAF 80/3723, *Minutes, Cardiganshire CWAEC*, 13 September 1940; MAF 80/3724, *Minutes, Cardiganshire CWAEC*, 4 July 1941, 2; 18 July 1941, 1; 25 July 1941, 1.
87 TNA, MAF 80/5001, *Minutes, Llanfyllin District Committee*, 28 May 1942.
88 *South Wales Gazette*, 'Mon. Beekeepers Association', 25 February 1944, 3.
89 TNA, MAF 80/3718, *Minutes, Caernarfonshire CWAEC*, 29 September 1942, 4; 24 February 1943, 7.
90 G. Lewis, *Henfryn, Radnorshire Hill Farming Life in the 1930s and 1940s* (Logaston Press, 2002), pp. 83–4.
91 *Land at War: The Official Story of British Farming, 1939–1944* (HMSO, 1945) pp. 7, 11, 37.
92 P. Brassley, 'Wartime policy and innovation', in Short, Watkins and Martin (eds), *The Front Line of Freedom*, pp. 36–54 (p. 54).

PART FOUR

RECONSTRUCTION, 1943–1947

9

SECONDARY MANUFACTURING

GOVERNING INDUSTRIAL RECONSTRUCTION THROUGHOUT BRITAIN

Although Churchill sought to avoid sensitive domestic issues that threatened the unity of his coalition,[1] a recast Regional Policy emerged after 1943. It was more ambitious than its inter-war predecessor but was not the fully integrated national approach called for by the Barlow Report in January 1940. The re-emergence of Regional Policy was driven instead by the success of wartime interventions. Political debates on the topic began before such success was apparent, while force of circumstances precluded progress. In December 1940 Minister of Works Sir John Reith asked the Cabinet to create a national authority to coordinate physical planning and industrial location. The topic was referred to Labour Minister without Portfolio Arthur Greenwood who chaired a Cabinet Committee on Reconstruction Problems. He created an inter-departmental Location of Industry sub-committee, but it met only three times and achieved little.[2]

Although Reith's pressure helped prompt the 1942 creation of a Ministry for Town and Country Planning, his attempts to create fully integrated planning encompassing industrial location failed given overlap with economic policy and military procurement, as these areas were guarded by other ministries whose opposition contributed to Reith's mid-1942 dismissal. Meanwhile, in early 1942 Greenwood was sacked as Minister without Portfolio and replaced with Labour's Sir William Jowitt. However, the most significant appointment in terms of post-war industrial location policy was Hugh Dalton as President of the Board of Trade in February 1942. He represented a 'Depressed Area' constituency in northeast England and had chaired Labour's pre-war commission on such areas.[3] Dalton's responsibilities included coal mining whose demands prompted his May 1942 diary entry on his struggles to 'get anywhere near my many other problems at the Board of Trade'.[4] Yet the June 1942 creation of a Ministry of Fuel and Power enabled him to focus on reconstruction, while by the end of that year, the turning tide of war combined with the popularity of W. H. Beveridge's report on social security to prompt the emergence of reconstruction as a central political theme.[5] In response, from 1943 Dalton developed an approach where building licences would prompt industrialists to locate factories in peripheral areas but precluded regulating all private investment.

However, Dalton had first to convince his ministerial colleagues, telling them in May 1943 that 'to secure full employment in the depressed areas ... some control of industrial location is essential'.[6] This comment foreshadowed debate over the contents of a White Paper on Employment where he was helped by personnel changes at HM Treasury. Chancellor Kingsley Wood had argued that maintaining nationwide demand and promoting labour mobility could prevent a repeat of the 1930s. Yet Wood died in September 1943 and his successor, Sir John Anderson, accepted that state intervention had a valid role in boosting regional employment. Political circumstances also helped Dalton as, although a Ministry of Reconstruction was created in November 1943, coalition tensions meant that it was restricted to a coordinating role with the new Minister chairing a Cabinet Reconstruction Committee scrutinising schemes promoted by other ministries.[7]

Dalton's approach progressed steadily through Whitehall and was approved by a Ministerial Committee on Post War

Employment in late 1943.[8] By early 1944 the more powerful Cabinet Reconstruction Committee had accepted his proposals that industrialists should be encouraged to locate in peripheral areas,[9] and the May 1944 White Paper on Employment committed the government to a 'primary aim' of maintaining 'high and stable' employment. Crucially, it contained a section entitled 'The Balanced Distribution of Industry and Labour' stating that an 'object of government policy' was to develop 'balanced industrial development in areas … unduly dependent on industries especially vulnerable to unemployment'.[10]

Dalton's lobbying was paralleled by his development of capacity within the Board of Trade. In September 1943 he appointed Douglas Jay to advise on post-war reconstruction. Jay had worked at the Ministry of Supply, where he argued that businesses should be awarded contracts based on labour availability, not pricing. Importantly, he stressed that 'wartime experience' could help prevent the 'curse of the Depressed Areas emerging after the war'. Within weeks of his appointment, he was anticipating a 'full machinery' to oversee regional industrial location.[11] Meanwhile, other elements of the wartime state were bringing forward ideas as to reconstruction. One was the Ministry of Production's Regional Division that in September 1943 proposed government-constructed advance factories to attract regional business investment. Another was the Factory and Storage Control Function that was comparing the lack of success of the 1930s Special Areas in obtaining industrial investment with wartime machinery, prompting arguments that such machinery could inspire a peacetime national location control system.[12]

The extent to which the development of post-war policy was concentrated within the Board of Trade contributed to the demise of a vehicle intended to formulate a more comprehensive approach, the Nuffield College Social Reconstruction Survey. Created by the Labour activist and author, G. D. H. Cole, it was based at the University of Oxford and was partially funded by the

Treasury. Its regional investigators produced a substantial body of commissioned research and recommendations for ministries, also arranging conferences on reconstruction. However, some civil servants became hostile as they resented what they saw as its intrusion into their responsibilities. Hostility prompted Board of Trade officials to tell Cole that the Board was 'very actively investigating a number of post-war problems' where its own staff 'under direct Ministerial guidance, must be the primary instrument'.[13] Concurrently, the Treasury accused the survey of producing poor work, an act characterised by a furious Cole as 'a stab in the back'.[14] The Treasury withdrew financial support in March 1943 and activity ceased subsequently.

In June 1944 Jay and Sir Phillip Warter, Controller of the Factory and Storage Control function, became joint heads of a Board of Trade department tasked with steering industry into peripheral areas. Warter negotiated with companies while Jay developed governance procedures.[15] In October the Board invited industrialists requiring more than 10,000 sq. ft of civilian factory space to apply for authorisation.[16] Other Ministries were also active, including the Ministry of Production that by August had increased the number of regional advance factories it wanted to construct throughout Britain to eighteen.

These policies, however, needed to be preserved for peacetime by a Distribution of Industry Act. Yet the bill had not been enacted when the coalition government broke up in May; but after Dalton threatened resignation,[17] it was supported by Lyttleton, Board President in the caretaker government in office between the dissolution of Churchill's administration and the July general election. The bill was finally enacted on the day of parliament's dissolution. It transferred responsibilities held by the Commissioner for Special Areas from the Ministry of Labour and National Service to the Board of Trade and extended them. While pre-war policy focused on transferring labour out of peripheral areas, the new approach built on wartime experience to transfer manufacturing into such areas.[18] The Board could now build factories in state-defined Development Areas (based on pre-war Special Areas but extended to adjacent, clear land made derelict by industry), construct key worker housing, and provide finance to companies subject to Treasury approval. Yet the most important element of the new Regional Policy was the continuation of building licences, repurposed from maximising nationwide munitions production to diverting industrial activity to increase regional employment. Although the Act did not constitute the all-embracing approach called for by the Barlow report as its provisions sought to balance regional employment with maintaining industrial efficiency, Dalton wrote in his diary that 'if the powers ... are strongly and sensibly used, there will never be any Depressed Areas again'.[19]

While the Board of Trade was to manage policy implementation centrally, the Act specified a regional organisation to 'bring together the representatives of government departments'.[20] The question was the extent to which it would be based on the Ministry of Production's Regional Boards whose responsibilities would disappear in peacetime. Debate on this issue ran parallel to broader discussions as to Regional Policy. Ministry of Production working parties in 1943 were unsurprisingly 'entirely convinced' of the need to retain their boards, arguing that their formation from representatives of government and both sides of industry enabled them to liaise successfully between all parties, but their future remained vague.[21] In September 1944 Regional Board Chairs asked the Ministry of Production for a 'statement on government policy on post-war planning'. Yet policies were still under what the Ministry called 'constant discussion at the highest level' and it was unable to provide guidance.[22] The reality, however, was that the Board of Trade had little interest in these Regional Boards given their focus on coordinating munitions procurement. A typically complex compromise was reached where Regional Distribution of Industry Committees were formed from members of the Regional Boards but without their industry or union representatives given the commercial sensitivities of industrial location. They were constituted temporarily as Regional Board Sub-committees chaired by the Board of Trade's Regional Controller pending the post-war abolition of the Ministry of Production and the transfer of its functions to the Board of Trade.[23]

In December 1944 the Board of Trade set out its post-war policy for factory building licences. It was to retain licences and grant priority to projects that would repair bomb damage, locate in Development Areas (the term used by 1944 to describe peripheral areas), or convert munitions factories for peacetime occupiers. The Ministry of Works administered licences but construction projects involving expenditure of more than £5,000 required approval by regional Distribution of Industry Sub-committees before a licence could be issued.[24] Regional structures sat within a national framework designed to capture and divert nationwide industrial expansion, described aptly by the Factory and Storage Control Function as 'somewhat complicated'.[25] All firms asking for permission to locate outside Development Areas had to outline 'adequate reasons why the scheme should not be in a Development Area'.[26] All large projects were also subject to approval by a Britain-wide 'Panel A', while a 'Panel B' considered applications to convert government-owned factories.

The Labour Party's landslide general election victory in July 1945 created a government determined to build on wartime planning to achieve full employment, reflected by its manifesto statement of 'we say, full employment in any case, and if we need to keep a firm public hand on industry in order to get jobs for all, very well'.[27] The government's ambitious programme included reconverting the economy and redistributing industrial employment. Dalton became Chancellor and in his 1946 budget speech promised to 'find, with a song in my heart, whatever money is necessary to finance useful and practical proposals for developing these [Development] areas', to bring 'them to a condition which they never had in the past, a condition of full and efficient and diversified economic activity'.[28]

The government's primary tool within Regional Policy was the building licences issued automatically by the Ministry of Works once the Board had approved projects. The new system meant that the Nil Certificate regime fell into disuse and was abolished in 1946.[29] Licences were used forcefully by newly appointed Board of Trade President Stafford Cripps. In 1946 the government stated that 'no factory building may take place anywhere in Great Britain unless there are strong national reasons for the choice of a particular locality'.[30] The Industries and Manufacturing Division at the Board of Trade had helped coordinate wartime building licences but the rapid increase in their volume prompted the Division to merge with the Factory and Storage Control Function to create a Distribution of Industry and Regional Division. Sir Cecil Weir, the Function's Controller-General until 1942, was to argue later that its repurposing to address post-war industrial distribution was a 'natural and logical development'.[31]

The Ministry of Production was abolished in July 1945 and its functions inherited by the Board of Trade, while the Ministry of Supply merged with the Ministry of Aircraft Production. The Board of Trade retained Regional Boards but renamed them in December 1945 as Regional Advisory Boards for Industry. They were given the vague roles of advising government on industrial conditions, keeping in 'close touch' with regional officials throughout government, and advising local authorities on the needs of industry.[32] Regional Distribution of Industry Panels ceased to be formally constituted as Regional Board sub-committees and met monthly to consider building licences applications, most of which were from firms steered to their area by centralised Board of Trade functions. Firms applying for building licences in Development Areas found that their applications were quickly processed and awarded by their Regional Distribution of Industry Committee. They were also often offered government-built factories that further reduced time needed to reach production. Finally, financial incentives were available although few industrial projects benefited, with only nine approved in 1947.[33] Meanwhile, companies wanting to expand outside Development Areas were generally referred to London where a cumbersome and time-consuming committee process awaited them.

All this meant that industrialists had a choice between either quickly obtaining permission to operate in a Development Area or wait to be processed slowly elsewhere. Moreover, even if permission was obtained to locate in more congested areas, scarce construction labour and material often prompted further delays.[34] The inevitable result was that many industrialists seeking to develop new production space chose a Development Area. Between 1945 and 1947 such areas gained 51.1 per cent of all industrial building in the UK, over double their 19.9 per cent share of the UK's insured population.[35]

However, the effectiveness of Regional Policy between 1945 and 1947 obscured potential problems. The most important was that interventions amounted to a successful but ad hoc containment of a nationwide industrial expansion that maximised job creation. Intervention increased employment but did little to create sustainable growth through clustering firms in related industries or prioritising those with greater potential.[36] The second was that the Board often lacked the commercial expertise to challenge financial projections made by applicant firms, while its administrative complexity often inadvertently supported larger firms that possessed the capacity to navigate government procedures successfully. Some large firms exploited these factors to secure permission on efficiency grounds to expand outside the Development Areas: examples in 1946 included Jaguar and Ford.[37] Finally, Regional Distribution of Industry Committees operated within a centralised system where the Regional Advisory Boards for Industry were sidelined, with their dissatisfaction prompting a 1947 inquiry into their significance.[38]

None of this mattered when the economic circumstances allowed the government to prioritise regional industrial growth. Yet 1947 was what Dalton described as an 'annus horrendus' culminating in August's crisis over sterling convertibility.[39] Crises prompted a need to increase earnings by boosting exports, and locating factories outside Development Areas became easier as the government was reluctant to impose constraints on export businesses. The proportion of industrial building in Development Areas more than halved between 1948 and 1951 when compared with 1945 to 1947, while advance factory construction ceased in 1947.[40] Cessation coincided with the 1947 Town and Country Planning Act's creation of a new system of Industrial Development Certificates requiring all new factories throughout the UK of 5,000 square feet or greater to obtain a certificate from the Board of Trade before planning permission could be granted.[41]

INDUSTRIAL RECONSTRUCTION IN WALES

The understandable lack of attention given to regional unemployment and post-war planning after 1940 was pronounced in Wales, where a Nuffield survey observed in early 1942 that the Commissioner for Special Areas had 'virtually gone out of business'.[42] Meanwhile, wartime industries had eliminated unemployment in once depressed industrial areas and boosted their prosperity. The 1942 Mass Observation study of Blaina and Nantyglo, for example, observed that 'the unemployment problem has disappeared, people have more money for saving and spending, are living better and ... more contentedly than for many years'.[43]

The lack of attention to regional reconstruction and the extent to which Whitehall was determined to retain control over policy was illustrated by the Wales Reconstruction Advisory Council (WRAC). Its emergence was prompted by the government appointing an advisory body in Scotland in 1941, leading to demands in Wales for an equivalent. Ministers resisted initially but Greenwood met with Welsh MPs in November 1941 when many pressed for a Welsh body. He agreed to create the WRAC to survey 'those problems of reconstruction which are of special application to Wales and Monmouthshire' and advise on them.[44] Yet its birth was protracted and difficult. After disputes as to who should sit on the Council, J. F. Rees, Principal of University College, Cardiff, was eventually appointed as chair.[45] By late 1942 the WRAC had spawned sub-committees including those for Industry, Agriculture, and Youth and Education that were issuing reports and recommendations for consideration by ministries.[46]

However, the WRAC's activity prompted concern within Whitehall that it was becoming too autonomous and producing recommendations that contrasted with government policy.[47] Concerns prompted a civil servant briefing a minister in June 1943 to argue that the council's requests for immediate actions risked distracting the government from its focus on the war.[48] All this prompted frustration and by mid-1943 the WRAC was complaining that ministries were barely considering its recommendations.[49] Its highest profile output was a December 1944 report on reconstruction noting that almost half of all workers in industries employed by new wartime industries were likely to lose their jobs when war ended. In response, it called for the recognition of Wales as a planning unit and argued that converting wartime plants and constructing factories to attract post-war industrialists was 'the only way in which industries can be brought to the people in many areas'.[50] Yet, although the report presaged many post-war policies, few officials were interested.

Developing plans for regional industrial location meant collecting data, a process that the Board of Trade was determined to control. Its disposal of the Nuffield Survey on the convenient grounds of poor work extended to Wales, where the survey produced detailed surveys of North, Central and South Wales in mid-1942. Reports foreshadowed later analysis, arguing that over half of the 80,140 jobs created in south Wales by new industries from 1936 to 1941 were provided by those that would close or contract at the end of the war.[51] Despite these findings, Board of Trade officials rushed to discredit the research by arguing that the south Wales report was 'rather too general to be really useful', objected to its attempts to influence policy by arguing for national control or ownership of industry, and condemned the Central Wales study as inconsistent and of 'little use'.[52]

In February 1943 Board of Trade officials met with Regional Controllers of Factory and Storage Space to inform them that 'the time had come ... to pay further attention to reconstruction' and that they should prepare reports on problem areas, setting out the impact of industrial mobilisation and recommending activities to secure peacetime full employment.[53] Over twenty reports on settlements across south Wales were produced with the assistance of University College Cardiff staff.[54] In north Wales, officials reported on towns including Wrexham and Blaenau Ffestiniog, while a March 1943 document set out policies needed to maintain full employment throughout the region and argued that a 'considerable amount of administrative experience' had been built in 'locating [wartime] factories where ... the needs are deserving and the facilities are right', recommending a similar approach in peacetime.[55]

Yet discontent continued. Regional Controller Brunning warned his headquarters in April 1943 about 'widespread uneasiness' as to the pace of industrial reconstruction planning and that if the 'separate and disparate efforts [throughout government] are not co-ordinated than into one clear channel, the results will be disastrous'.[56] Moreover, while Chambers of Commerce and local authorities could be avoided, MPs were different. They met ministers including Jowitt and Minister of Supply Sir Andrew Duncan to argue that 'nothing in fact was being done' on reconstruction and that 'planning and early action' was needed.[57]

However, by early 1944 Ministry of Production officials recognised the Board of Trade's tightening grip on industrial location, prompting their observation that the government 'intends to deal sympathetically' with peripheral areas.[58] Grip was symbolised by Dalton's instructions to his Board of Trade Regional Controllers that the problem faced by areas including south Wales was 'very simple' as they had too few factories, and therefore needed 'more factories to [be] put in them' to drive a diversification from primary industries.[59] Activity was also spurred by the dire warnings from the Factory and Storage Control Function that it estimated that only 27,440 of the new 97,940 jobs created in factories throughout south Wales were likely to be permanent.[60] Brunning noted in February 1944 that although local authority representatives visited his office to complain that they knew little about government preparations for post-war industrial location and express fears that their towns would be overlooked, the increasing pace of activity meant that he was 'generally able to leave them very satisfied on both counts'.[61]

Nevertheless, concern did not abate until mid-1944 when the White Paper on Employment was published. By this time, three elements of intervention were shaping. The first was direct intervention from Dalton's office to steer industrial investment to south Wales. Jay, for example, communicated with Brunning as to whether Chepstow in Monmouthshire merited inclusion as a priority area for intervention.[62] The result was that the priority area was extended from the coalfield to include Cardiff, Swansea and Newport,[63] areas more attractive to industrialists. One example of direct intervention was British Nylon Spinners (BNS), a wartime joint venture between ICI and Courtaulds.[64] It produced parachute yarn at factories in Coventry and Suffolk but by 1943 was planning expansion. The company bought a site near Banbury, but Dalton refused to issue a building licence.

He instead offered the company data on peripheral areas, telling its management that if they chose one as a site for their factory, a license would arrive 'by return of post'.[65] BNS eventually selected a site near Pontypool in south Wales.[66] Dalton's office remained closely involved as the Ministry of Supply refused initially to dismantle hostels housing ROF workers occupying part of the site until Jay brokered a compromise enabling construction to commence.[67] Meanwhile, Factory and Storage Control regional officers had been meeting with industrialists since early 1943 to discuss peacetime requirements, but these meetings increased in volume throughout 1944. In total, regional officers met 105 industrialists to discuss their requests for factory space in Wales often after they had met officials in London who encouraged them to consider peripheral areas.

The second element was advance factory construction coupled with planning the conversion of ROF buildings. In south Wales six advance factories were allocated to companies keen to produce goods ranging from watches to electric components.[68] One company was Pullman Springs whose furniture factory in London had been requisitioned. In 1944 it chose a government factory in Ammanford where it eventually employed 1,100 workers.[69] The most important element, however, was ROF conversions. In March 1945 the Board of Trade engineered the transfer of the facilities at Hirwaun and Bridgend to the South Wales and Monmouthshire Trading Estate Company, responsible for factories constructed under the Special Areas Acts of the 1930s, for their conversion into industrial estates.[70]

The final element was adapting regional governance machinery. The Wales Regional Board of the Ministry of Production was working well, and its constituent parts wanted to continue. In December 1944 for example, both the East Wales and West Wales district sub-committees argued for their retention; that for West Wales argued that it brought together both sides of industry to offset conflict, while both argued for an expansion of their remits to cover industries apart from munitions.[71] Nevertheless, the Regional Distribution of Industry Committee met for the first time in October 1944 although its influence was initially limited as building permits were allocated centrally.[72] Its meetings in 1944 and early 1945 considered a list of companies applying for post-war space at the Newport ROF, made a recommendation to the responsible Board of Trade panel, and referred decisions as to the wartime occupation of standard factories to the Regional Board.[73] However, the Committee accrued influence and by February 1945 was authorising building licences.

By August 1944 Brunning could tell Jay that the Mayor, Town Clerk and Surveyor of Merthyr Tydfil had left his office 'perfectly satisfied' about what was being done in 'post-war affairs connected to the town'.[74] Dalton toured south Wales in March 1945, noting that he looked forward to a 'full employment' in peacetime that could 'only be achieved by a one-way policy of steering new industries to the places where they were most needed'.[75] By April 1945 momentum was such that the Ministry of Town and Country Planning had surveyed and approved some 2,500 acres for new industrial buildings, with a further 1,200 acres held in reserve.

In 1946 the government extended Development Areas to include Wrexham and its former ROF, meaning that around 85 per cent of employees in Wales resided in such areas.[76] Meanwhile, the regional Board of Trade Office in Cardiff ended the war with only 23 staff, but promptly trebled to administer the industrial influx.[77] It set out two aims in August 1945 when hosting a tour for journalists. One was to find employment for workers facing unemployment and the other was to reduce dependence on a 'few basic industries liable to depression'. This was to be achieved through expansion of existing factories while 'English firms' wanting to develop new factories were to be 'induced' to select locations with surplus labour capacity. The policy was to focus on maximising employment as opposed to building sustainable industrial clusters, as the factories to be 'steered' towards south Wales would be those that could 'economically' be located there.[78]

Nevertheless, the rapid drop in munitions production had an immediate and negative impact. Some alternatives were found with 3,000 workers at former aircraft component factories producing prefabricated aluminium houses by mid-1946 including those at Ratcliffe's Llandudno plant,[79] but closures were widespread. Employment at Treforest Industrial Estate fell by almost half to some 8,000, and most ROFs had closed by mid-1947.[80] Unemployment approached pre-war levels in some areas, reaching 26 per cent in Merthyr Tydfil in June and a 'substantial proportion' in Pontypridd.[81] Yet the transition to peacetime production and the implementation of Regional Policy prompted expansion as unemployment throughout Wales halved from February 1946 to September 1947, while its economy grew faster than the UK throughout the late 1940s.[82]

Repurposed wartime machinery was part of an administrative package that operated to divert businesses to Development Areas. The Board's headquarters in London helped steer large projects to Wales, including a large Hoover factory that was encouraged to locate in Merthyr Tydfil in 1946 even though its management had preferred a location in the south of England. Nevertheless, an important element of this approach was delay as industrialists could choose a Development Area and quickly receive a building licence or apply to locate elsewhere and wait as a slow and cumbersome administrative process unfolded.[83] Repurposed wartime factories were often those on former ROF sites where the Board of Trade reimbursed management costs incurred by the Wales and Monmouthshire Industrial Estates Ltd (WMIE). WMIE was the renamed South Wales and Monmouthshire Trading Estates Ltd that was established in the 1930s to discharge the property functions of the Commissioner for Special Areas. Increased activity meant that such reimbursements grew from £1,263 in 1945–6 to £25,689 in the subsequent year.[84] As peacetime commenced, the few Ministry of Supply staff remaining at Bridgend ROF included those selling or transferring office furniture to new tenants.[85] Meanwhile, many pre-existing government owned factories were allocated to their wartime occupiers. One example was Birmingham-based Joseph Lucas Ltd that had manufactured wartime aircraft components in a 419,000 sq. ft factory in Cwmbran, before being allocated the same factory to produce car components in peacetime.[86]

The WMIE began to build an industrial estate in Swansea from mid-1945 but by December officials were worried that the influx would not reach more peripheral locations without further intervention. The WMIE promptly authorised 200,000 square feet of factories in areas less attractive to industry such as Rhondda and Pembroke Dock, adding thirty-one in the subsequent year.[87] By mid-1946 the WMIE was constructing 125 government-financed factories in the Development Areas.[88] The Board also benefited from the continuation of a permit-driven economy into the immediate post-war years. These benefits flowed from its ability to help firms obtain the permits necessary to obtain construction materials as well as the raw materials necessary to commence production. The final element was financial support in the form of loans from HM Treasury's Development Areas Advisory Committee. These were few, however, although Polikoff's received £150,000 to double its Rhondda clothing factory from 1,500 employees to 3,000.

These activities combined to prompt a remarkable surge of investment in the Wales Development Areas. By the end of 1947-8 the government-financed programme in these areas comprised 168 factories covering some 5.8 million square feet, of which all but twenty-seven had been allocated to tenants. Meanwhile, it had also approved 121 privately financed factories totalling 10.2 million square feet, of which all but twenty-one were occupied or under construction.[89]

Although rising unemployment in 1946 prompted the South Wales Evening Post to warn of 'disaster', levels fell subsequently as factories opened.[90] Yet Regional Policy's implementation obscured two problems. One was that the interventions in Wales as throughout Britain focused on the immediate creation of employment, not enabling sustainable regional industrial economies, even as a jubilant government announced that the new factories were introducing 'a wide measure of diversity' to Wales by producing many different types of consumer goods.[91] The other was that the Board remained mindful of the need to boost nationwide economic efficiency, stating in 1945 that factories to be 'steered' towards Development Areas in Wales would only be those that could 'economically' be located there. Many managers promptly argued that the overall efficiency of their businesses would be harmed if one of their factories was directed to one of these areas.[92] The post-war government initially ignored such problems to prioritise regional employment growth, but economic crises of 1947 forced it to instead emphasise export growth and ease its industrial location policies to enable businesses greater discretion over factory location.

CONCLUSION

While reconstruction topics such as industrial location were understandably overlooked during the early years of the war, the experiences of the 1930s meant that they were never entirely absent. Once the fortunes of war began to favour the allies, attention within government turned towards reconstruction. Spearheaded by Dalton, an approach emerged that sought to capture industrial reconversion and divert it to the regions to avoid any return to the high unemployment of the interwar period. By the end of 1947–8 over 16 million square feet within 289 privately or state-funded factory projects was either progressing or had received authorisation throughout the Wales Development Areas.[93] All this meant that between 1945 and

1951 Wales obtained 27 per cent of all British inter-regional factory moves.[94]

The lead time for construction and equipping factories meant that many of the projects directed to Wales before Regional Policy was downgraded in 1947 opened subsequently. Of the 243 factories opened in Wales between 1945 and 1949 by firms headquartered elsewhere, 104 began production after 1947.[95] Examples included BNS and Hoover, both of which were constructed from 1946 onwards before opening in 1948. Their combined employment peaked at over 13,000 in the 1960s. However, the influx was not solely attributable to Regional Policy. If industrialists had been able to locate factories in more congested areas, they would have been hampered there by shortages of labour and materials. Such delay would have risked losing market share to competitors, prompting some to locate in areas such as Wales regardless of government policies. Nevertheless, policy additionality is indicated by the extent to which few industrialists chose to locate their factories in Wales during the 1930s, and how many showed a similar reluctance after 1947.

The frenetic burst of state intervention within industrial location helped ensure that the economic legacies of war in Wales were retained, namely industrial diversification, full employment, and increased female participation in the paid labour force. Readjustment to peacetime had been largely completed by 1948 when manufacturing employment in Wales had grown by over 70,000 when compared to 1939, an increase of 56 per cent compared to 15 per cent for Great Britain.[96] By this year, unemployment throughout Wales averaged 4.9 per cent, lower than any year since comparable data were available after 1923.[97] Crucially, the composition of the industrial labour force shifted as secondary manufacturing employment grew from 13 per cent to 18 per cent. Also noticeable was the retention and expansion of gains in female labour as 235,000 women were employed in 1948, compared to 219,000 in 1944 but only 94,000 in 1939.[98]

In 1948 Dalton could justifiably describe regional employment throughout the UK as representing 'victory indeed ... my dreams of twenty years ago ... were coming true at last'.[99] Although Regional Policy's short-lived initial phase created secondary manufacturing economies dominated by 'branch plants', it enabled a surge of investment to remodel post-war regions using methods informed by the war's upending of the relationship between business and state.

Notes

1. Jeffreys, *The Churchill Coalition*, pp. 112–13. Parts of this chapter draw on material within: Gooberman, 'The Emergence of Regional Industrial Policy in Britain: The Case of Wales, 1939 to 1947', *Enterprise and Society* (2023). Published online before print.
2. Parsons, *The Political Economy of British Regional Policy*, p. 56.
3. *Report of the Labour Party's Commission into Depressed Areas: South Wales* (Labour Party, 1937).
4. Ben Pimlott (ed.), *The Second World War Diary of Hugh Dalton* (Johnathan Cape, 1986), p. 431.
5. Jeffreys, *The Churchill Coalition*, p. 112.
6. Pimlott, *Hugh Dalton*, p. 401.
7. Jeffreys, *The Churchill Coalition*, p. 125.
8. A. Booth, 'The Second World War and the Development of Modern Regional Policy', *Economy and Society*, 11/1 (1988), 1–21 (13–14).
9. B. Pimlott, *The Second World War Diary of Hugh Dalton, 1940–1945* (Jonathan Cape, 1986), p. 700.
10. *Employment Policy* (Cmd 6527) (HMSO, 1944), 3, 11.
11. Jay, *Change and Fortune*, p. 108; TNA, BT 106/16, Note by D. P. T. Jay, 8 November 1943.
12. TNA, BT 131/28, *Location of Industry, 21 September 1943*, 7, 14.
13. NA, BT 64/3157, *Letter to G. D. H. Cole*, 22 April 1943.
14. NA, BT 64/3157, *G. D. H. Cole to Board of Trade*, 6 March 1943.
15. Jay, *Change and Fortune*, pp. 113–14.
16. TNA, BT 168/204, *Press Notice*, 10 October 1944.
17. LSE Digital Library, DL1HD01, *Diary of Hugh Dalton*, 6 February 1945.
18. Booth, 'The Second World War and the Development of Modern Regional Policy', 8.

19 Pimlott, *The Second World War Diary of Hugh Dalton*, p. 866.
20 HMSO, *Employment Policy*, May 1944, 13.
21 TNA, BT 168/209, *Future Regional Organization Committee Report*, 3 November 1943, 1.
22 TNA, BT 168/209, *Note to Regional Controllers*, 4 September 1944.
23 TNA, BT 168/210, *Ministry of Production, Balanced Distribution of Industry, Regional Production*, October 1944, 1.
24 TNA, BT 64/1946, *Memorandum*, 1 December 1944.
25 TNA, BT 64/1946, *Letter to Ministry of Works*, 14 February 1945.
26 TNA, BT 64/1946, *Applications for Building Licences, Post War Aspects*, 28 December 1944.
27 *Let Us Face the Future* (The Labour Party, 1945).
28 Hansard (Commons), *9 April 1946, vol. 421, col. 1808*.
29 TNA, BT 64/1946, *Building Schemes*, 19 December 1945; BT 106/16, *Circular*, July 1946.
30 *Government Action 1st August 1946–31st July 1947*, 16–17.
31 Weir, *Civilian Assignment*, p. 56.
32 TNA, BT 168/224, *Statement by Chairman, Treasury Committee on Regional Organisation*, 6 December 1945.
33 *Second Report from the Select Committee on Estimates: Development Areas, Session 1955–56* (HMSO, 1956), 23.
34 S. Rosevear, 'Balancing Business and the Regions: British distribution of industry policy and the Board of Trade, 1945–51', *Business History* 40:1 (1998), 77-99 (84, 86).
35 *Second Report from the Select Committee on Estimates: Development Areas, Session 1955-56*, vii.
36 P. Scott, 'British Regional Policy 1945–51: A Lost Opportunity', *Twentieth Century British History*, 8/3(1997), 358–82 (373).
37 Rosevear, 'Balancing Business and the Regions', 84–8.
38 Parsons, *The Political Economy of British Regional Policy*, p. 79.
39 H. Dalton, *High Tide and After* (Frederick Muller, 1962), p. 187.
40 Parsons, *The Political Economy of British Regional Policy*, p. 82.
41 McCrone, *Regional Policy in Britain*, p. 111.
42 TNA, BT 63/315, *Nuffield College Reconstruction Survey, South Wales, Part, II*, March 1942, 11.
43 Mass Observation, *Mining Town 1942*, 5.
44 Hansard (Commons), *30 June 1942, vol. 381, cols 27–9*.
45 TNA, CAB 117/254, *Herbert Morrison to Sir William Jowitt*, 20 May 1942; CAB 117/255, *Secretary of Association of Welsh Local Authorities to Sir William Jowitt*, 12 October 1942.
46 TNA, CAB 117/255, *Discussion with Principal Rees*, 25 November 1943.
47 TNA, CAB 117/255, *Note to Minister*, 6 March 1943.
48 TNA, CAB 117/259, *Meeting with Welsh Reconstruction Advisory Council, Notes for the Minister*, 7 June 1941, 1.

49 TNA, CAB 117/258, *Secretary of Welsh Reconstruction Advisory Council to Reconstruction Secretariat*, 7 July 1943.
50 Welsh Reconstruction Advisory Council, *First Report*, 69.
51 TNA, BT 63/315, *Nuffield College Reconstruction Survey, South Wales, Part, II*, 13.
52 TNA BT 64/3134, *Board of Trade, Note on Nuffield Central Wales Survey Report*, 1 March 1943; BT 64/ 3153, *Board of Trade Note*, 14 May 1943.
53 TNA, BT 106/17, *Post-war Reconstruction, Note by the Board of Trade*, 10 February 1943.
54 Percival, *The Government's Industrial Estates in Wales 1936–1975*, p. 45.
55 TNA, BT 106/17, *North Wales, Post War Reconstruction*, 8 March 1943, 8.
56 TNA, BT 64/ 3129, *Factory and Storage Control (Wales) to Board of Trade*, 22 April 1943.
57 TNA, CAB 117/258, *Note of Deputation of Welsh Members of Parliament of 19 October 1943*, 2.
58 TNA, BT 168/205, *Wales Regional Board Comments on Minister's Brief on Reconversion*, 6 January 1944, 1.
59 LSE Digital Library, DL1HD01, *Diary of Hugh Dalton*, 30 March 1944.
60 TNA, BT 64/3392, *South Wales, Employment in New War Factories*.
61 TNA, BT 64/3239, *Brunning to Board of Trade*, 11 February 1944.
62 TNA, BT 64/3395, *Jay to Brunning*, 3 October 1944.
63 Pimlott, *The Second World War Diary of Hugh Dalton*, p. 700.
64 W. J. Reader, *Imperial Chemical Industries, Volume II: The First Quarter Century 1926–1952* (Oxford: Oxford University Press, 1975), p. 374.
65 H. Dalton, *The Fateful Years* (Frederick Muller, 1953), pp. 437–8.
66 L. Gooberman and B. Curtis, 'The Age of Factories: The Rise and Fall of Manufacturing in South Wales, 1945–1985', in L. Miskell (ed.), *New Perspectives on Welsh Industrial History* (University of Wales Press, 2020), pp. 181–206 (pp. 188–9).
67 Jay, *Change and Fortune*, pp. 115–16.
68 Percival, *The Government's Industrial Estates in Wales*, p. 47.
69 S. Town, *After the Mines: Changing Employment Opportunities in a South Wales Valley* (University of Wales Press, 1978), p. 59.
70 Jay, *Change and Fortune*, p. 119.
71 TNA, BT 168/203, *West Wales District Committee Memorandum*, 7 December 1944, 1; *Extract from East Wales Advisory District Committee Meeting*, 11 December 1944.
72 TNA, BT 168/213, *Wales Regional Board to Ministry of Production*, 31 October 1944.
73 TNA, BT 208/65, *Regional Distribution of Industry Committee, Minutes of Third Meeting*, 4 December 1944, 4; *Minutes of Fifth Meeting*, 8 January 1945, 2; *Minutes of Sixth Meeting*, 5 February 1945, 4.
74 TNA, BT 64/3229, *Brunning to Jay*, 3 August 1944.
75 *Pontypridd Observer*, 'Mr Dalton Visits the Trading Estate', 3 March 1945.
76 *Distribution of Industry* (Cmd 7540) (HMSO, 1945), Appendix 5.
77 Percival, *The Government's Industrial Estates in Wales 1936–1975*, p. 47.

78 TNA, BT 64/3559, *Editors' Tour*, 1 August 1945, 1.
79 *Wales and Monmouthshire: A Summary of Government Action 1st August 1945–31st July 1946* (Cmd 6938) (HMSO, 1946), 18; *North Wales Weekly News*, 'Output for Peace', 16 August 1945.
80 Percival, *The Government's Industrial Estates in Wales 1936–1975*, p. 49.
81 Thomas, 'War and the Economy: The South Wales Experience', in Baber and Williams (eds), *Modern South Wales: Essays in Economic History*, pp. 251–77 (p. 259); *Pontypridd Observer*, 'Jobs and Unemployment', 6 July 1946.
82 Williams, *DWHS, vol. 1*, pp. 147–8; E. Nevin, A. R. Roe and J. I. Round, *The Structure of the Welsh Economy* (Cardiff: University of Wales Press, 1966), p. 6.
83 Rowlands, *Something Must be Done*, p. 184.
84 Glamorgan Archives, DIEC 11, *South Wales and Monmouthshire Trading Estates Limited, Report of Directors, 1946–1947*, 2.
85 NLW, MS 23071E, *Women in World War 2, Manuscript Accounts, Interview with Mair Davies*.
86 *Wales and Monmouthshire: A Summary of Government Action 1st August 1945–31st July 1946*, 65.
87 Percival, *The Government's Industrial Estates in Wales 1936–1975*, pp. 53–4.
88 *Wales and Monmouthshire: Report of Government Action for the Year ended 30th June 1947*, 20.
89 *Wales and Monmouthshire: Report of Government Action for the Year ended 30th June 1948* (Cmd 7532) (HMSO, 1948), 60–1, 63; TNA, 117/1110, Note on Polikoff's, 7 August 1946; Application to D. I. Panel, undated.
90 Williams, *DWHS, vol. 1*, pp. 147–8; NLW, GB 0210, *Letter to Emrys Price*, 12 December 1945.
91 *Wales and Monmouthshire: A Summary of Government Action 1st August 1945–31st July 1946*, 8–9.
92 TNA, BT 64/3559, *Editors' Tour*, 1 August 1945, 1.
93 *Wales and Monmouthshire: Report of Government Action for the Year ended 30th June 1948*, 60–1.
94 B. Ashcroft and J. Taylor, 'The Effect of Regional Policy on the Movement of Industry in Great Britain', in D. Maclennan and J. Parr (eds), *Regional Policy: Past Experience and New Directions*, pp. 43–64, (p. 46).
95 *Commission on the Constitution, Research Paper 8: Survey of the Welsh Economy* (HMSO, 1973), 58.
96 *Western Mail*, 'Plans to Attract Workers back to Wales', 17 December 1946; Thomas, 'War and the Economy: The South Wales Experience', in Baber and Williams (eds), *Modern South Wales: Essays in Economic History*, pp. 251–77 (pp. 264–5).
97 Williams, *DWHS, vol. 1*, pp. 142–8.
98 Williams, *DWHS, vol. 1*, p. 138; B. Thomas, 'Post-war Expansion', in Thomas (ed.), *The Welsh Economy: Studies in Expansion*, pp. 30–1.
99 Parsons, *Political Economy of British Regional Policy*, p. 84.

10

NATURAL RESOURCE INDUSTRIES

Nationalisation was central to the Labour government's commitment to economic planning, but its purpose and practicalities were unclear. Justifications included helping to plan the national economy, raising levels of industrial efficiency, and radically shifting the balance of power to advance socialism. The weight given to each varied over time and across industries but a common argument by 1945 was that large state-owned industrial entities would feature improved technology and working conditions that would in turn prompt greater efficiency.[1] These technocratic views prompted Labour's election manifesto to declare that the 'basic industries [were] ripe and over-ripe for public ownership and management in the direct service of the nation' and promised to nationalise those including coal and power, although agriculture was to be left in private hands, albeit 'planned' by the state.[2]

The new government planned to constitute nationalised industries as public corporations. These were known as 'Morrisonian' corporations as they shared the approach embodied by the London Passenger Transport Board, created in the 1930s by Labour's Herbert Morrison to combine what he defined as 'public ownership, public accountability, and business management for public ends'.[3] They were overseen by boards appointed by government for their members' commercial and technical expertise, not as interest group representatives. However, the speed and ambition of Labour's programme meant that the structural and operational details of nationalisation remained vague, prompting TUC secretary

Walter Citrine to argue later that it 'had not been thought out with any precision'.[4]

Yet the lack of detail was obscured by how the scale of Labour's general election victory offered the prospect of a fundamental break with pre-war norms. The government had an ambitious programme of maintaining full employment, creating a welfare state, nationalisation, and redistributing industrial employment. At the same time, it had to steer the conversion of wartime industries, repair bomb damage, revitalise domestic industries, and find employment for demobilised service personnel. As if this was not enough, it also had to contend with the sudden ending of lend-lease in 1945, food precarity, extreme weather, and the balance of payments and convertibility crises of 1947. Ambition and turbulence interacted to prompt different governance approaches to each of the three resource-based industries.

COAL

Throughout the war the Labour Party and miners' unions were committed to public control while the Conservative Party and mine owners sought to maintain the status quo. The result was deadlock and although the state gradually extended its governance over the industry, albeit with mixed results, its structure and ownership remained unchanged. However, the poor state of the industry inevitably prompted debates on reform while scepticism within the civil service grew as to its ability to reform itself.[5] By 1945 successive crises had prompted a growing acceptance throughout the industry and beyond that reform was inevitable; the official wartime history noted that 'no other major British industry carried so many problems into the war; none brought more out', while wartime circumstances had prompted a 'confused national awakening to the true magnitude of these problems'.[6] National solutions needed national bodies and the creation of national bargaining systems in 1944 prompted regional unions to merge into a National Union of Mineworkers (NUM) in early 1945. Meanwhile, the Miners Association of Great Britain reluctantly discussed reforms. In early 1945 its Chair Robert Foot produced a plan proposing a national board of coal owners to coordinate the industry, only for it to be widely condemned as inadequate and overly corporatist.

Yet even as the Foot Plan was being prepared, the government had appointed mining engineers with managerial experience to the Reid Committee, tasked to assess the industry's technical potential and identify the necessary organisational reforms. Minister for Fuel and Power Gwilym Lloyd George signalled his support by placing his regional coal control staff at 'the disposal of the committee' to help meet what he defined as the contemporary 'urge' to reform far more apparent than in 1939 given the 'different circumstances prevailing'.[7] The plan that emerged in March 1945 identified reforms that 'cannot be carried through by the industry organised as it is today' and shifted the national debate from industrial relations towards industrial efficiency.[8] While the Reid Report did not propose nationalisation, it argued for amalgamations and modernisation under a central authority, conclusions accepted in May 1945 by the owners and the Conservative caretaker government.[9] Labour's manifesto concurred, arguing that 'amalgamation under public ownership will bring great economies in operation and make it possible to modernise production methods, and to raise safety standards in every colliery'.[10]

The Labour government acted quickly by introducing a Coal Nationalisation Bill in December 1945. The Mining Association of Great Britain agreed not to oppose the bill,[11] and the Conservatives did not criticise its principles. Yet wartime struggles around productivity and output inevitably continued, prompting Horner to argue later that while the bill was 'pursuing its long course through Parliament, we ... regarded it as our duty to push up production as much as possible'.[12] The

NUM seconded Horner to the Ministry of Fuel and Power in September 1945 as National Production Officer and he toured the coalfields to urge managers and employees to make better use of Pit and Area Production Committees. Meanwhile, the NUM argued that recruitment difficulties were prompted by poor employment terms and conditions, arguing in favour of its 'Miner's Charter' where improvements such as a five-day working week and two weeks' paid annual holiday would aid recruitment to drive greater production.[13]

The Coal Industry Nationalisation Bill received royal assent in August 1946 and created the National Coal Board (NCB), a technocratic corporation under arm's-length ministerial guidance that took control of the industry on 1 January 1947, known as 'Vesting Day'. The NCB was governed by a chairman and eight members with functional responsibilities, while its board reflected its business-like nature; its Chair, Lord Hyndley, was a former managing director of Powell Duffryn, while only two members, TUC Chair Citrine and NUM Secretary Ebby Edward, were trade union leaders and both left their posts to serve as individuals.[14]

The NCB was immediately plunged into a fuel crisis when the cold weather of early 1947 impeded coal deliveries, prompting industrial layoffs and emergency efforts to boost production. Its longer-term aim, however, was to enable greater productivity through investment and structural reform; *The Economist* argued that 'although labour relations have the limelight at present, it will be the investment policy of the Board that will tell in the long run'.[15] Yet in April 1947 Horner led a delegation to Downing Street to argue that operating inefficient collieries to maximise short-term output was depressing productivity, and that the NCB's rationalisation efforts were 'too leisurely'. In response, Atlee observed that the NCB was carrying out a survey to inform planning, while Manny Shinwell, Minister of Fuel and Power, argued that the NUM should use the consultation processes set out within the Act to influence the Board. An unimpressed

Horner responded that 'we have got a production committee, but we cannot get on' due to the 'resentment' of some NCB board members to discuss production.[16] Nationalising the industry was relatively straightforward, but boosting its productivity was far more difficult.

In south Wales, Horner had long argued that the only solution 'this side of socialism' to industrial problems was a UK-wide nationalised entity.[17] Some mine owners accepted that reform was inevitable; one told his association that the 'present methods [of governance] could not continue after the war'.[18] Unsurprisingly, the NUM's South Wales Division argued in its 1945 general election statement that only a Labour government could 'ensure that resources shall be available and used to fulfil the needs of people in peace as they were made available to organise victory over the fascist powers'. Moreover, the south Wales colliery managers association stated before the election that its members would work with a Labour government to ensure a successful transition,[19] while the importance of the coalfield was reflected by three of its MPs becoming cabinet ministers, and Horner's election as NUM General Secretary in July 1946.[20] Meanwhile, the South Wales NUM returned to its wartime role of seeking to boost production amidst what Horner called a 'coal crisis deeper and sharper' than 'at any time since the commencement of the war'.[21] Being seen as actively working to boost production had political advantages; the south Wales NUM newsletter argued that the UK-wide 'ruling class' expected the new government to fail, requiring 'the conscious determination of every worker to ensure that production is intensified' to increase the government's chances of success.[22]

As the NCB was being established, geography combined with centralist tendencies to preclude a unified Wales-specific governance structure, and the southern coalfield was grouped with the Somerset and Forest of Dean coalfields to form the NCB's South-Western Division. The division was divided into seven districts, the six in south Wales employing 115,500 miners in 1947.²³ The 8,808 miners of the north Wales coalfield were grouped with Lancashire into a North-Western Division. The South-Western Board met for the first time in November 1946 when its Labour Director stated ominously that he had attended a meeting in London to be told that 'no finality' had been reached on national policies on industrial relations or training.²⁴ Finally, the South West Divisional Chair General Godwin-Austen admitted honestly if unhelpfully that he had 'little knowledge' of either south Wales or the coal industry; the south Wales NUM responded by declaring their lack of confidence in him before pressure from national leadership prompted a reversal.²⁵

Vesting day was met with pithead speeches as the NCB flag was hoisted but workforce views were tempered by the technocratic nature of the new corporation, as although the NUM lodge chairman at Cwm Colliery hailed the flag as one 'of victory' there was no sudden change in working relationships.²⁶ Five of the seven members of the Divisional Production Board were former managers of the Powell Duffryn combine, the legal and statistical staff of the Monmouthshire and South Wales Coal Owners' Association all transferred to the NCB, and the Powell Duffryn General Manager for Pontypridd and Rhondda was appointed NCB manager for Monmouthshire.²⁷ Continuity prompted NUM South Wales President Emlyn Williams to argue later that there was 'little difference except that the mines were nationalised. As far as management were concerned, as far as the system was concerned, there was no change at all'.²⁸ Nevertheless, working conditions improved as the board introduced a five-day working week, replaced the wartime Pit Production Committees with similar Colliery Consultative Committees, and created a Divisional Consultative Council.²⁹ Goodwill was reflected by many south Wales miners suspending the five-day week during the fuel crisis to enable weekend shifts.³⁰

The industry, however, was exhausted. A review of the south Wales coalfield commissioned by the government as part of the Reid Report found that most of the 155 collieries employing more than 250 miners had been operating for more than forty years, with only eleven sunk in the previous twenty-five years. A key problem was the lack of mechanisation as only 32 per cent of output was machine cut in 1944, hampered by many factors including difficult geology, persistent absenteeism, turbulent industrial relations hampering the introduction of new working practices, and the preference of some mine owners for cheaper pneumatic picks instead of more efficient but more expensive coal-cutting machinery.[31]

Faced with these problems, the NCB began to rationalise and invest. Rationalisation was built into nationalisation as the board owned but did not usually operate mines employing fewer than fifty miners; these were instead operated privately under licence to reduce the management burden on the new Board.[32] In north Wales, half of the sixteen mines operating in 1946 employed fewer than fifty miners and by 1948 the NCB operated only the eight larger collieries.[33] Once established, the Board sought further rationalisations and closed twelve south Wales collieries in its first year; 1,700 of the 2,000 miners affected were transferred to more productive mines.[34] Both methods meant that, while there were 322 collieries in south Wales in 1943, the NCB operated 203 in 1948.[35] Finally, investment began with, for example, two Nantgarw collieries modernised to benefit from production 'methods new to this country' and new coke ovens.[36] Mechanisation also proceeded elsewhere as the percentage of coal cut mechanically rose from 36.3 per cent in 1947 to 43 per cent in the following year.[37]

Although Hyndley visited Cardiff in late 1946 to ask miners and managers to 'wipe out the past and let us get on with the great task in front of us',[38] the NCB faced familiar problems of turbulent industrial relations and poor financial performance. While the number of days lost in 1945 was the lowest since 1939, relative peace did not last as those in 1947 reached levels comparable to 1942 and 1943 (see Figure 1 in Appendix); in one week in June, there were thirteen disputes involving 1,162 miners.[39] In June 1947 Shinwell met the south Wales NUM in Cardiff where there was 'general agreement' that coalfield output was 'not satisfactory' and, although productivity and attendance had improved following the introduction of the five-day week, output per shift remained below 1938 levels. The NUM responded by condemning what they argued was a lack of consultation, the centralised nature of decision making, and a rigid approach to dispute resolution.[40] Meanwhile, low productivity meant that all south Wales Areas made heavy losses in 1947 when the Divisional Chair argued that the coalfield was 'in a terrible state financially', while the north Wales Area was also loss-making.[41]

All this indicated that dissatisfaction with working conditions and enmity between production and labour remained salient. Salience was symbolised by a board discussion on the Gwaen-Cae-Gurwen area when the Divisional Production Director, a former colliery manager, condemned miners as militant and 'making as little effort as possible'. Such comments prompted the Divisional Labour Director, a former union official, to respond that, while conditions had improved, the previous frequency of pneumoconiosis and silicosis had prompted miners to assume that 'their lives would be of short duration, and they therefore should not exert themselves unduly'.[42] While the NCB was making progress, public governance was no panacea for its deep-rooted problems.

METAL MANUFACTURING

The steel industry was one of the more successful examples of wartime state control, with the Ministry of Supply loosely governing the Iron and Steel Control to allow operational autonomy. Although wartime steel output barely grew, government and businesses recognised that post-war growth was necessary to supply an expanded secondary manufacturing sector. Coordinated planning began in 1943 when the British Steel Industry Federation worked with the Iron and Steel Control to assess post-war requirements. In the following year, the Federation began to prepare an industry-wide national development plan and vet investment schemes proposed by its member firms. In mid-1945 the caretaker government asked the Federation to complete the plan quickly, and the document emerged in 1946 to argue that the UK's industry should be remodelled to increase output by a fifth through constructing new plants and closing or modernising others.[43]

From mid-1945 many Control staff returned to their companies and there was a brief transition when oversight was shared between the Federation and the Control, until the latter was wound up in October 1946. Yet coordinated governance continued and was generally accepted by the industry as wartime controls had been successful and offered an alternative to nationalisation. Governance was shared by two bodies. One was a reconstituted Federation formed from sectoral trade associations; those who wrote its new constitution argued for a corporatist approach of 'self-government within the framework of government policy'.[44] It promptly created a Development Committee formed from Chairs or Managing Directors of the larger steel firms to examine and comment on all schemes brought forward as part of the development plan issued in 1946.[45]

The other was a Control Board formed from representatives of both sides of industry to succeed the Iron and Steel Control as an interim measure before nationalisation. Chaired by Sir Archibald Forbes, an industrialist who had worked at the Ministry of Aircraft Production,[46] it was tasked with reviewing and supervising investments within the context of the national plan, supervising the industry, and advising on the government's price controls. Yet its powers were negative in that while it vetted the investment plans of members, it could not plan new capacity or rationalisations. It instead interacted between the state and trade associations within a system featuring centralised control over imports of raw materials and semi-finished goods. Meanwhile, the Federation continued to operate the wartime steel allocation system.[47]

The backdrop to this opaque system was Labour's commitment to nationalise the industry. This promise was a late insertion into the 1945 manifesto amidst much opposition, as while nationalisations elsewhere were more easily justifiable given their status as utilities, or poor performances, steel was profitable and an important exporter.[48] Many Labour politicians were uncertain, including Board of Trade President Cripps who in 1944 had opposed nationalising light metal as 'we have learned in the war that we can control industry'.[49] Civil servants were also unconvinced, prompting Franks's 1946 refusal to prepare a paper on steel nationalisation unless ordered formally, arguing that there were 'no good administrative reasons' for the policy that was instead 'a purely political matter'.[50] Debate continued as the industry believed that nationalisation would achieve little beyond that already achieved by state supervision, prompting GKN Chair Samuel Beale to argue that a 'cumbersome, slow moving and doctrinaire' government would struggle to control the 'highly complex' industry.[51] Nevertheless, in mid-1947 the Cabinet rejected endowing the Control Board with greater powers while keeping the industry in private hands, and the government began to prepare nationalisation. However, it decided against amalgamating the entire industry into one body in favour of an Iron and Steel Corporation holding the securities of most large firms, thus maintaining a semblance of the existing industrial structure under state ownership.[52]

In Wales the immediate post-war dynamic of 'self-government within the framework of government policy' was obvious, as was the importance of the industry. South Wales plants had since the mid-1930s produced over a fifth of all the UK's steel, almost all its tinplate, and around half of its sheet steel. The 1946 plan proposed investment of some £41 million, the largest of any UK region, and by 1947 the Ministry of Supply had approved schemes of some £37 million to boost production from 2.38 million tons in 1945 to 3.25 million tons.[53] While dominated by a new plant at Port Talbot, modernisations and expansions took place elsewhere including at Cardiff, Ebbw Vale and Newport. Expansion was not confined to south Wales as from 1946 a six-year programme at John Summer's plant at Shotton included new coke ovens, a blast furnace and an open-hearth steel plant to create a fully integrated plant with annual ingot capacity of a million tons.[54] Its scale was illustrated by the dredging of six million tons of sand from the Dee estuary to create a 280-acre platform for the new facilities.[55]

Aside from steel, aluminium retained much of its localised wartime importance as production or rolling imported ingots continued at three plants. Meanwhile, the Ministry of Supply sold the aluminium plant constructed at Newport with financial support from the Ministry of Aircraft Production to its operators, the Canadian firm of Northern Aluminium. Other smaller factories including those in Cardiff were declared surplus and allocated to other industries.[56]

The impact of the state-business modernising dynamic, described aptly by a history of the British iron and steel industry as 'protracted and extremely complicated',[57] was demonstrated by a new strip mill at Port Talbot. It was designed to produce sheet steel for uses including tinplate and automotive manufacturing and was to become the UK's largest steelworks.[58] The context was the modernisation of the tinplate industry, concentrated in south Wales but comprised largely of obsolete hand rolling mills. Although one strip mill was constructed in the 1930s at Ebbw Vale, a second was needed and companies made tentative proposals before being interrupted by war. Their inability to agree the most suitable site and ownership structure for a new strip mill eventually prompted state involvement. In 1943 the Iron and Steel Control recommended the construction of a mill that could produce 80-inch strips, wider than current capacity. Although the Board of Trade did not formally control industrial decision making, it wanted to ensure that the location of the new works took account of social needs, an aim helped by the industry realising that the cost savings of new production techniques would more than offset the costs of locating the plant in a marginally less favourable location.[59]

The Board's most important lever was its ability to reject concentration schemes given their incorporation of tax-exempt compensation for the owners of closed plants. The industry finally submitted a scheme in 1944, only for it to be rejected by Dalton who complained that neither the tinplate manufacturers nor the British Steel Industry Federation had told him where the new plants would be sited, and that he would not consider their scheme unless the new factories were placed 'in accord with the public interest'.[60] However, once reassured in early 1945 that Port Talbot was to be chosen, he noted that this would help 'secure a balanced distribution of industry' and approved a concentration scheme and associated levy on tinplate.[61] It aimed to remove around a third of capacity at what the Control Board described as inefficient hand mills in poor condition.[62] Dalton also announced that a new tinplate plant would be located in the Llanelli area unless 'some insuperable technical or economic difficulty is encountered'.[63]

The project formed a central element of the 1946 Development Plan,[64] while the Welsh Plate and Steel Manufacturers' Association warned that the industry had five years to replace the 'doomed' hand mills with a strip mill to retain competitiveness against overseas producers.[65] In early 1947 a business consortium obtained approvals from the Control Board, the Regional Distribution of Industry Committee, and the nationwide Panel A, and merged to create the Steel Company of Wales. The new company was to deliver a project formed from two elements.

One was producing sheet steel at a new Abbey Works at Port Talbot formed from coke ovens, blast furnaces, steel melting shops, and a continuous hot strip mill, while two existing works at Port Talbot and Margam were to be modernised and amalgamated into the new works. While larger sheets could be sold to the car industry, tinplate required the other element of the project: new works to process and tinplate sheet steel. Although the Abbey Works would boost sheet steel employment in south Wales, new tinplate plants would reduce total employment in that industry by almost 4,000 as hand mills closed. The Steel Company of Wales noted that one worker using modern processes could produce the same as six did in the hand mills.[66] The Control argued in 1947 that their most efficient location was adjacent to the new works to reduce transport costs but that 'sociological considerations' favoured other sites, while the added transport costs would not have a 'serious' impact on production cost per unit, given the efficiency of the new plants.[67] Such considerations meant that one plant was to be located in the Swansea area and the other around Llanelli.

Having influenced locations, the state also helped with funding. Most capital was provided by the Finance Corporation for Industry, created in 1945 with support from the Bank of England to provide long-term finance to government-supported projects. Moreover, the share issues for the project were approved by the Bank of England's Capital Issues Committee, created in 1946 to authorise large-scale capital issues.[68] Although civil servants noted that debt raised privately was more expensive than that raised by the state after nationalisation, meaning that a few years' delay would reduce costs, Ministry of Supply officials noted that they were 'under great pressure from ministers not to hold up these development schemes', prompting Treasury agreement to the required dollar expenditure even as the balance of payments crisis loomed, and the project proceeded.[69]

Meanwhile, domestic demand for canned products prompted the UK-wide output of tinplate to grow from 512,000 tons in 1945 to 664,000 in 1947.[70] The government addressed the shortage of workers through funding training and enabling the employment of workers from Poland and Italy, although unions secured undertakings that these would be dismissed first should fewer workers be required in future.[71] Despite such schemes, in late 1946 the Society of Motor Manufacturers and Traders complained that a lack of sheet steel supplies could force their members' factories to reduce production.[72] In response, plans to close smaller sheet steel and tinplate plants were delayed, and some that had closed during the war were reopened.[73] Finally, the extent to which policies were driven by employment considerations was again demonstrated when the site being prepared north of Swansea for a tinplate plant was discarded in favour of one near Llanelli. The new site was further from the Abbey Works but was closer to communities affected by tinplate redundancies and was favoured by influential Labour MPs, although the Swansea site was retained for future development.

Overall, the state-enabled post-war transformation of the steel and tinplate industries was underway by August 1947 when the site for the tinplate works was being prepared while 2,100 workers were driving 25,000 piles to support the Abbey Works.[74] The Steel Company of Wales claimed that the project amounted to a nationally important 'City of Steel' as 'without steel to meet the tremendous demands and competition of the post-war world, Britain would perish'. Although this assertion tended towards hyperbole, the project did symbolise the government's determination to support regional and national industrial rejuvenation.[75]

AGRICULTURE

Wartime intervention restored prosperity and stability to agriculture, while the success of cooperation between government and agricultural interests prompted eleven interest groups, including the NFU and trade unions, to issue a statement on 'post war agricultural policy' in 1944. They proposed a corporatist system where farmers would accept an obligation to achieve a 'reasonable standard of good husbandry' in return for the state guaranteeing output prices.[76] During the 1945 election campaign the Conservative Party argued that the state should help ensure stable markets and prices but Labour was more forthright, arguing that 'people need food at prices they can afford to pay – this means our food supplies have to be planned' and pledging that the CWEACs would 'continue in peacetime'.[77] Nevertheless, Labour's earlier insistence on land nationalisation was rejected as unnecessary given the success of wartime governance.[78] Labour instead argued that farmers should be relieved of concern for markets and prices to concentrate on improving efficiency to prompt greater output. Overall, the policy was sponsorship and guidance, not direct control.

Policy was also shaped by worsening food supply symbolised by the introduction of bread rationing in 1946, a step avoided during wartime. Even the weather harmed production as an early summer drought in the same year was followed by an unusually wet summer and an arctic winter featuring prolonged and severe snowfalls requiring hay to be dropped from bombers to sustain isolated hill farms,[79] and, finally, flooding as snow thawed. All this prompted the Ministry to tell CWAEC chairs at an April 1947 conference that the food situation was 'more serious than at any point during the war years'.[80]

The government had two options. It could import food or import feedstuffs to boost livestock and poultry numbers while reducing arable acreage. Influenced by the need to conserve foreign currency, it chose the latter and in 1947 set out plans to raise UK-wide output by 20 per cent through measures including raising prices and increasing livestock subsidies. Meanwhile, the Ministry of Food continued to purchase commodities directly from farmers, while the need to conserve foreign currency led to import reductions that in turn prompted it to cut consumer rations including those of bacon, ham and fat to levels below those of wartime.[81]

Planning required a legislative framework to replace the defence regulations enabling wartime control. This new framework was formed mostly from two Acts in 1946 and 1947. One was the 1946 Hill Farming Act that set out grants to extend livestock farming and provide half the cost of farm improvement schemes including farmhouses, cottages, roads, bridges, drainage and installing private electricity schemes, although raising even half the cost was beyond the reach of many upland farmers.[82] The other and more significant was the 1947 Agriculture Act that aimed to ensure stability, greater efficiency and higher outputs through combining state support with self-regulation. Annual price reviews continued to set prices, while the state guaranteed markets and prices paid to farmers for around three-quarters of their outputs, operating a deficiency payments system to grant them the difference between guaranteed and market prices. Moreover, the Ministry of Food continued to purchase most output for disposal to the wholesale and retail trade, assisted by demand for most commodities exceeding output.[83] Finally, the government continued and expanded the wartime systems of grants and subsidies to boost farm efficiency.

The Act also abolished CWAECs and replaced them with County Agricultural Executive Committees (CAECs) to help farmers increase productivity through better working practices. The immediate needs of the post-war period differed little from wartime: Herbert Morrison told CAEC Chairs that 'today the assault is economic, but none the less deadly'.[84] The CAECs continued to issue cultivation orders, and regulated the continued rationing of feedstuffs and fertilisers, as well as contract services such as ploughing, pest control and labour. Other provisions of the Act enabled the Ministry to set out legal minimum standards of land husbandry and farms failing to achieve these could be subjected to direction followed by dispossession.

Nevertheless, there were departures from wartime approaches. While wartime committee boards were formed from members appointed as individuals, their successors were led by twelve members appointed by the Minister, of whom seven were nominees put forward by representatives of farmers, workers and landowners, granting authority to the NFU, the county landowners association and unions. NFU nominations, for example, were ratified by its central headquarters.[85] Moreover, government responded to concerns that some CWAECs had been over-zealous by creating bodies to temper their behaviour. An Agricultural Land Tribunal acted as a final court of appeal against CAEC decisions, an Agricultural Land Commission acquired and managed land that was not being managed efficiently, while a National Agricultural Advisory Service promoted best practice.[86] All this created a type of generalised 'productivism' that focused on intensive, industrially driven and expansionist agriculture where state and industrial institutions were bound together in ways not seen in other privately held industries.

In post-war Wales, the CWAECs operated initially in a manner like wartime. The minutes of the Radnorshire CWAEC and its sub-committees of one meeting in April 1947 comprised thirty-eight pages on topics including surveying farms, pest control, deploying labour and machinery, and supervising subsidy schemes.[87] Systems of similar complexity continued elsewhere such as in Cardiganshire, whose CWAEC employed an 'investigating shepherd' to expose discrepancies between the number of sheep he counted on hill farms and those claimed for through the hill sheep subsidy scheme.[88] Meanwhile, CWAECs continued to recruit Labour Camp Officers, Drainage Officers and Machinery Officers.[89]

However, food precarity meant that their most important activity remained cultivation orders, prompting the Minister for Agriculture to write to all CWAECs in February 1946 calling for greater food production, while in 1947 one hill farmer in Radnorshire noted that high snowfall meant that 'grass was never seen from ... January until the first week of May'.[90] In November 1945, for example, the Aberystwyth District Sub-committee of the Cardiganshire CWAEC issued fifty-six cultivation orders for 194 while continuing the minutiae of control; in August 1946 the committee ordered a farmer at Tresaith to destroy an unauthorised crop of ragwort in three fields otherwise it would carry out the task itself and charge the cost. Others were called to appear before the committee and their farms were visited by the chairman and his staff to ensure compliance, supported by threatening to ask the Ministry to authorise 'prosecution and dispossession' where lacking.[91] Nevertheless, the shape of agriculture began to evolve away from its wartime form. Grassland acreage and animal numbers grew as, although 'ploughing up' grants continued, the cultivation of wheat, barley and oats in some of the more marginal land used during wartime ceased.[92] Such acreages in Radnorshire dropped noticeably in the 1945 harvest.[93]

Other tasks continued although CWAECs' approaches continued to vary: the Pembrokeshire CWAEC and its nineteen sub-committees remained less likely to seize land than other committees, preferring to use such threats as a lever to ensure compliance in exceptional cases such as when a large farm was to split into small units in a way that might impact efficiency.[94] Inevitably, the efforts of many CWAECs were not always appreciated with a dispute in Merioneth prompting a councillor to accuse one of 'breeding little Hitlers'.[95]

The 1947 Act retained the Welsh Department of the Ministry of Agriculture, its status reflected by the establishment of separate Welsh functions for the new executive bodies. Aberystwyth remained an important administrative centre,[96] as the Headquarters of the National Advisory Service for Wales opened at Trawscoed near Aberystwyth incorporating a large farm as a demonstration centre, while the Agricultural Land Commission included a sub-commission for Wales.[97] Landowners could appeal to the Land Commissioner if dissatisfied with the compensation offered for land requisitioned, with, for example, the commissioner assessing fifteen cases in Denbighshire in 1947.[98]

The new system jointly discharged three functions. The first was supervising the maintenance of agricultural standards, imposing sanctions where necessary up to and including eviction. Yet sanctions remained a last resort given their unpopularity, and voluntary compliance by farmers was expected and commonplace, while the CAECs increasingly focused on monitoring and advising rather than direct intervention. Moreover, the CEACs initially retained most of their wartime activities such as their marshalling of a varied labour force throughout Wales. In mid-1947 it still included 8,000 prisoners of war, although 250 European volunteer workers were being recruited, as were 1,400 'gang workers' including 600 from Development Areas.[99] Cultivation orders remained in use in 1947 although the Ministry of Agriculture's Parliamentary Secretary had told the Pembroke CWAEC in the previous May that their future use would depend on the government's assessment of food supply. In late 1947 the Ministry told the same committee that it would be expected to make orders in at least the subsequent year to avoid too much arable land reverting to grassland.[100]

The second was administering subsidies, grants and regulations. In 1947 these included subsidies for hill sheep, hill cattle; bulls, boars and heavy horses kept for breeding purposes; as well as water supply. Some 3,000 ploughing grants were awarded in 1947 while in 1945–6, prior to the introduction of the CAECs, 51 per cent of hill sheep and hill cattle subsidies throughout England and Wales were made in Wales, covering some 1.3 million animals. Much of this routine work was carried out by officers of the National Agricultural Advisory Service, who worked at county level under the auspices of the CAECs.[101] Such activities took up most of the committees' time as they were well placed to intervene in disputes and manage the local administration of often complex regulations such as those covering milk production.

The third was responsibility for technical advice, again via the National Agricultural Advisory Service to whom some

CEAC staff were transferred.[102] This service aimed to extend the advisory work previously carried out by universities and colleges, combine it with those services provided by county councils, with coordination to be provided by CEAC district officers, and with adverts telling farmers that he was 'the man you must get to know' when seeking advice.[103] Finally, the work of surveying continued to identify farms most in need of guidance. Surveys were usually conducted by officers of the National Agricultural Advisory Service, but if surveys identified farmers requiring warnings or advice, then these activities were carried out by their local committees.

CONCLUSION

The government brought resource-based industries under its control but used different approaches across each. In coal, wartime intervention failed to increase productivity and served instead to demonstrate the inability of the industry to govern itself to the point that by 1945 few observers inside or outside the industry were arguing credibly against nationalisation. Moreover, while the need for efficiency encapsulated by the Reid Report was widely accepted, the history of the industry meant that social justice was never absent in debate. These factors combined to prompt the amalgamation of the industry under a Morrissonian public corporation that excluded unions from formal management structures within an approach described aptly by Harold Macmillan as 'not socialism' but 'state capitalism'.[104] Nationalisation, however, was more of a reaction to wartime failure than a fully developed plan. It did little to immediately calm industrial relations while the linked problem of often poor productivity could only be addressed over the long term through rationalisation coupled with large-scale investment.

In agriculture, state-sponsored wartime modernisation prompted the abandonment of nationalisation in favour of consolidating and refining wartime achievements. Consolidation meant replacing wartime committees with those that carried out many of the same tasks. Refinement meant implicit corporatism as the occasional excesses of wartime committees was addressed by reconstituting them as regulated bodies formed from interest representatives, whose activities were conducted in tandem with new bodies such as the Agricultural Land Tribunal. Importantly, the NFU was unique among privately held British industries in having a statutory right to consultation over prices received for their products,[105] while finally, the industry was enveloped in a system of state financial support.

In the steel industry, the success of the quasi-corporatist wartime controls relying on voluntary cooperation prompted an attempt at continuation through the Control Board. Although this approach was successful and the remodelling and modernisation of the south Wales steel industry progressed, the inclusion of the industry in the 1945 manifesto as a target for nationalisation meant that the cabinet eventually agreed to bring forward a bill to take the industry into public ownership, although the model adopted was the least disruptive.

All this meant that the process of recasting governance across different industries was uneven.[106] Such unevenness was the final legacy of wartime industrial governance as the state retained a central role, but its development of governance mechanisms was pragmatic and flexible, characterised by incremental experimentation and ceaseless debate.

Notes

1 J. Tomlinson, *Democratic Socialism and Economic Policy: The Atlee Years, 1945–1951* (Cambridge University Press, 1997), pp. 99–100.
2 The Labour Party, *Let Us Face the Future* (Labour Party, 1945).
3 *Herbert Morrison, Socialization and Transport* (1933), p. 149; cited in Tomlinson, *Democratic Socialism and Economic Policy*, p. 96.

4   Lord Citrine, *Two Careers* (Hutchinson, 1967), p. 263.
5   Supple, *History of the British Coal Industry*, pp. 611–12.
6   Court, *Coal*, p. 391.
7   TNA, POWE 37/77, *Technical Advisory Committee*, 15–16 November, 5; 21 September 1944, 1.
8   *Coal Mining: Report of the Technical Advisory Committee* (Cmd 6610) (HMSO, 1945), 2.
9   Supple, *History of the British Coal Industry*, p. 625.
10 The Labour Party, *Let Us Face the Future*.
11 Arnot, *The Miners*, pp. 127–8.
12 A. Horner, *Incorrigible Rebel* (MacGibbon and Kee, 1960), p. 179.
13 N. Fishman, *Arthur Horner, Volume 2* (Lawrence & Wishart, 2010) pp. 656, 662, 665.
14 K. O. Morgan, *Labour in Power* (Oxford University Press, 1985), p. 105; Citrine, *Two Careers*, pp. 247–8.
15 *Economist*, 'The Coal Board Takes Over', 20 July 1945, 108.
16 TNA, POWE 22/179, *Extracts from Notes of NUM Deputation to the Prime Minister*, 16 April 1947, 1–2.
17 SWML, *SWMF Annual Conference Report 1944, Presidential Address*, 22.
18 NLW, *MSWCOA General Meeting Minutes*, 22 February 1944.
19 I. Zweiniger-Bargielowska, 'Colliery Managers and Nationalisation: The Experience in South Wales', *Business History*, 34/4 (1992), 59–78 (68).
20 Francis and Smith, *The Fed*, pp. 433–5.
21 Fishman, *Arthur Horner, Volume 2*, p. 646.
22 *The Miner*, vol. 1, June/July 1945, *Editor's Notes, The General Election*, 3.
23 Williams (ed.), *DWHS 1700–1974, vol. 1*, pp. 307–8.
24 TNA, COAL 6/151, *NCB South Western Divisional Board Minutes*, 5 November 1946.
25 TNA, POWE 22/179, *Unofficial Stoppages*, 19 June 1947; *Western Mail*, 'Coal General Asks for Square Deal', 14 December 1946.
26 *Pontypridd Observer*, 'Miners' Dream a Reality', 4 January 1947; I. Zweiniger-Bargielowska, 'South Wales miners' attitudes towards nationalization: an essay in oral history', *Llafur* 6/3 (1994) 70–84 (79).
27 TNA, COAL 6/151, *NCB South Western Divisional Board Minutes*, 7 January 1947; *Pontypridd Observer*, 'Coal Board Appointment', 28 December 1947.
28 S. Broomfield, 'South Wales During the Second World War: The Coal Industry and its Community' (unpublished doctoral dissertation, University of Wales, 1979), 661.
29 TNA, POWE 22/179, *NCB Chair to Minister of Fuel and Power*, 15 May 1947; COAL 6/151, *NCB South Western Divisional Board Minutes*, 13 May 1947.
30 *Western Mail*, 'Welsh Miners' Sunday Work', 18 February 1947.
31 *South Wales Coalfield, Regional Survey Report, 1946*, 60–1, 64–7.
32 *Annual Report and Statement of Accounts of the National Coal Board, 1946–7* (HMSO, 1948), 84.
33 Jones, 'Coal', in Thomas (ed.), *Studies in Expansion*, pp. 89–110 (p. 109).

34 *Government Action, 1947–8*, 6; *Annual Report and Statement of Accounts of the National Coal Board, 1946–47*, 10.
35 *South Wales Coalfield, Regional Survey Report, 1946*, 59; Jones, 'Coal', in Thomas (ed.), *Studies in Expansion*, pp. 89–110 (p. 93).
36 *Wales and Monmouthshire: Report of Government Action for the Year ended 30 June 1947* (Cmd 7267) (HMSO, 1947), 9; TNA, COAL 6/151, *NCB South Western Divisional Board Minutes*, 19 November 1947.
37 *DWHS*, vol. 1, p. 336.
38 *Western Mail*, 'Coal: Hyndley Calls Wales to the Great Task', 23 September 1946.
39 TNA, POWE 22/179, *Dispute Notice*, 6 June 1947.
40 TNA, POWE 22/179, *Note on Minister's Meeting with the Executive Committee of the South Wales NUM*, 9 June 1947, 1.
41 *Annual Report and Statement of Accounts of the National Coal Board, 1946–47*, 174–5, 182–3; *Western Mail*, 'Coal: Wales Up to Second Place', 20 October 1947.
42 TNA, COAL 6/152, *NCB South Western Divisional Board Minutes*, 23 November 1948.
43 Burn, *The Steel Industry, 1939–1959*, pp. 78, 173; *Iron and Steel Industry: Reports by the British Iron and Steel Federation and the Joint Iron Council* (Cmd 6811) (HMSO, 1946).
44 Burn, *The Steel Industry, 1939–1959*, p. 69.
45 Keeling and Wright, *The Development of the Modern British Steel Industry*, p. 146.
46 *Western Mail*, '£170 a Week Chief for Steel Board', 6 September 1946.
47 Keeling and Wright, *The Development of the Modern British Steel Industry*, p. 100.
48 Morgan, *Labour in Power*, pp. 110–11.
49 P. Clarke, *The Cripps Version* (Allen Lane, 2002), p. 383.
50 A. Danchev, *Oliver Franks, Founding Father* (Clarendon Press, 1993), p. 54.
51 Lorenz, *GKN*, p. 86.
52 R. Ranieri, 'The Government's Decision to Nationalize Steel', in R. Millward and J. Singleton, *The Political Economy of Nationalization in Britain, 1920–1950* (Cambridge University Press, 1995), pp. 275–308 (pp. 292–5).
53 *Iron and Steel Industry: Reports by the British Iron and Steel Federation and the Joint Iron Council*, 13; *Wales and Monmouthshire: Report of Government Action for the Year ended 30 June 1947*, 11–13.
54 *Iron and Coal Trades Review, Technical Survey of the Hawarden Bridge Steelworks of John Summers and Sons Limited*, 1953, 5.
55 Smith, *A Century of Shotton Steel*, p. 39.
56 *Wales and Monmouthshire: A Summary of Government Action 1st August, 1945–31st July, 1946*, 16.
57 K. Warren, *The British Iron and Steel Industry since 1840* (G. Bell and Son, 1970), p. 205.
58 J. Driscoll, 'Steel', in Thomas, *The Welsh Economy*, pp. 114–37 (p. 117).
59 Warren, *The British Iron and Steel Sheet Industry Since 1840*, p. 210.
60 Hansard (Commons), *17 October 1944, vol. 403, col. 2323*.
61 LSE Digital Library, DL1HD01, *Diary of Hugh Dalton*, 27 January 1945.

62 TNA, BE 1/379, *Scheme for the Modernisation and Development of Sheet and Tinplate Production in South Wales*, April 1947, 5.
63 *Western Mail*, 'Strip Mill for Port Talbot', 29 January 1945.
64 *Iron and Steel Industry: Reports by the British Iron and Steel Federation and the Joint Iron Council*, 13–17.
65 *Western Mail*, 'Scrap Old Mills or Welsh Tin Trade "Doomed"', 3 May 1946.
66 TNA, BE 1/379, *Scheme for the Modernisation and Development of Sheet and Tinplate Production in South Wales*, April 1947, 3; The Tinplate Division of the Steel Company of Wales Ltd, *Trostre and Velindre Works: An Illustrated Description of Plant and Process*, 1.
67 TNA, BE 1/379, *Scheme for the Modernisation and Development of Sheet and Tinplate Production in South Wales*, April 1947, 8.
68 TNA, T 228/147, *Lazards to Governor of the Bank of England*, 9 December 1946; Richard Saville, 'Commanding Heights: The Nationalization Programme', in *Labour's High Noon: The Government and the Economy, 1945–51* (Lawrence & Wishart: 1993), pp. 37–60 (p. 46).
69 TNA, T 228/147, *F. Lee, Ministry of Supply, to HM Treasury*, 20 June 1947, 2; J. Bamford, *HM Treasury, to Ministry of Supply*, 24 June 1947.
70 *DWHS*, vol. 1, p. 356.
71 Minchanton, *The British Tinplate Industry*, p. 239; Glamorgan Archives, DITSC/30, *Iron and Steel Trade Confederation Reports*, 30 September 1946, 161.
72 Warren, *The British Iron and Steel Sheet Industry*, p. 247.
73 *Wales and Monmouthshire: Government Action, 1947*, 12.
74 Warren, *The British Iron and Steel Sheet Industry*, p. 242.
75 Steel Company of Wales, *The City of Steel* (Steel Company of Wales, undated), 2–3.
76 G. Cox, P. Lowe and M. Winter, 'From State Direction to Self-regulation: The Historical Development of Corporatism in British Agriculture', *Policy & Politics*, 14/4 (1986), 475–90 (479).
77 Labour Party, *Let Us Face the Future*.
78 M. Tichelar, 'The Labour Party, Agricultural Policy and the Retreat from Rural Land Nationalisation During the Second World War', *The Agricultural History Review*, 51/ 2 (2003), 209–25 (219–22).
79 Smith, *Hawarden*, p. 37.
80 TNA, MAF 80/4161, *Radnorshire County War Executive Agricultural Committee Minutes*, 29 April 1947, 267.
81 Martin, *The Development of Modern Agriculture*, p. 73; I. Zweiniger-Bargielowska, *Austerity in Britain: Rationing, Controls, and Consumption, 1939–1955* (Oxford University Press, 2000), p. 218.
82 *Wales and Monmouthshire: Government Action, 1947*, 24; Moore-Colyer, *Farming in Wales*, p. 60.
83 Martin, *The Development of Modern Agriculture*, pp. 70–1.
84 Short, *Battle of the Fields*, p. 377.
85 Cox et al., 'From State Direction to Self-regulation', p. 481.
86 R. Colyer-Moore, *Mans' Proper Study* (Gomer Press, 1982) pp. 66–7.

87 TNA, MAF 80/4161, *Radnorshire County War Executive Agricultural Committee Minutes*.
88 TNA, MAF 80/3728, *Emergency Meeting of the Executive Committee*, 28 November 1945.
89 As examples, see *Western Mail*, 'Public Appointments', 2 May 1947, 18 May 1946, 17 July 1946.
90 Lewis, *Henfryn*, p. 106; TNA, MAF 80/4641, *Painscastle District Committee Minutes*, 28 February 1946, 487.
91 TNA, MAF 80/3728, *Cardiganshire County War Executive Agricultural Committee, Executive Committee Meeting*, 22 November 1945, 4; 2 August 1946, 2; 8 June 1946, 3.
92 *DWHS, vol. 1*, p. 200.
93 TNA, MAF 80/4161, *Radnorshire County War Executive Agricultural Committee minutes*, 25 February 1946.
94 TNA, MAF 80/4124, *Pembroke County War Executive Agricultural Committee, Executive Committee Meeting*, 18 December 1946, 2 January 1947.
95 *Western Mail*, 'Housing Site was Ploughed', 23 June 1947.
96 *Wales and Monmouthshire: Report of Government Action for the Year ended 30th June 1948*, 18.
97 *Western Mail*, 'Welsh Land Commission', 9 December 1947.
98 TNA, MAF 112/102, *Lands Taken Over*, 29 August 1947.
99 *Government Action 1946–47*, 21.
100 TNA, MAF 80/4124, *Pembroke County War Executive Agricultural Committee, Executive Committee Meeting*, 1 May 1947, 4; 7 May 1946, 2; 9 July 1947, 1.
101 *Wales and Monmouthshire: A Summary of Government Action 1st August 1945–31st July 1946*, 21; *Wales and Monmouthshire: Government Action 1947*, 21, 23.
102 TNA, MAF 80/4124, *Pembroke County War Executive Agricultural Committee, Executive Committee Meeting*, 1 October 1946, 2.
103 J. Coggins, 'Science and the Farmer; the Development of Agriculture in West Wales, 1900–1950' (unpublished doctoral dissertation, University of Wales, Trinity St Davids, 2018), 276; *Western Mail*, 'A Farmer's Service', 28 December 1946.
104 Hansard (Commons), *20 May 1946, vol. 423, cols 44–153 (col. 133)*.
105 Bowers, 'British Agricultural Policy since the Second World War', 67.
106 Edgerton, *Warfare State*, p. 95.

CONCLUSION

This book argues that the governance of industrial mobilisation throughout regional Britain during rearmament, wartime and reconversion has been neglected, and that a case study of Wales illuminates its processes and achievements. It began by setting out three aims: to map mobilisation; to detail the governance of mobilisation; and to assess the extent to which wartime governance influenced post-war industrial policy.

The book makes three arguments whose contours are reflected across other regions, helping to explain the broader trajectory of the state's mobilisation of industry throughout Britain across war and peace. The first is that mobilisation was protracted but ultimately successful. Pre-war rearmament barely impacted on Wales, where unemployment at the end of 1938 was double the UK average. Limited impact stemmed from discontinuities between the structure of the Welsh economy and how the requirements of rearmament tended towards aircraft construction and shipbuilding. Meanwhile, perceptions in Whitehall and of many industrialists were that Wales was unsuitable for secondary industries. The result was that, while demand for raw materials produced there was buoyant, few factories were under construction by the end of 1938 and even these were often the result of protracted disputes. Notably, the only aircraft factory in Wales, Vickers-Armstrong at Broughton, was located so close to the border that both management and officials knew it as the 'Chester factory'. None of this was helped by the absence of formal representation within Whitehall governing structures, in contrast to Scotland whose interests were assisted by its more diversified economy and administrative presence via the Scottish Office.

These dynamics evolved as war broke out. One change was the activation of the CWAECs and their state-sponsored marshalling and modernisation of agriculture. Meanwhile, metal manufacturing plants were at full capacity under their Ministry of Supply mandated Control functions, although little changed within the restive coal mining industry that was left in its peacetime shape. Finally, more secondary manufacturing activity arrived but, even in early 1940, industrialists were complaining furiously about the lack of contracts, and poor or non-existent governance over munitions production.

Nevertheless, by mid-1940 the end of the 'phoney war' combined with the formation of the coalition government and air raids on major cities to prompt an upsurge in munitions manufacturing as new factories joined the few existing plants switching from peacetime goods. The air raid threat declined subsequently but inflows to Wales continued given the availability there of labour reserves formed primarily from unoccupied females who could be directed towards industrial employment. From 1942 ammunition surpluses prompted employment to fall in most state-owned ROFs, but the emergence of coordinated governance meant that such declines could be offset by the continued inflow of manufacturing businesses often contracted to and financially supported by the Ministry of Aircraft Production. The dynamic of the 1930s where industrialists were reluctant to locate in Wales reversed and by 1944 many thousands of munitions employees worked for a mass of private employers. However, the low starting point meant that reaching peak munitions production was a protracted process, reflecting broader trends throughout Britain where production did not peak until 1944.

Meanwhile, metal manufacturing plants continued at full capacity and, although no new steel plants were constructed, the state supported the modernisation of some facilities as well as the construction of aluminium plants. The enforced run-down of tinplate proved contentious given its localised importance as an employer but was completed successfully. Within agriculture, although much of the increased output was spurred by the reallocation of land towards arable production as opposed to rising crop yields, this was still a significant achievement marshalled by the CWAECS. The exception to success was, however, coal mining whose productivity and output declined continuously. Effective intervention proved too difficult given the combination of a militant and well-organised labour force facing poor pay and conditions, intransigent owners, and a divided government unable to impose reforms on either side of industry. Nevertheless, unemployment and strike data both reflect the overall success of industrial mobilisation throughout the economy, as do the rapid increases in nationwide production. Unemployment in Wales was eliminated while industrial action was concentrated within coal mining and tinplate, and was largely absent elsewhere.

The second argument is that the development of wartime governance was characterised by piecemeal and pragmatic advances driven by force of circumstances around individual industries, each subjected to different approaches. Summarising these structures is challenging given their complexity and variety, but Table 1 sets out a typology of their primary components by industry.

Table 1: Wartime industrial governance

	Munitions	Coal	Metal Manufacturing	Agriculture
Industrial ownership	Mainly private	Private	Private	Private
Date of effective implementation	1942	n/a	Varied	1939
Ministerial responsibility	Cross-ministerial	Ministry of Fuel and Power (post-1942)	Ministry of Supply (and Raw Material Controls)	Ministry of Agriculture (and CWAECs)
Regional structures	Yes	Yes	No	Yes
Regional administrative boundaries	Civil defence regions	Coalfield groupings	N/A	Counties

One commonality is that most industrial activity remained privately owned but under state direction. The only partial exception was munitions manufacturing where the Ministry of Supply owned and managed ROFs, while some other plants were owned and managed by the Admiralty. In Wales, this division of ownership meant that around one-third of munitions manufacturing employees worked for state concerns while the rest worked for private businesses. Meanwhile, workers within metal manufacture, coal mining and agriculture were all employed by private concerns, or often self-employed in the latter industry. Nevertheless, the state dominated the overall production environment. It controlled prices and profits as well as the allocation of raw materials and was usually the sole or primary purchaser of items produced. Moreover, businesses often received financial support either directly from the state or via state mandated industry-specific redistributive systems.

In munitions manufacture, the Ministry of Supply provided agency factories and paid management fees, most notably for ICI while the Ministry of Aircraft Production often financed machine tools and other equipment. Coal mining became increasingly dependent on financial support channelled by the coal charges account. While this system was not designed as a system of state subsidy but rather to redistribute resources within the industry, it was administered after 1942 by the Ministry of Fuel and Power. Within steel, some businesses received government financial support while an industry-run levy on purchases that subsidised raw material and machinery imports was repurposed in 1941 to subsidise high-cost firms subject to profitability caps. Yet this approach became increasingly dependent on state subsidies within a system notable for its opaqueness and complexity. Finally, farmers benefited from state financial support managed by the CWAECS that included credit for agricultural improvements, and subsidies including those covering hill farms and drainage.

Crucially, the pace at which governance was implemented varied substantially by industry. Two industries began the war with approaches that, if not finalised, had reached an advanced stage. One was agriculture, where the Ministry of Agriculture prepared a county committee structure for wartime implementation. The other was metals manufacturing, where repurposed trade associations buttressed with industry secondees and statutory control orders were also ready to be activated, although their operational specifics were left to wartime experimentation.

Governance structures, however, were less advanced elsewhere. In munitions manufacture, disputes between the three supply ministries meant that attempts to coordinate production failed, apart from the Factory and Control Function created in 1941 and placed in the Board of Trade to ensure administrative neutrality. The three supply ministries ignored regional coordinating structures until labour constraints in 1942 incentivised their participation in the Ministry of Production's Regional Boards. Yet, in coal mining, attempts to govern the industry emerged slowly and ultimately failed. The problem was that both sides of industry were implacable opponents, and each could deploy political allies influential within the governing coalition. Wholesale structural reform was politically impossible, and the government initially refused to intervene. Nevertheless, the deteriorating state of the industry eventually forced intervention through a cumbersome system of 'Dual Control' that achieved little apart from highlighting the industry's shortcomings.

All this meant that the processes used to govern wartime industries were remarkably varied and complex, often developing haphazardly and protractedly. Looking at individual industries: munitions manufacture was eventually corralled by intra-ministerial regional committees without executive authority; coal mining was never successfully controlled as its post-1942 Regional Controllers could be ignored by owners on 'safety' grounds; agriculture was controlled by committees of rural worthies; and most metal manufacture was governed by rebadged trade associations operating autonomously to the point of effective independence. Variety within industries was common. Farmers' experiences depended on their location as Committee behaviour ranged from benevolent paternalism to quasi feudalism, while the various metals controls experimented with different mechanisms to control their sub-sectors before autonomously settling on the approach that they decided was the most effective. Their activities flexed according to circumstances. One example was how allocating metals for manufacturing end uses varied widely. Meanwhile, some metal manufacturing businesses were subject to concentration schemes to remove excess capacity, others were encouraged to amalgamate to drive greater productivity, while where capacity was lacking the state often funded expansions or new plants.

In December 1944 *The Economist* published a gently satirical assessment entitled 'Lessons of Five Years' of the government's approach to industrial governance. It identified a four-stage process. The first stage opened when an 'outside critic' identified an approaching problem within production and suggested a remedy, to which the government responded by arguing that the problem 'may never arise' and that the proposed solution was 'politically impossible and administratively unworkable'. The second stage began when the problem arrived. The government responded that 'surprises are inevitable in war' before appealing for voluntary cooperation as there is 'no time to deal with the matter thoroughly'. The third stage was the 'belated acceptance, under further pressure' by the government of the remedy suggested earlier. The final stage occurred later when a White Paper was issued to 'illustrate the magnificent results obtained by the energy and forethought of His Majesty's Government'.[1]

Much of this portrait is accurate. While the lessons of the First World War prompted the pre-war development of a comprehensive system of agricultural control, departures elsewhere from the 'business as normal' approach that characterised much of 1930s rearmament were gradual and reluctant. The state gradually extended its authority over production, but usually only after voluntarist approaches to solve capacity constraints had failed as governance structures were either absent or lacked sufficient coordinating authority. These dynamics meant that governance developed at varying speeds. This was most apparent within munitions manufacture, but in all activities apart from agriculture the state was consistently reluctant to impose centralised solutions featuring powerful executive bodies who could deploy statutory authority. A similar dynamic was apparent within labour governance, where control was extended gradually as Bevin preferred to use voluntarist approaches, although the unchallenged position of his ministry within labour policy combined with his own status across the labour movement to ensure that this process was far less fraught than that within munitions production. The general preference for administrative experimentation and voluntarism was prompted by factors including lessons learnt from the First World War such as those within agriculture, political imperatives such as those surrounding coal mining, but the most important impulse was reacting to force of circumstances.

In 1947 former wartime Ministry of Supply Permanent Secretary Oliver Franks reflected on the dynamic and fluent nature of wartime governance. While accepting that the war was a 'prolonged exercise in central planning and control', he argued against any notion of his Ministry being a 'great machine' responding to government priorities through issuing a 'cloud of detailed instructions to manufacturers'. Instead, the process was 'dialectical' and the Ministry 'worked by no calm and established routine … it was full of intellectual energy and the clash of competing ideas … few ideas survived long unexamined and uncontested'.[2] Furious and protracted arguments were a constant feature within and across the administrative machines governing production. While this is common within government organs and can prompt sclerosis, the shared commitment to the war effort meant that, apart from coal mining, such arguments eventually resulted in structures at all levels, ranging from the Lord President's Committee to the Wales Regional Board, that could marshal and direct production.

Crucially, *The Economist* also argued correctly that the 'machine' of state-mandated industrial mobilisation 'does run, and to good purpose'.[3] All types of munitions manufacture increased more than sixfold between the end of 1939 and the production peak of early 1944. Meanwhile, arable production grew rapidly, and steel production remained sufficient to meet requirements, although the exception to success was coal mining whose productivity and output declined steadily. Although Edgerton highlights the undeniable importance of imports and the UK's central position within its global trading network to the war effort,[4] there is no doubt as to the overall effectiveness of industrial mobilisation.

Administrative improvisation means that while regional structures eventually played an important role within mobilisation, their shapes varied. The most successful example was within munitions manufacturing where Regional Boards eventually emerged under the Ministry of Production as effective agents of industrial planning. They unified the diverse strands of governance existing within ministries involved with munitions manufacturing into manageable units where information could be shared to enable private businesses to be coordinated, while identifying and exploiting local pockets of labour capacity. The evolution of these structures was paralleled by the changing nature of relationships between businesses and the state. In 1940 factory relocations barely required permits or official authorisations. By the following year, however, relocations required authorisation from the Factory and Storage Control Function and were also subject from mid-1942 to the cross-departmental remit of the Wales Regional Board. Nevertheless, the basis of their operations was the consent of the ministries whose representatives formed each board, while they did not influence the formation of national production priorities and programmes which by necessity remained centralised.

Successful localised governance was also apparent within agriculture, constituted at county level and overseen by Wales-specific Ministry of Agriculture functions. While there were tensions between the CWAECS and those that they governed, and their impact on crop yields may have been less than often assumed, their 'ploughing up' campaigns were effective in increasing arable output. Far less successful, however, were regional functions within coal mining, hobbled by the reluctance of either side of industry to cooperate as well as by their lack of powers. A voluntaristic approach was effective when labour supply constraints incentivised supply ministries to cooperate but failed in coal mining. Finally, regional structures were absent from metal manufacturing controls as there was no need to vertically sub-divide governance by geography within governance functions already horizontally sub-divided by industrial specialisation.

The third argument is that wartime governance experiences influenced the creation of the post-war economic settlement, even if the absence of the motivating and unifying impacts of war would progressively reduce the effectiveness of governmental administrative machinery. Although the outbreak of war prompted the government's suspension of Regional Policy, the need to maximise munitions production eventually gave rise to complex machinery governing industrial location. Their success meant that Dalton adapted wartime mechanisms when developing regional policy for the post-war environment that would help achieve his goal of full employment. But post-war policy did not represent an acceptance of the Barlow Report's proposal for an all-powerful national body to direct industry, instead owing its genesis to the incremental, complex and opaque nature of wartime industrial governance.[5]

Links between wartime circumstances and the post-war iteration of Regional Policy were reflected by its implementation before the war ended. Two years before the war ended, the Factory and Storage Control Function was handling investment queries from industrialists and asking them to locate in Wales. Its investment promotion activities increased in the last year of the war and were reinforced by the Ministry of Production's construction of advance factories. Handling queries and constructing factories in a similar manner later emerged as key activities of state bodies far into the future, such as the Development Corporation for Wales from 1958 and the Welsh Development Agency from 1976. Finally, the effectiveness of such wartime activities was enhanced by the forceful interventions of Dalton's office directing companies to locate their new investment projects to Wales.

Linkages gained further importance after the war ended. The government repurposed wartime building licences into instruments guiding industrial location. Repurposing meant that the nil certificate regime was redundant, prompting its 1946 abolition even though they resembled the Industrial Development Certificates introduced subsequently. Regional Policy instruments such as WMIE were often manged by those who had carried out similar responsibilities in wartime. Finally, the survival of a permit-driven economy into the immediate post-war period supported the Board of Trade as it could help businesses locating in Development Areas obtain the factories, construction materials and raw materials needed to commence production. While not formally part of Regional Policy, assisting companies to obtain goods helped its successful implementation to attract a large volume of secondary industry within the Wales Development Area in a remarkably short period.

In agriculture, the wartime success of state-sponsored modernisation and control meant that state guidance was accepted throughout the industry and continued, although the occasional excesses of some wartime committees meant that they were subject to greater oversight. However, the wartime success of the arm's-length controls over metal manufacturing prompted pressure for a more corporatist approach short of nationalisation, but political dynamics within the Labour Party eventually led to nationalisation. The opposite lesson was learned from the failure to govern the coal industry. All sides accepted that structural reforms were inevitable, and it was quickly nationalised under a public corporation with little opposition.

Overall, the war prompted the creation of large-scale secondary manufacturing in Wales that helped eliminate unemployment while employing many women. It also legitimised state intervention throughout the UK, prompting arguments that if the state could create full employment in wartime, it should take responsibility for ensuring it in peacetime. From 1945 the newly formed Labour Government solidified intervention across primary and secondary industries across the UK, as well as agriculture, all the while learning from, and acting on, wartime experiences. The war years and their immediate aftermath solidified a new consensus as to state involvement, as the economy transitioned from a failing pre-war approach focused on businesses operating within a laissez-faire environment, towards one characterised by state intervention described by Egerton as a 'low-key war economy which was very slowly liberalised'.[6]

Even as the post-war consensus unravelled in the 1970s, the architects of its replacement recognised the war's importance in its creation. In 1976 Keith Joseph, a leading adviser to Margaret Thatcher, set out the foundations of a new approach to economic governance while arguing that the war had 'not only further increased the actual role of the state, but also increased belief in the efficacy, indeed the virtual omnicompetence of state intervention'.[7] Crucial aspects of this state-focused and regionally aware approach survived for some thirty years until replaced by one featuring impulses to reduce governmental interventions within tradable goods and services, prompting the return of deep and prolonged regional inequalities.

Notes

1 *The Economist*, 'Lessons of Five Years', 9 December 1944.
2 Franks, *Central Planning in War and Peace*, pp. 8–10.
3 *The Economist*, 'Lessons of Five Years', 9 December 1944.
4 Edgerton, *Britain's War Machine*.
5 Gooberman, 'Public Governance of Private Munitions Businesses in Regional Britain'.
6 Edgerton, *Warfare State*, p. 95.
7 Margaret Thatcher Foundation Archives, *Sir Keith Joseph, Stockton Lecture, 'Monetarism is not enough'*, 1976 (online). Available at *https://www.margaretthatcher.org/document/110796* (accessed 2 October 2024).

APPENDIX

Table 2: Labour force distribution, UK (000s)

	Jun-40		Jun-43		Change	
	Men	Women	Men	Women	Men	Women
Services	2,218	55	4,300	462	2,082	407
Civil defence, fire, police	292	53	253	70	-39	17
Group I	2,885	674	3,305	1,928	420	1,254
Group II	3,902	716	3,686	1,341	-216	625
Group III	5,373	3,863	3,430	3,431	-1,943	-432
Unemployed	434	211	44	16	-390	-195
Totals	**15,104**	**5,572**	**15,018**	**7,248**	**-86**	**1,676**

Notes:

Group I: Munitions industries, metal and metal-goods manufacture, engineering, motors, aircraft and other vehicles, shipbuilding and repairing, chemicals, explosives, oil, etc.

Group II: Basic industries, agriculture, mining, national and local government services, gas, water, and electricity supply, transport, and shipping.

Group III: Other manufacturing and services.

Source: Gowing, M. 'The Organisation of Manpower in Britain during the Second World War', *Journal of Contemporary History*, 7(1/2) (1972), 147–67 (150).

Figure 1: Days lost to industrial action, Wales, 1939–1947

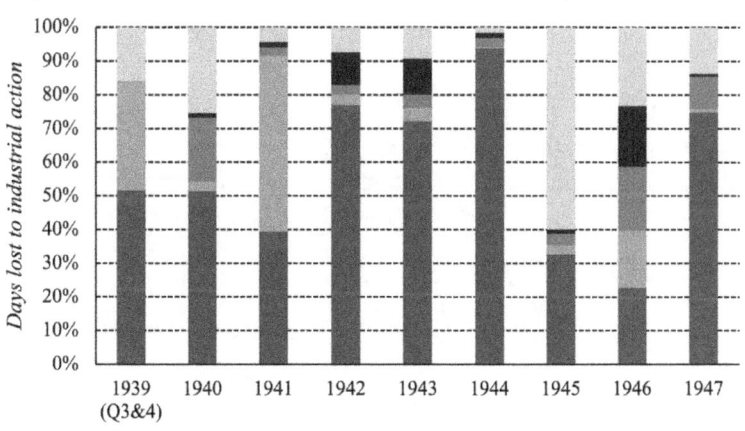

Source: TNA, LAB 34/56, *Trade Disputes, 1939* to LAB 34/62 *Trade Disputes, 1947*.

Figure 2: Days lost to industrial action, Wales, 1940–1945

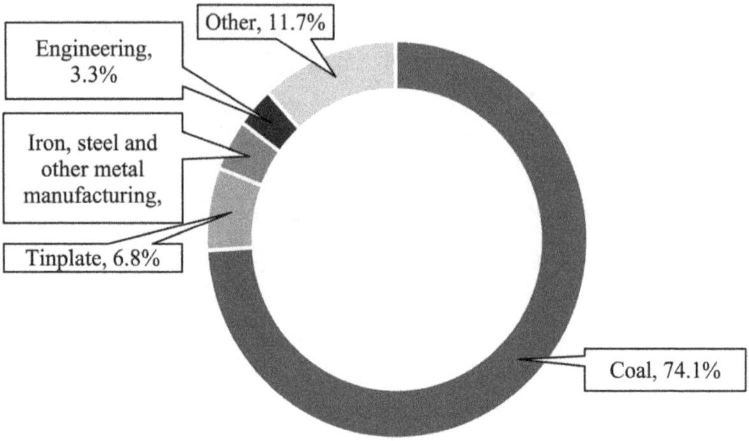

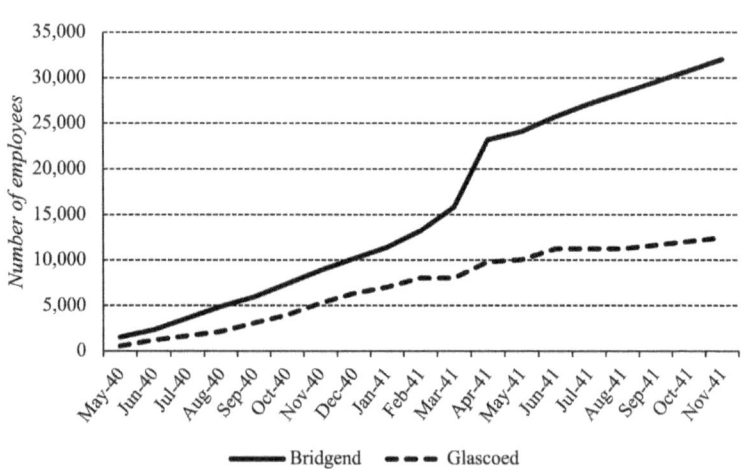

Source: TNA, LAB 34/57, *Trade Disputes, 1940*; 34/54 – LAB 34/60 *Trade Disputes, 1945.*

Figure 3: Employees at Bridgend and Glascoed ROFs, June 1940– November 1941

Note: Ordnance inspectors excluded from Bridgend data until April 1941.
Source: TNA, LAB 12/82, *Ministry of Labour Monthly Reports, Wales*

Table 3: ROF employees, 1939–1943

Type/ location	Number employed (December)					Peak employment		
	1939	1940	1941	1942	1943	Date	Number	Per cent female
Filling								
Bridgend	28	10,383	28,368	23,853	19,928	1942, March	32,570	59
Glascoed	0	6,691	11,482	10,829	10,902	1942, May	11,900	46
Explosive								
Pembrey	571	2,174	3,015	2,804	2,293	1942, April	3,050	0.4
Wrexham	0	531	8,435	8,247	4,438	1942, March	10,250	47
Engineering								
Cardiff	0	436	2,723	3,705	3,759	1943, August	4,020	43
Newport	0	707	2,223	2,405	2,340	1942, March	2,440	53
Hirwaun	0	0	0	4,830	8,453	1944, March	8,600	54
Totals	**599**	**20,922**	**56,246**	**56,673**	**52,113**		**72,830**	

Note: Construction workforce excluded.

Source: TNA, 102/272, *Employment at ROFs, 1939–1943; Females employed in ROFs.*

Figure 4: Production and output per head in the coal mining industry, UK, 1940–1945

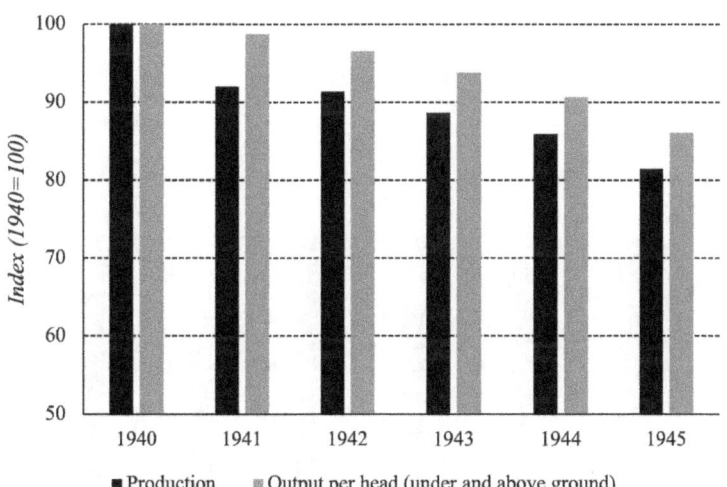

■ Production ■ Output per head (under and above ground)

Note: Data on productivity per coal face worker not available for Wales. Graph uses alternative measure of per head average output for all workers.

Source: Statistical Digest of the War, 75, 81.

Figure 5: Production and output per head in the coal mining industry, Wales, 1940–1945

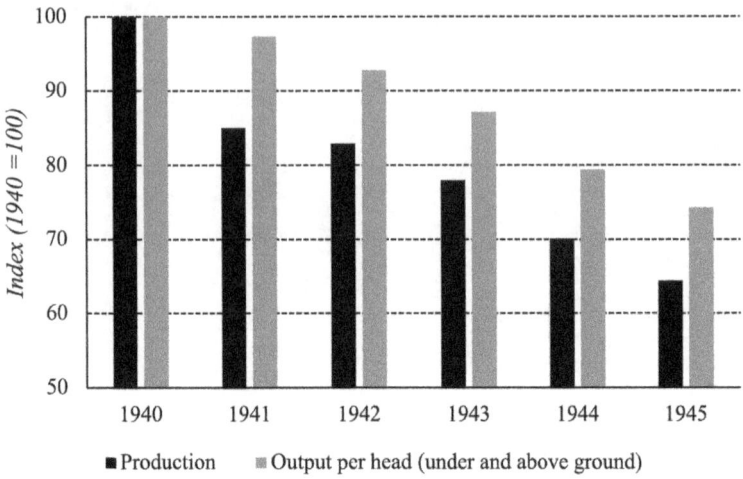

Note: Data on productivity per coal face worker not available.
Source: DWHS, vol. 1.

Figure 6: Production and deliveries of crude steel, UK, 1940–1945

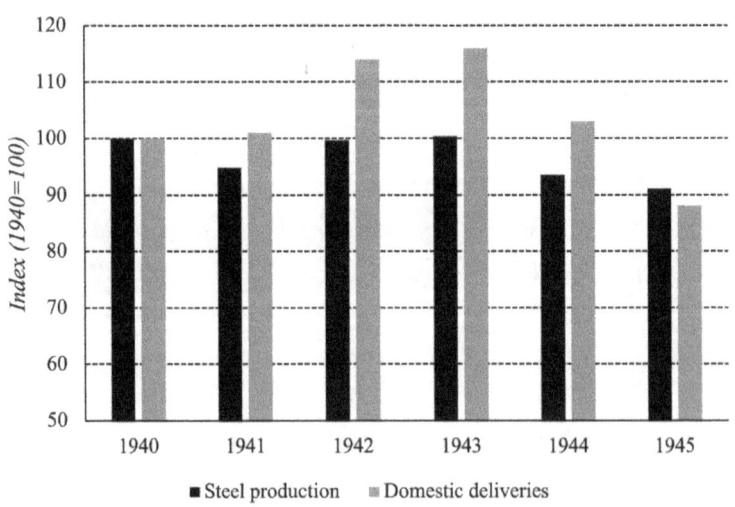

Source: Keeling and Wright, *The Development of the Modern British Steel Industry,* 60.

Figure 7: Production of steel ingots and castings, south Wales, 1940–1945

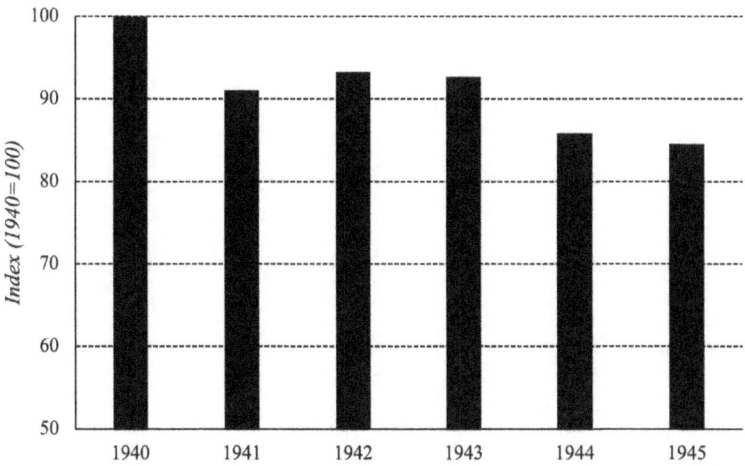

Note: Data not available for north Wales.

Source: DWHS, vol. 1, 355.

Table 4: Agricultural output (selected types), Britain, 1940–1944

Output type		1940	1944	Change	Percentage change
Wheat		1,628	3,134	1,506	93%
Barley	*Tons*	1,089	1,737	648	60%
Potatoes	*('000s)*	5,375	8,026	2,651	49%
Vegetables		2,596	3,387	791	30%
Cattle	*Number*	8,361	8,616	255	3%
Sheep and lambs	*on*	25,465	19,435	-6,030	-24%
Pigs	*holdings*	3,631	1,631	-2,000	-55%
Poultry	*('000s)*	62,121	38,481	-23,640	-38%

Source: *Statistical Digest of the War*, 59, 61.

Figure 8: Agricultural governance structures

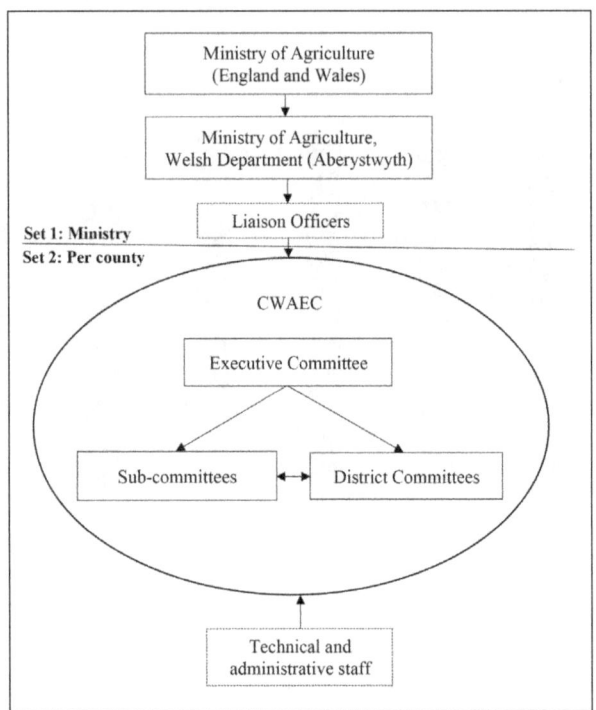

Source: Author's assessment.

Table 5: Agricultural output (selected types), Wales, 1940–1944

Output type		1940	1944	Change	Percentage change
Wheat		27	100	73	270%
Barley	*Tons*	26	61	35	135%
Potatoes	*('000s)*	138	390	252	183%
Turnips and swedes		322	469	147	46%
Cattle	*Number*	844	938	94	11%
Sheep and lambs	*on*	4,512	3,947	-565	-13%
Pigs	*holdings*	204	109	-95	-47%
Poultry	*('000s)*	3,884	3,314	-570	-15%

Source: DWHS, vol. 1, 217, 219, 221, 223, 235.

BIBLIOGRAPHY

ARCHIVES (main holdings consulted)

The National Archives
CAB, Cabinet Office Papers
LAB, Ministry of Labour and National Service, and related bodies
MAF, Ministry of Agriculture
BT, Board of Trade
T, Treasury
COAL, National Coal Board and related bodies
POWE, Ministry of Power and related bodies
SUPP, Ministry of Supply and successors
AVIA, Air Ministry and successor bodies, including the Ministry of Aircraft Production

National Library of Wales
Monmouthshire and South Wales Coalowners' Association
Women in World War 2, Manuscript Accounts

Gwent Archives
GKN Cwmbran

Glamorgan Archives
Iron and Steel Trades Confederation
Wales Industrial Estates Corporation

South Wales Miners' Library
South Wales Miners' Federation

London School of Economics
Diary of Hugh Dalton

AUTOBIOGRAPHIES AND MEMOIRS

Citrine, *Two Careers* (Hutchinson, 1967).
Dalton, H. *High Tide and After* (Frederick Muller, 1962).
Dalton, H. *The Fateful Years* (Frederick Muller, 1953).
Horner, A. *Incorrigible Rebel* (MacGibbon and Kee, 1960).
Jay, D. *Change and Fortune* (Hutchinson, 1980).
Lewis, G. *Henfryn, Radnorshire Hill Farming Life in the 1930s and 1940s* (Logaston Press, 2002).
Lyttleton, O. *The Memoirs of Lord Chandos* (The Bodley Head, 1962).
Pride, E. *Tinman's Progress* (University College Swansea, 1959).
Thomas, P. *Pupil to President, Memoirs of an Architect* (F. Lewis, 1963).

HANSARD

Volume 270, 10 November 1932
Volume 309, 2 March 1936
Volume 339, 6 October 1938
Volume 368, 21 January 1941
Volume 336, 23 May 1941
Volume 378, 24 March 1942
Volume 389, 13 May 1942
Volume 380, 11 June 1942
Volume 381, 30 June 1942
Volume 382, 5 August 1942
Volume 392, 13 October 1942
Volume 403, 17 August 1944
Volume 421, 9 April 1946
Volume 423, 20 May 1946
Volume 428, 28 October 1946

NEWSPAPERS

Birmingham Gazette
Caerphilly Journal
Economist
Flintshire Herald
Merthyr Express
Neath Guardian
North Wales Weekly News
Pontypridd Observer
Rhos Herald
South Wales Gazette
Times
Western Mail

OFFICIAL PUBLICATIONS

Annual Report of the National Coal Board 1947 (HMSO, 1948).
Ashworth, W. *Contracts and Finance* (HMSO, 1953).
Coal Mining. Report of the Technical Advisory Committee (Cmd. 6610) (HMSO, 1945).
Commission on the Constitution, Research Paper 8, Survey of the Welsh Economy (HMSO, 1973).
Court, W.H.B. *Coal* (HMSO, 1951).
Distribution of Industry (Cmd. 7540) (HMSO, 1945).
Eleventh Report from the Select Committee on National Expenditure (HMSO, 1942).
Employment Policy (Cmd. 6527) (HMSO, 1944).
Gibbs, N. *Grand Strategy*. (HMSO, 1956).
Hornby, W. *Factories and Plant* (HMSO, 1958).
Hurstfield, J. *The Control of Raw Materials* (HMSO, 1953).
Inman, P. *Labour in the Munition Industries* (HMSO, 1957).
Iron and Steel Industry-Reports by the British Iron and Steel Federation and The Joint Iron Council (Cmd. 6811) (HMSO, 1946).

Land at War, The Official Story of British Farming, 1939–1944 (HMSO, 1945).
Murray, K. A. H. *Agriculture* (HMSO, 1955).
Office of the Minister of Production (Cmd. 6337) (HMSO, 1942).
Parker, H. M. D. *Manpower* (HMSO, 1957).
Postan, M. M. *British War Production* (HMSO, 1952).
Report of the Committee on Regional Boards (Cmd. 6360) (HMSO, 1942).
Reports of Investigations into the Industrial Conditions in Certain Depressed Areas (Cmd. 4728) (HMSO, 1934).
Royal Commission on the Distribution of the Industrial Population (Cmd. 6153) (HMSO, 1940).
Scott J. D. and Hughes, R. *The Administration of War Production* (HMSO, 1955).
Second Report from the Select Committee on Estimates: Development Areas, Session 1955–56 (HMSO, 1956).
South Wales Coalfield, Regional Survey Report (Ministry of Fuel and Power, 1946).
Statement Relating to Defence (Cmd. 4827) (HMSO, 1935).
Tenth Report from the Select Committee on National Expenditure (HMSO, 1941).
Third Report of the Commissioner for Special Areas (Cmd. 5303) (HMSO, 1936).
Wales and Monmouthshire. A Summary of Government Action 1st August 1945–31st July 1946 (Cmd. 6938) (HMSO, 1946).
Wales and Monmouthshire. Report of Government Action for the Year ended 30 June 1947 (Cmd. 7267) (HMSO, 1947).
Wales and Monmouthshire. Report of Government Action for the Year ended 30th June 1948 (Cmd. 7532) (HMSO, 1948).
Welsh Reconstruction Advisory Council, *First Report* (HMSO, 1944).
Williams, L. J. *Digest of Welsh Historical Statistics 1700–1974, Vol. 1* (Welsh Office, 1985).
Williams, L. J. *Digest of Welsh Historical Statistics 1700–1974, Vol. 2* (Welsh Office, 1985).

REPORTS

Iron and Coal Trades Review. *Technical Survey of the Hawarden Bridge Steelworks of John Summers and Sons Limited*, 1953.

Labour Party, *Report of the Labour Party's Commission into Depressed Areas: South Wales*, 1937.

Mass Observation, *Mining Town*, 1942.

SECONDARY LITERATURE

Arnot, R. P., *The Miners in Crisis and War* (Allen and Unwin, 1961).

Ashcroft, B. and Taylor, J., 'The Effect of Regional Policy on the Movement of Industry in Great Britain', in D. Maclennan and J. Parr (eds), *Regional Policy, Past Experience and New Directions* (Wiley-Blackwell, 1979), pp. 43–64.

Baber, C. and Thomas, D., 'The Glamorgan Economy, 1914–1945', in A. H. John and G. Williams (eds), *Glamorgan County History, Volume V* (Glamorgan County History Trust, 1980), pp. 519–75.

Berryman, D., *North Wales Airfields in the Second World War* (Countryside Books, 2013).

Booth, A., 'The Second World War and the Development of Modern Regional Policy', *Economy and Society*, 11/1 (1988), 1–21.

Bowers, J. K., 'British Agricultural Policy Since the Second World War', *The Agricultural History Review*, 33/1 (1985), 66–76.

Brassley, P., 'Wartime policy and innovation', in Short, Watkins and Martin (eds), *The Front Line of Freedom*, pp. 36–54.

Broadberry, S. and Howlett, P., 'The United Kingdom: 'Victory at All Costs', in M. Harrison (ed.). *The Economics of World War II: Six Great Powers in International Comparison* (Cambridge University Press, 1998), pp. 43–80.

Broomfield, S., 'The Apprentice Boys Strikes of the Second World War', *Llafur*, 3/2 (1981), 53–67.

Bullock, A., *The Life and Times of Ernest Bevin, II, Minister of Labour, 1940–1945* (Heinemann, 1967).

Burn, D., *The Steel Industry, 1939–1959* (Cambridge University Press, 1961).

Calder, A., *The People's War, Britain 1939–1945* (Random House, 2012).

Carr, J. C. and Taplin, W., *History of the British Steel Industry* (Basil Blackwell, 1962).

Chambers, R., *Bless 'Em All* (Bridge Books, 1995).
Christensen, M., 'Royal Ordnance Factory, Cardiff (Llanishen), Part 1', *Quarterly Journal for British Industrial and Transport History*, 33 (2002), 31–42.
Christensen, M., 'Royal Ordnance Factory, Llanishen, Part 2', *Quarterly Journal for British Industrial and Transport History*, 34 (2002), 24–45.
Clegg, A., *History of British Trade Unions, Vol. 3* (Clarendon Press, 1994).
Clubb, M. J., *The Welsh Arsenal* (Bridgend, 2007).
Coombs, B. *British Tank Production and the War Economy, 1934–1945* (A&C Black, 2013).
Cox, G., Lowe, P. and Winter, M.. 'From State Direction to Self-regulation: the Historical Development of Corporatism in British Agriculture', *Policy & Politics*, 14/ 4 (1986), 475–90.
Crafts, N. and Mills, T. C., 'Rearmament to the Rescue? New Estimates of the Impact of "Keynesian" Policies in 1930s' Britain', *Journal of Economic History*, 73/4, 1077–1104.
Crafts, N., *Forging Ahead, Falling Behind and Fighting Back* (Cambridge University Press, 2018).
Crowcroft, R., '"Making a Reality of Collective Responsibility': The Lord President's Committee, Coalition, and the British State at War, 1941–42', *Contemporary British History*, 29/4 (2015), 539–62.
Danchev, A., *Oliver Franks, Founding Father* (Clarendon Press, 1993).
Davies, J., *A History of Wales* (Penguin, 1994).
Davies, J. D., *Britannia's Dragon: A Naval History of Wales* (The History Press, 2013).
Driscoll, J., 'Steel', in B. Thomas (ed.), *The Welsh Economy, Studies in Expansion* (University of Wales Press, 1962).
Edgerton, D., 'Technical Innovation, Industrial Capacity and Efficiency: Public Ownership and the British Military Aircraft Industry, 1935–48', *Business History*, 26/3 (1984), 247–79.
Edgerton, D., *Britain's War Machine* (Penguin, 2012).
Edgerton, D., *Warfare State: Britain, 1920–1970* (Cambridge University Press, 2005).
Elliot J. and Deneen, C., 'Iron, Steel and Aluminium', in C. Williams and A. Croll (eds), *The Gwent County History* (University of Wales Press, 2013).
Fishman, N., *Arthur Horner, Volume 2* (Lawrence and Wishart, 2010).

Forbes, N., 'Democracy at a Disadvantage? British Rearmament, the Shadow Factory Scheme and the Coming of War, 1936–40', *Economic History Yearbook/Jahrbuch für Wirtschaftsgeschichte* (2014), 49–70.

Francis, H. and Smith, D., *The Fed* (Lawrence and Wishart, 1980).

Franks, O., *Central Planning and Control and War and Peace* (London School of Economics, 1947).

French, D., *Raising Churchill's Army: The British Army and the War against Germany 1919–1945* (Oxford University Press, 2001).

Gildart, K., 'Coal Strikes on the Home Front: Miners' Militancy and Socialist Politics in the Second World War', *Twentieth Century British History*, 20/2 (2009), 121–51.

Gooberman, L., '"Revolution in the Coalfields": Industrial Relations in Wartime South Wales, 1939–45', *Labor History*, 63/1 (2022), 55–72.

Gooberman, L., 'Public Governance of Private Munitions Businesses in Regional Britain, the Case of Wales, 1938 to 1945', *Business History* (2021), 1–20.

Gooberman, L., 'The Emergence of Regional Industrial Policy in Britain, the Case of Wales, 1939 to 1947', *Enterprise and Society* (2023), published online before print.

Gooberman, L., *From Depression to Devolution, Government and Economy in Wales, 1934–2006* (University of Wales Press, 2017).

Gooberman L. and Curtis, B., 'The Age of Factories: the Rise and Fall of Manufacturing in South Wales, 1945–1985', in L. Miskell (ed.), *New Perspectives on Welsh Industrial History* (University of Wales Press, 2020), pp. 181–206.

Gordon, G. A. H., *British Seapower and Procurement Between the Wars* (Naval Institute Press, 1988).

Gowing, M., 'The Organisation of Manpower in Britain during the Second World War', *Journal of Contemporary History*, 7/1–2 (1972), 147–67.

Gray, S., *Steam Power and Sea Power, Coal, The Royal Navy and the British Empire, c.1870–1914* (Palgrave Macmillan, 2018).

Gwyn, D., *Welsh Slate, Archaeology and History of an Industry* (RCAHMW, 2015).

Harris, C., *Redundancy and Recession in South Wales* (Basil Blackford, 1986).

Harrison, M., 'A Volume Index of the Total Munitions Output of the United Kingdom, 1939–1944', *Economic History Review*, 43 (1990), 657–66.

Hobsbawn, E., *Industry and Empire* (Penguin, 1969).

Holman, B., 'The Air Panic of 1935: British Press Opinion between Disarmament and Rearmament', *Journal of Contemporary History*, 46/2 (2011), 288–307.

Holmes, G., 'The First World War and Government Control', in C. Baber and L. J. Williams (eds), *Modern South Wales: Essays in Economic History* (University of Wales Press, 1986), pp. 206–21.

Hoover Ltd, *The Official Opening of the Hoover Factory at Pentrebach, Merthyr Tydfil* (Hoover, 1948).

Howell, C., 'Hidden Labours: The Domestic Service Industry in South Wales, 1871–1921', in L. Miskell (ed.), *New Perspectives on Welsh Industrial History* (University of Wales Press, 2022), pp. 75–102.

Howell, D., '"All or Nowt": The politics of the MFGB', in A. Campbell, N. Fishman and D. Howell (eds), *Miners, Unions, and Politics 1919–1947* (Routledge, 1996).

Howlett, P., 'New light through old windows: A new perspective on the British economy in the Second World War', *Journal of Contemporary History*, 28/2 (1993), 361–79.

Howlett, P., 'Resource Allocation in Wartime Britain: The Case of Steel, 1939–45', *Journal of Contemporary History*, 29/3 (1994), 523–44.

Hughes, A., *The Second World War in the Borough of Conwy* (Conwy Town Council, 2019).

Hutton, J., *An Illustrated History of Cardiff Docks, Vol. 3: Cardiff Railway Company and the Docks at War* (Silver Link Publishing, 2008).

Jeffreys, K., *The Churchill Coalition and Wartime Politics, 1940–1945* (Manchester University Press, 1995).

Jenkins, P., *Twenty by Fourteen, A History of the South Wales Tinplate Industry, 1700–1961* (Gomer, 1995).

Jones, E., *A History of GKN, Volume 2, 1918–1945* (Macmillan, 1990).

Jones, L., 'Coal', in Thomas (ed.), *Studies in Expansion*, pp. 89–110.

Keeling, B. S. and Wright, A. E. G., *The Development of the Modern British Steel Industry* (Longmans, 1964).

Lowe, C., *Colwyn Bay Accredited, The Wartime Experience* (Bridge Books, 2010).

MacKenzie, A., '"Public-spirited men": Economic Unionist Nationalism in Inter-War Scotland', *The Scottish Historical Review*, Vol. XCVI, 1/242 (2017), 87–109.

Macve, J., 'The search for Zinc Blende in Mid Cardiganshire during World War 2', *Ceredigion*, 11/3 (1992), 271–88.

Martin, J., 'The structural transformation of British agriculture: the resurgence of progressive high-input arable farming', in Short, Watkins and Martin (eds), *The Front Line of Freedom, British Farming in the Second World War*.

Martin, J., *The Development of Modern Agriculture; British Farming Since 1931* (Palgrave Macmillan, 2000).

Mass Observation, *An Enquiry into British War Production, Part 1, People in Production* (Penguin, 1942).

McCamley, N. J., *Disasters Underground* (Pen and Sword, 2004).

McCrone, G., *Regional Policy in Britain* (George Allen and Unwin, 1971).

McIlroy, J. and Campbell, A., 'Beyond Betteshanger: Order 1305 in the Scottish Coalfields during the Second World War, Part 1: Politics, Prosecutions and Protest', *Historical Studies in Industrial Relations*, 15 (2003), 27–72.

Medwyn Parry, R., *A History of the Royal Navy Propellant Factory, Caerwent* (pamphlet, undated).

Miller, C., *Planning and Profits, British Naval Armaments Manufacture and the Military Industrial Complex, 1918–1941* (Liverpool University Press, 2018).

Miller, C., *Planning and Profits: British Naval Armaments Manufacture and the Military-Industrial Complex 1918–1941* (Oxford University Press, 2018).

Minchanton, W. E., *The British Tinplate Industry* (Clarendon Press, 1957).

Montagu and Burgess-Wise, D., *Daimler Century* (Haynes Publishing, 1995).

Moore, B. C., Rhodes, J. and Tyler, P., 'Urban/rural Shift and the Evaluation of Regional Policy', *Regional Science and Urban Economics* 12/1 (1982), 139–57.

Moore, B., and Rhodes, J., 'Evaluating the Effects of British Regional Economic Policy', *The Economic Journal* 83/329 (1973), 87–110.

Moore-Colyer, R., 'The County War Agricultural Executive Committees: The Welsh Experience, 1939–45', *Welsh History Review*, 22 (2005), 558–87.

Moore-Colyer, R., *Farming in Wales, 1936–2011* (Y Lolfa, 2011).

Morgan, K. O., *Labour in Power* (Oxford University Press, 1985).

Ollerenshaw, P., *Northern Ireland in the Second World War: Politics, Economic Mobilisation and Society, 1939–45* (Manchester University Press, 2013).

Ollerenshaw. P., 'War, Industrial Mobilisation and Society in Northern Ireland, 1939–1945', *Contemporary European History*, 16/2 (2007), 169–97.

Parsons, D., *The Political Economy of British Regional Policy* (Routledge, 1988).

Peden, G., *Arms, Economics and British strategy: From Dreadnoughts to Hydrogen bombs.* (Cambridge University Press, 2007).

Peden, G., *British Rearmament and the Treasury, 1932–1939* (Scottish Academic Press, 1979).

Percival, G., *The Government's Industrial Estates in Wales 1936–1975* (WDA, 1978).

Phillips, L., *Pembroke Dockyard and the Old Navy, A Bicentennial History* (The History Press, 2014).

Pimlott, B. (ed.), *The Second World War Diary of Hugh Dalton* (Johnathan Cape, 1986).

Pimlott, B., *Hugh Dalton* (Johnathan Cape, 1985).

Pitfield, D. E., 'Regional Policy and the Long Run: Innovation and Location in the Iron and Steel Industry', *Business History*, 16/2 (1974), 160–74 (162–165).

Ranieri, R., 'The Government's Decision to Nationalize Steel', in R. Millward and J. Singleton, *The Political Economy of Nationalization in Britain, 1920–1950* (Cambridge University Press, 1995), pp. 275–308.

Reader, W. J., *Imperial Chemical Industries, Vol. II, The First Quarter Century 1926–1952* (Oxford University Press, 1975).

Redhead B. and Goodie, S., *The Summers of Shotton* (Hodder and Stoughton, 1987).

Robinson, A. G., 'The Overall Allocation of Resources', in D. N. Chester (ed.), *Lessons of the British War Economy* (Cambridge University Press, 1951), pp. 34–57.

Rollings, N., 'Whitehall and the Control of Prices and Profits in a Major War, 1919–1939', *The Historical Journal*, 44/2 (2001), 517–40.

Rosevear, S., 'Balancing Business and the Regions: British Distribution of Industry Policy and the Board of Trade, 1945–51', *Business History*, 40/1 (1998), 77–99.

Rowlands, T., *'Something Must Be Done'; South Wales V Whitehall, 1921–1951* (TTC Books, 2000).

Saville, R., 'Commanding Heights: the Nationalization Programme', in *Labour's High Noon, The Government and the Economy, 1945-51* (Lawrence and Wishart: 1993), 37–60 (46).

Scott, P., 'British Regional Policy 1945–51: A Lost Opportunity', *Twentieth Century British History*, 8/3 (1997), 358–82.

Scott, P., *Triumph of the South, A Regional Economic History of Early Twentieth Century* Britain (Ashgate, 2007).

Scranton, P. and Fridenson, P., *Reimagining Business History* (Johns Hopkins University Press, 2013).

Shay, R., *British Rearmament in the Thirties* (Princeton University Press, 1977).

Short, B., Watkins, C. and Martin, J. (eds), *The Front Line of Freedom; British Farming in the Second World War* (British Agricultural History Society, 2006).

Short, B., *The Battle of the Fields* (Boydell Press, 2014).

Skidelsky, R., *John Maynard Keynes* (Penguin, 2005).

Smith, D., *Hawarden, A Welsh Airfield, 1939–1979* (Clarington Press, 1980).

Smith, G., *A Century of Shotton Steel* (British Steel, 1996).

Steel Company of Wales, *The City of Steel* (Steel Company of Wales, undated)

Supple, B., *History of the British Coal Industry, Vol. 4* (Oxford University Press, 1987).

Taylor, A. J. P., *Beaverbrook* (Hamish Hamilton, 1972).

Thomas, B. (ed.), *The Welsh Economy: Studies in Expansion* (University of Wales Press, 1962).

Thomas, B., 'Post-war Expansion', in Thomas (ed.), *The Welsh Economy: Studies in Expansion*, pp. 30–50.

Thomas, B., 'Wales and the Atlantic Economy', in Thomas (ed.), *The Welsh Economy: Studies in Expansion*, pp. 1–30.

Thomas, D. A., 'War and the Economy: The South Wales Experience', in Baber and Williams (eds), *Modern South Wales: Essays in Economic History*, pp. 251–77.

Thomas, M., 'Rearmament and Economic Recovery in the late 1930s', *The Economic History Review*, 36/4 (1983), 552–79.

Thorpe, D. R., *Supermac, the Life of Harold Macmillan* (Pimlico, 2011).

Tichelar, M., 'The Labour Party, Agricultural Policy and the Retreat from Rural Land Nationalisation During the Second World War', *The Agricultural History Review*, 51/2 (2003), 209–25.

Todman, D., *Britain's War, A New World, 1942–1947* (Penguin, 2016).

Todman, D., *Britain's War, Into Battle, 1937–1941* (Penguin, 2016).

Tomlinson, J., *Democratic Socialism and Economic Policy, The Attlee Years, 1945–1951* (Cambridge University Press, 1997).

Tooze, A., *The Wages of Destruction: the Making and Breaking of the Nazi Economy* (Penguin, 2007).

Town, S., *After the Mines, Changing Employment Opportunities in a South Wales Valley*, (University of Wales Press, 1978).

Verrill-Rhys L. and Beddoe, D. (eds), *Parachutes and Petticoats* (Honno, 2003).

Warren, K., *The British Iron and Steel Industry since 1840* (G. Bell and Son, 1970).

Weir, C., *Civilian Assignment* (Methuen, 1953).

Williams, J., *Was Wales Industrialised?* (Gomer, 1995).

Williams, M., *A Forgotten Army, Female Munitions Workers of South Wales, 1939–1945* (University of Wales Press, 2002).

Wilt, A. F., *Food for War; Agriculture and Rearmament in Britain before the Second World War* (Oxford University Press, 2001).

Wren, C., *Industrial Subsidies, The UK Experience* (Springer, 1996).

Zweiniger-Bargielowska, I., 'Colliery Managers and Nationalisation: The Experience in South Wales', *Business History*, 34/4 (1992), 59–78.

Zweiniger-Bargielowska, I., 'South Wales Miners' Attitudes towards Nationalization: an Essay in Oral History', *Llafur*, 6/3 (1994), 70–84.

Zweiniger-Bargielowska, I., *Austerity in Britain: Rationing, Controls, and Consumption, 1939–1955* (Oxford University Press, 2000).

UNPUBLISHED THESES

Parry, S., *History of the Steel Industry in the Port Talbot Area* (Leeds University, 2011).

Howells, K., *A View from Below: Tradition, Experience and Nationalization in the South Wales Coalfield, 1937–1957* (University of Warwick, 1979).

Broomfield, S., *South Wales During the Second World War: The Coal Industry and its Community* (University of Wales, 1979).

Coggins, J., *Science and the Farmer; the Development of Agriculture in West Wales, 1900–1950* (University of Wales Trinity Saint David, 2018).

INDEX

A
A. R. Adams and Sons (Newport), 106
Aberdare, 107, 117
Abergavenny, 113
Aberystwyth
  CWAEC District sub-committee, 241
  Ministry of Agriculture's Welsh Department, 34, 179
  Nanteos Estate, 192
  National Library of Wales, 11
  Post-war location for government's agricultural services, 242
  University College of Wales, Aberystwyth, 33, 182, 185, 189
Abyssinia, 20
Act of Union, 1
Admiralty
  Two-power standard, 22
  Procurement, 45, 160
  Employment of Regional Officers, 46
  Structure, 69–70
  Regional organisation, 75–6
  Reluctance to share office space, 81
Agricultural Land Commission, 241, 242
Agricultural Land Tribunal, 241
Agriculture Act (1947), 240
Air Council, 26
Air Ministry
  Aircraft specifications, 22
  Contracts in Wales, 50, 115–16
  Procurement, 69
  Trecwn depot, 115
Alexander, Hubert, 57
Ammanford, 134
Anderson, John, 90, 204
Area Boards, *see* Ministry of Supply, Production Council, Production Executive, Ministry of Production
Army, 19, 127
Austria, 39

B
Baldwin, Stanley, 20, 21
Baldwins 53, 163 (Swansea, Gowerton, Neath and Panteg), 159
Balfour, Arthur, 29
Banbury, 214
Bangor, 82, 119
Bank of England, 237
Barlow Commission and report, 43, 203, 207, 259
Beale, Samuel, 234
Beaverbrook, Max, 68, 69, 70, 74
Benallt (manganese mine), 164
Bevan, Aneurin, 72, 138
Beveridge, William, 24, 33, 128, 204
Bevin Boys, 131, 143
Bevin, Ernest
  Denounces striking miners, 132
  Iron ore mining industrial relations, 162
  Labour regulation, 89, 91, 93, 102, 257
  Minister of Labour and National Service, 67
  Role of Production Executive, 70
  Sees prosecuting strikers as inflammatory, 125
  Threatens resignation, 74
  Wages settlement within metal manufacturing, 156

Birmingham Small Arms (Merthyr Tydfil), 106
Birmingham, 112, 155
Blaenavon, 137, 140
Blaina, 2, 98
BNS, 214, 215, 220
Board of Trade, 8, 9, 80
   Cardiff office, 216
   Determined to control data, 206, 212
   Dispersal of aircraft industry, 112
   Estimates of factory openings in 1930s, 47
   Mines Department, 56, 116, 126, 134
   Regional Advisory Boards for Industry, 209, 210
   Regional Distribution of Industry Committee, 209, 216, 236
   Sheet steel concentration, 158
   Strike data, 165, 170
   Suppression of peacetime manufacturing, 153, 155
   Tinplate concentration, 167, 169, 236
   see also Hugh Dalton, Development Areas, Factory and Storage Control Function, Douglas Jay, and Regional Policy
Bolivia, 169
Brazil, 154
Bridgend ROF
   Construction, 47–8
   Industrial relations, 99
   Operations, 108–9
   Post-war use, 218
   Recruitment and employment, 28, 47–8, 97, 264, 265
   Site choice, 28
   Transfer to Board of Trade, 215
   Wages, 97, 135, 136
   Within regional structure, 110
   Unions, 99
Bristol Aeroplane Co., 30
Bristol Channel, 2
British Expeditionary Force, 41, 42
British Aluminium Company, 56, 164
British Industrial Solvents (Kenfig), 51
British Iron and Steel Federation, 32, 53, 154
British Overseas Aircraft Corporation (Treforest), 113
British Steel Industry Federation, 233, 236
Brittania Foundry (Porthmadog), 159
Broadhaven, 190
Brown, Ernest, 44
Brown, William, 53–4
Brunning, 213, 214, 216
Brymbo steelworks, 159, 163
Bryner Jones, Cadwaldr, 34, 179, 188
Buckinghamshire, 155
Burgin, Leslie, 45
Robert Byness (Swansea), 164

C

Caernarfon, 112
Caernavonshire, 164
Caerwent Royal Navy Propellent Factory, 28, 115, 116
Canada, 133
Canadian Army, 140
Cardiff
   Admiralty reluctance to release office space, 81
   Aluminium plants (general), 164, 235
   Board of Trade regional Office, 216
   Chamberlain speech, 40
   Companies contracted to supply

ministries, 116–17
Curran Metal Works, 26, 117
Development Area, 214
Efficiency of metal works, 32, 54
Engineering ROF, 50, 98, 109, 265
Factory and Storage Space Control Function, 79
GKB, 161
GKN Castle Works, 160
International Alloys, 164
Lord Hyndley visits, 231
Machine Products, 101–102.
Ministry of Labour and National Service Regional Controller, 96
Shinwell meets NUM, 232
Steel plants (general), 159, 235
Swastika over City Hall, 39
University College Cardiff, 212, 213
Castlemartin, 185
Central Council of Colliery Owners, 126
Central Wages Board (agriculture), 59
Ceredigion, 164
Charles, A. G., 56, 154
Chepstow, 116, 119, 214
Chorley, 27
Churchill, Winston
　Addresses miners, 130
　Appeasement, 40
　Avoids sensitive domestic policies, 203
　Becomes Prime Minister, 43, 67
　Chair of Lord President's Committee, 67
　Chancellor, 19–20
　Creation of Ministry of Supply, 44
　First Lord of the Admiralty, 42
　Norway debate, 43
　Overrules Beaverbrook, 71
　Rearmament, 22
　Rules out nationalisation of coal mining, 131
　Ten-year-rule, 19
　Views on bombing, 21
　Wilderness years, 21
Citrine, Walter (and Citrine Commission), 75–6, 80, 226
Coal Charges Account, 129, 141
Coal Industry Nationalization Bill (1946), 228
Coal Owners Association, 137
Coal Production Council, 126, 129, 134, 135
Coal Production Council, 56
Cole, G. D. H., 205, 206
Colwyn Bay, 44, 107, 175
Collieries
　Aberaman (absenteeism), 141
　Abergorki (dissatisfaction), 142
　Bersham (disputes), 137
　Black Park (disputes), 137
　Blaenclydach (accident), 136
　Caerphilly (loss of labour), 56
　Cwm (vesting day), 230
　Ffaldau (poor wages), 136
　Glanaman (cessation of financial support), 135
　Glynogwr (absenteeism), 141
　Gresford, 141, (recruitment), 135
　Gresham (disputes), 137
　Hafod (disputes), 137
　Nantgarw (NCB investment), 231
　Penallta (collapse of Pit Production Committee), 142
　Penrhiwceiber (dispute), 139
　Point of Ayr, 137, 139, (poor sentiment) 143, (absenteeism), 145
　Seven Sisters (Essential Work Order), 141
　Tower Colliery (clerical staff), 145
　West Blaina (dispute), 56
Conditions of employment

national arbitration order, 125
Conservative Party
  1945 election campaign, 239
  Backbench discontent as to
    Labour influence, 128
  Caretaker Government, 227
  Monmouth CWAEC Chair, 181
  Nationalisation of coal mining
    industry, 227
  Support for mineowners, 146, 226
Cookes Explosives
  (Penrhyndeudraeth), 52, 107
Corbett, 111
County Agricultural Executive
  Committees (CAECs), 240,
  243, 244
Courtauld's, 214
Coventry, 112
County War Executive Committees
  (CWAECs)
  Anglesey (Lord Anglesey) 181,
    (Malltraeth) 185
  Authority, 177–8, 252
  Breconshire (farm grading), 187
  Caernarfonshire (pest control)
    182, 192, (cultivation orders)
    184, (farm survey) 187,
    (labour) 189, (machinery)
    191, (mobile film van) 193
  Cardigan, 58, (circulars) 179,
    (chair) 180, (prosecutions)
    183–4, (cultivation orders)
    184, (Borth bog) 185,
    (cultivation orders) 241
  Carmarthenshire, 58, (cultivation
    orders) 184, (machinery) 191
  Chairs alerted (in 1939), 57
  Creation, 33
  Cultivation Orders, 182
  Denbighshire (drainage) 186,
    (farm grading) 187, (labour)
    189
  Flintshire (drainage) 186, (farm

survey) 188, (labour) 190,
  (machinery) 190
Glamorgan (pest control) 182
Governance, 179–82
Meirioneth ('little Hitlers') 242
Monmouthshire (labour), 190
  (fireside chats) 193
Montgomeryshire (Chair) 180,
  (seizes land) 183, (prosecutions)
  184–5, (clearance) 185,
  (farm grading) 187,
  (Llanfyllin district committee)
  188, (fireside chats) 193
Pembrokeshire (Letterston District
  Committee) 181, (machinery)
  182, 191, (recruitment) 184,
  (farm grading) 187, (drainage)
  193, (land seizure) 242
Ploughing up, 58, 182
Post-war developments, 239–40
Radnorshire (prosecutions) 183,
  (snow), 241
Crete, 72
Cripps, Stafford, 85, 209, 233
Crown Compositions (Swansea),
  116
Curran Metal Works (Cardiff), 26,
  117
Czechoslovakia, 39, 41

D
Daimler (Bangor/Penrhyn Castle),
  113
Dalton, Hugh
  Anger at coal owners, 147
  Announces Llanelli location for
    tinplate plant, 236
  'Annus horredus' (1947), 211
  At Board of Trade, 204–7, 216,
    219, 221, 259–60
  Becomes Chancellor, 208
  General approach, 259
  Intervention in factory location,

214, 215
Proposals on coal mining, 128
Rejects tinplate concentration, 236
Role within Regional Policy, 219, 221, 260
Davies, H. Leighton, 167
Davies, S. O., 83
Denbighshire, 242
Denmark, 43
Development Areas
Building licences in, 209
Creation, 207–8
Diversion of businesses to, 217, 219, 260
Expanding outside, 210, 211
Extension of, 216
Government factories and loans, 218
Development Corporation for Wales, 260
D. G. Hall and Co. (Newport), 116
Dinorwic, 112
Distribution of Industry Act (1945), 10, 206
District Production Committees, 126
Dolgarrog, 55, 164, 184
Dowlais, 106
Duncan, Andrew, 213
Duncan, Oliver, 74

E
Elliot, Walter, 33
Emergency Powers Act, 67, 89
Essential Work Order, 90, 98, 127, 141
Employment of Women (Control of Engagement) Order, 91
Edmonds, Reg, 111
Elliot Equipment (Cardiff), 116
Egypt, 126
Edwards, Ebby, 129, 130, 228
Essendon Committee, 167

Elba Mill (Swansea), 170
Eppynt, 185
Ebbw Vale, 4, 32, 72, 138, 159, 165–6, 235

F
Factory and Storage Space Control Function
Activities, 258, 260
Admiralty, 116
Allocates floorspace, 79–82
Creation, 71
Impact on manufacturing, 118
Joins Regional Boards, 77
MAP, 112
Preparing for peacetime, 205–6, 208, 209, 213, 214, 215
Reason for creation, 84
Tinplate, 167–9
Ferndale, 59
Finance Corporation for Industry, 237
First World War
Agriculture, 33, 256, 257
Disrupts global trade, 3
Food shortages, 33
Government control of coal mining, 31, 32
Government desire to avoid repeat experience within coal mining, 146
Loss of export markets, 32
Low defence expenditure after victory, 19, 20
Pembrey factory, 28
Women's Land Army, 57
Flex Fasteners (Porth), 107
Foot, Robert, 227
Forbes, Archibald, 233
Ford, 210
Forest of Dean coalfield, 229
Foster-Stedman, L., 181
France, 133, 175

Franks, Oliver
  Ministry of Supply, 74
  On governing metal manufacturing, 152
  On governing raw materials, 171
  Reflects on wartime governance, 257
  Refuses to draft paper on steel nationalisation, 234
French North Africa, 154
Freshwater West, 192
Frys Chocolates (Bristol), 111

G
Geneva Disarmament Conference, 20
Germany, 20, 22
Gesford Lodge, 107
Glascoed ROF
  Construction, 48
  Operations, 109, 110
  Recruitment, 98, 108, 264–5
  Site choice, 28
  Wages, 97, 98, 135–6
GKB Briton Ferry, 161
GKB Port Talbot/Margam, 159, 160, 165
GKN Cardiff, 159, 160, 161
GKN Cwmbran, 11, 160, 161
GKN Newport, 165
Glamorgan Archives, 11
Glamorgan, 2, 43, 97
Godwin-Austen, Reade, 230
Gold Standard, 3
Gorseinon, 167
Great Depression, 3
Greene Board, 130
Greenwood, Arthur, 203
Grenfell, David, 128, 134
Gretna, 27
Griffiths, Jim, 138, 168
Gwaun-Cae-Gurwen, 232
Gwent Archives, 11

H
Hitler, Adolf, 20
Hurricane (aircraft), 22, 40, 42
Horner, Arthur, 56, 134, 228, 229
Hiles, Herbert, 79
Hirwaun ROF, 99, 110, 215, 265
Hill Farming Act (1946), 240
Hereford, 110
Heliwells (Treforest), 113
Halkyn, 164
Hudson, Robert, 175
Hoover, 217, 220
Hyndley, Lord, 228

I
Imperial Chemical Industries (ICI), 31
  Agency fees, 52
  Billingham, 30, 31
  BNS joint venture with Courtauld's, 214
  Dowlais, 52, 107
  Kenfig, 51
  Pembrey, 52, 107
  Rhydymwyn (Valley Works), 52, 107–8
  Swansea, 53, 164
Industrial Development Certificate, 211, 260
Industrial Transference Board, 4
Inskip, Thomas, 21, 24
International Alloys (Cardiff), 164
Ireland, 176, 190
Iron and Steel Control
  Benefits larger firms, 160
  Controls distribution, 155
  Creation, 53
  Declares capacity sufficient, 171
  Expands alloy production, 163
  Issues occupation list for women, 158
  Organisation, 155
  Post-war planning, 252

Sheet steel concentration, 166
Successor to, 235
Successor wartime control, 232
Supports efficiency drives, 161
Supports modernisation and expansion, 159
Iron and Steel Trade Confederation, 153
Italy, 20, 238

J
Jaguar, 210
Japan, 19, 20, 22
Jay, Douglas
   At Board of Trade, 205, 206, 216
   Conflict between ministries, 90
   Conflict within Ministry of Supply, 91
   Influences BNS location, 214
   Intervenes within Ministry of Supply, 215
   Merthyr Tydfil, 215
Jeffreys, David, 142
Jones, Garro, 83
Jones, J. Morgan, 180
Jones, William, 143
Joseph, Keith, 261
Jowlitt, William, 204, 213

K
Kenfig, 51
Kent, 125
Keynes, John Maynard, 42

L
Labour Party
   Commission on Depressed Areas, 204
   Merthyr Tydfil, 83
   Mineowners dismayed, 134
   Nationalisation, 225–7
   Nationalisation of coal mining, 227–9
   Nationalisation of land rejected, 239
   Nationalisation of metal manufacturing, 234
   Participation in coalition government, 74, 128
   Post-war intervention, 5, 6, 261
   Support for miners, 146, 147
   Victory at 1945 general election, 208
J. Lysaught (Newport), 166
Lancaster (aircraft), 114
Landore (Baldwins), 161
Landore, 116
League of Nations, 20
Leamington Spa, 155
Lee, Laurie, 194
Lewis, George, 193
Limited liability, 23
Lithgow, James, 29
Llanberis, 5, 100
Llanelli
   Industrialists urged to consider, 113
   Morris Motors, 101, 114
   Steel furnaces, 159
   Strikes, 165–6
   Tinplate, 166–8, 236–8
Llandrindod Wells, 82
Llanfyllin, 193
Llangennech, 168
Llanharry (iron ore mine), 162
Lloyd George, Gwilym, 129, 131, 147, 227
London
   Air defence, 23
   Air raid risk, 26
   Businesses flee air raids, 68, 112, 113
   Churchill addresses mass meeting of miners, 130
   Delegations to, 83
   Dispatch of sheet steel to, 54

Drift of population towards, 43
Factory openings, 25
Industrial governance, 75
Iron and Steel Control, 53, 155
Ministry of Agriculture, 179, 186
NCB meeting, 230
Regional Policy, 210, 215, 217
Sourcing labour for Bridgend ROF, 48
London Passenger Transport Board, 225
Lord President's Committee, 8, 67, 70, 258
Lucas, Joseph (Cwmbran), 114, 218
Luftwaffe, 42
Lyttleton, Oliver, 8, 70, 72, 76, 80, 206

M

Machine Products (Cardiff), 101
Macmillan, Harold, 68, 70, 244
Magnesium Metal Corporation (Swansea), 164
Mainwaring, W. M., 98
Malaya, 169
Manchester, 185
Manchuria, 19
Marconi Wireless Company, 52–3
Mass Observation, 3, 72, 98, 100, 101, 137, 142, 211
McDonald, Gordon, 143, 145
McDonald, Ramsey, 28
Merioneth, 164
Metal Box (Neath), 108
Metal Pressing (Caldicot), 53
Merthyr Tydfil
  Commissioner for Special Areas' factories, 25
  Hoover, 217
  ICI, 31
  Labourers transferred from, 96
  Memorandum from Minister of Health and Minister for Labour, 34
  Ministry of Supply contracts, 106
  Post-war planning, 83
  Post-war unemployment, 217
  Rotax, 114
Milford Haven, 115, 116
Miners' Federation, 129, 132
Mines Department, 56
Mining Association of Great Britain, 129, 130
Ministry of Agriculture
  Goods and Services scheme, 191
  Governance, 178, 259
  Hill Cattle Subsidy Scheme, 192
  Hill Sheep Subsidy Scheme, 192
  Ploughing up, 176
  Welsh Department, 34, 59, 179, 186, 242
  Within governance, 253, 255
  see also CWAECs
Ministry of Aircraft Production
  Asks sub-contractors to release labour for coal industry, 127
  Creation, 69, 84
  Dispersal of production, 111–12
  Governance, 254
  Lack of state managed factories, 111
  Light Metals Control, 152, 154, 155, 163, 164
  Merges with Ministry of Supply, 209
  Premises in Pontypool, 168
  Procurement and contracts, 160
  Regional organisation, 75
  Sir Archibald Forbes, 233
Ministry of Food
  Concordat with Ministry of Agriculture, 175
  Contracts, 116
  Evacuation to Colwyn Bay, 44, 175
  Fixed prices, 177

INDEX

Food purchases, 59, 239–40
Import substitution, 176
Ministry of Food and Agriculture, 33
Ministry of Fuel and Power
   Dual Control, 128
   Governance, 253, 254
   Miners on productive work, 140
   Regional Controllers, 128, 138, 143, 255
Ministry of Information, 115, 193
Ministry of Labour and National Service
   Authority over coal miners, 127
   District Manpower Boards, 95, 98
   Employment exchanges, 94, 96, 127, 136
   Governing labour, 89–91
   Joint Consultative Committee, 93
   Joint Production Committees, 93, 100, 163
   Labour supply in south Wales coalfield, 57
   Manpower budgeting, 92
   Membership of Regional Board, 80
   Metal manufacturing labour transfers, 163
   Pit Production Committees, 142
   Regional Industrial Relations Officer, 144
   Regional Preference Committees, 95
   Ring Fence Scheme, 156
   Role in labour market, 8
   Transfer of Regional Policy from, 206
Ministry of Production
   Abolished, 203, 208, 209
   Advance factories, 260
   Creation, 74
   Headquarters Preference Committee, 75, 92, 95
   Location of Industry Committee, 75
   Materials Committee, 153
   Merthyr Tydfil, 83
   Regional Boards, 76, 77, 81, 85, 96, 155–6, 205, 207, 255, 258
   Wales Regional Board, 100, 101–2, 215
Ministry of Reconstruction, 204
Ministry of Supply
   392 Register, 45, 69, 71
   Approves post-war metal manufacturing schemes, 235
   Area Boards, 46, 68, 78
   Creation of Raw Materials Controls, 53, 55
   Creation, 44
   Employment of Regional Officers, 46
   Governance, 253, 254
   Iron ore mining industrial relations, 162
   Materials Committee, 152, 153
   Merges with Ministry of Aircraft Production, 209
   Non-Ferrous Metal Control, 55, 154, 155, 163, 164
   Light Metals Control, 152, 154, 155, 156, 163, 164
   Pressure to agree steel development schemes, 237
   Procurement and contracts, 45, 69, 77, 106–7, 159, 160
   Refuses to dismantle hostels, 215
   Regional Organisation, 76
   ROF Construction, 47
   ROF governance, 69
   ROF recruitment, 96
   ROF regional structure, 110–11
   Role of, 43–4, 118
   Sells aluminium plant at Newport, 235
   see also individual ROFs, Iron and Steel Control

Ministry of Works and Buildings, 116, 208, 209
Monmouthshire and South Wales Coal Owners Association, 130, 230
Monmouthshire, 1, 2
Montgomery, General Bernard, 107, 139
Morgan, Denis, 79
Morris Motors (Llanelli), 114
Morrison, Herbert, 225, 240
Munich, 40

N
Nanteos estate, 192
Nantyglo, 98
National Agricultural Advisory Service, 241, 242, 243, 244
National Archives, 11
National Coal Board (1942), 129, 139
National Coal Board (1947), 228–32
National Farmers' Union, 181, 238, 241, 245
National Production Advisory Council, 77
National Service Act, 91
National Union of Mineworkers, 132, 227, 229, 232
Neath Steel Sheet, 159
Neath Valley, 133
Neath, 82, 159, 166
NECACO (Llanberis), 112
Newgale, 190
Newport
  Admiralty contracts, 116
  Development Area, 214
  Engineering ROF, 29, 50, 110, 216, 265
  GKN, 165
  J. Lysaught, 166
  Ministry of Supply contracts, 106

Northern Aluminium (Rogerstone), 50, 56, 164, 235
Post-war metal manufacturing, 235
Newtown (Accles and Pollock), 113
North Africa, 190
Northampton, 134
Northern Aluminium (Rogerstone), 50, 56, 164, 235
Northern Ireland, 6, 9
Norway, 43, 154
Nottingham, 29
Nuffield College Social Reconstruction Survey, 81, 205, 206, 211–12

O
Oran and Ward (Cardiff), 116
Orb Works (Newport), 164
Oswestry, 27

P
Pembrey ROF
  Site choice, 28
  Recruitment, 99, 265
  Industrial Relations, 99
  Wages, 97, 98, 135
Pembroke Dock, 218
Pembroke, 29
Pembrokeshire, 96, 101
Penrhyndeudraeth, 52
Penygroes, 193
Persian Gulf, 2
Pit Production Committees, 93
  Creation, 56, 93
  Deadlocked, 135, 144
  Interviews absentees, 127, 129
  Lapse in 1940, 126
  Miners' distrust of, 136, 142, 146
  Observes absenteeism, 145
  Replacement of, 230
  see also Collieries
Poland, 40, 238
Polikoffs (Rhondda), 107, 218

Pontardawe, 159, 166
Pontypool, 166, 168, 214
Porter Award, 131
Porth, 59, 107
Porthcawl, 48
Powell Duffryn, 143, 146, 228
Prague, 40
Prestigne, 113
Pride, Emrys, 79, 82
Production Council
　Area Boards, 68, 69, 70
　Creation, 67
　Replacement with Production Executive, 70
　Wales Area Board, 71, 78
Production Executive
　Area Boards, 70, 71
　Creation, 70
　Regional Boards, 71, 79–80
　Wales Area Board, 78, 168
　West Wales Advisory Panel, 169
Pullman Springs (Ammanford), 215
Purnell, Oliver, 39

Q
Queensferry, 27

R
Radnorshire, 193
Railways, 3
Ratcliffe Tool and Guage (Colywn Bay), 113, 217
Reading, 30
Regional Policy, 9, 10, 11
　1930s Origins, 4
　Implementation, 213–21
　Instruments, 208–11
　South Wales Commissioners, 24, 52
　Transfer of power from Commissioners, 206
　Wartime re-emergence, 203–7
Rees, Edgar, 155

Rees, J. F., 212
Regional Boards *see* Production Executive and Ministry of Production
Registration of Employment Order, 91, 98
Reid Report, 227, 230, 244
Reith, Sir John, 203
Resolven, 56
Rhineland, 20
Rhondda
　Apprentice strike, 138
　Polikoff, 107, 218
　Post-war factories, 218
　Pre-war depression, 5
　Transport problems faced by ROF workers, 97
Rhydymwyn *see* ICI
Robinson, Arthur, 27
Rodgers, John, 30
Rollaston Aircraft Services (Croydon), 112
Rootes, 30
Rotax (Merthyr Tydfil), 114
Rothschild, Victor, 143
Royal Air Force, 19, 127
Royal Navy, 2, 19
Royal Ordnance Factories (ROFs)
　Role within munitions production, 26–9
　Enfield, 27
　Governance, 69
　Recruiting labour, 96–9
　Wages, 135–6, 162
　Waltham Abbey, 27
　Woolwich, 27, 111
　see also Bridgend, Cardiff, Glasgoed, Hirwaun, Newport, Pembrey, Wrexham
Royal Welsh Factory (Newtown), 105
Rugby, 155
Russia, 107
Ruthin, 79

S

Sarn, 193
Saunders Roe (Isle of Wight/ Beaumaris), 112
Schedule of Reserved Occupations, 46
Scotland, 6, 251
Scottish Office, 25, 252
Severn Estuary, 112
Sheetmakers Conference, 166
Shepard and Sons (Bridgend), 106
Shinwell, Manny, 228, 232
Simon, John, 41
Sinclair, Robert, 77
Singapore, 72
Slate industry, 2, 5, 112
Slough, 4
Society of British Aircraft Constructors, 55
Society of Motor Manufactures and Traders, 238
Somerset coalfield, 229
Somerset Wire Products, 161
South America, 126
South Wales and Monmouthshire Trading Estate Company, 25, 215
South Wales Miners Federation (SWMF)
  Attempts to broker a settlement, 139
  Complaints of Blaenavon section, 137
  Defuses tensions, 135
  Iron ore miners, 162
  Opposes transfers, 134
  Orders speech printed, 57
  Porter award strikes, 144
  Seeks state support for colliery (1939), 56
  Supports war effort, 142
South Wales Miners' Library, 11
South Wales Special Area Commissioners *see* Regional Policy
Spitfire (aircraft), 22, 40, 42
Stanhope, Earl, 41
Steel Company of Wales (Port Talbot), 236–8
Stewart, Malcolm, 24
Sudetenland, 39
John Summers (Shotton)
  1930s, 3
  Anderson shelters, 54
  Employment, 159
  Female workers, 163
  Post-war expansion, 235
  Sheet steel, 166
Swansea
  Admiralty contracts, 116
  Baldwins, 159
  Development Area, 214
  ICI (Metals), 53, 164
  Industrial estate, 218
  Industrialists asked to consider as location, 113
  Ministry of Supply contracts, 106
  Non-Ferrous Metal Control office, 155
  South Wales Miners' Library, 11
  Tinplate, 166, 169, 170, 237, 238
  Town Council, 168
Sweden, 154

T

Treforest Industrial Estate
  Aircraft components, 113, 118
  Creation, 25
  Factories (in 1939), 52
  Firms displaced from, 107
  Post-war, 217
  Rents, 82
Thatcher, Margaret, 261
Thomas, Percy, 78, 80
Tinplate
  1930s, 32

Concentration of, 166–70
Postwar modernisation, 235–8
Strikes, 100, 165
see also Ministry of Supply, Iron and Steel Control
Trawscoed, 242
Treasury
　Approves Cardiff ROF, 50
　Delays approval for ROFs, 28
　Financial rationing, 40, 41, 47, 48
　Funds farm surveys, 33
　Orthodox view, 3
Tonypandy, 59
Trade Unions
　1938–40, 46–7, 53–4, 56
　Agriculture, 241
　Coal mining in the First World War, 31
　Company backed union, 137, 139
　Density and industrial action in secondary manufacturing, 99, 100
　Dilution, 46
　Exclusion from public corporation boards, 244
　Joint Production Committees, 100
　Lobbying on Merthyr Tydfil, 83
　Metal manufacturing, 153, 156, 158, 164–5, 238
　Protests over labour transfers, 140
　Regional Board, 80
　Regional Distribution of Industry Committees, 207
　Regional mining unions, 9
　Voluntarist approaches, 89–90, 93, 96
　see also South Wales Miners' Federation, National Union of Mineworkers, Trades Union Congress
Trades Union Congress (TUC), 46, 75, 93, 126

Richard Thomas & Co. (Ebbw Vale), 139, 165, 166
Tredegar Estate, 181
Town and Country Planning Act (1947), 211
Tresaith, 242

U

Unemployment, 28, 29
　Inter-war levels, 3, 34, 59
　Wartime levels, 5
Undertakings (Restriction on Engagement) Order, 90
United States, 169, 185

V

Vickers Armstrong (Broughton), 251
　Industrial Relations, 100
　Operations, 50–1, 114–15
　Site choice, 30

W

Wales and Monmouthshire Industrial Estates Ltd, 217
Wales Reconstruction Advisory Committee, 212
Walters, Richard, 79, 169
War Office, 45
Warter, Philip, 206
Weir, Cecil, 71–2, 209
Weir, William, 25, 29
Wellington (aircraft), 30, 50
Welsh Development Agency, 260
Welsh Metals Industries (Caerphilly), 106
Welsh Plate and Steel Manufacturers Association, 236
West Africa, 169
Weybridge, 51
White Paper on Employment (1944), 205, 214
White, Professor, 180

William Thomas and Sons
    (Wrexham), 106
Williams, Emlyn, 230
Willians, Evan, 129, 147
Women in the labour force
    Brinley Thomas's observations, 5
    Importance to workforce
        mobilisation, 92–3
    Labour governance, 90–1
    Lancashire, 27
    Metal manufacturing, 158, 168
    Miners' disquiet, 136
    Pre-war, 96
    Recruitment to factories, 96–9,
        101, 103
    ROFs, 108, 109–10
    Transfers, 95
    TUC against night working, 46
    Unoccupied in Merthyr Tydfil, 83
    Workforce expansion, 90, 220
    see also Women's Land Army
Women's Land Army, 57, 58, 181,
    190
Wood, Kingsley, 204
Wrexham ROF
    Operations, 109
    Post-war use, 216
    Recruitment and employment,
        97, 265
    Rejection as location, 27
    Site choice, 49
Wright, Charles, 53, 157